Cataclysms

Cataclysms

A History of the Twentieth Century from Europe's Edge

Dan Diner

Translated by
William Templer
with
Joel Golb

THE UNIVERSITY OF WISCONSIN PRESS

This book was published with the support of
the GEORGE L. MOSSE PROGRAM
at the University of Wisconsin–Madison.

The University of Wisconsin Press
1930 Monroe Street
Madison, Wisconsin 53711

www.wisc.edu /wisconsinpress /

3 Henrietta Street
London WC2E 8LU, England

Originally published in Germany as *Das Jahrhundert verstehen,*
copyright © 1999 Dan Diner
Translation copyright © 2008 The Board of Regents
of the University of Wisconsin System

1   3   5   4   2

Printed in the United States of America

Library of Congress Cataloging-in-Publication Data
Diner, Dan, 1946–
[Das Jahrhundert verstehen. English]
Cataclysms : a history of the twentieth century
from Europe's edge / Dan Diner;
translated by William Templer with Joel Golb.
p.   cm. — (George L. Mosse series in modern European cultural and
intellectual history)
Includes bibliographical references and index.
ISBN 0-299-22350-7 (cloth: alk. paper)
1. History, Modern — 20th century.
I. Golb, Joel David.   II. Title.   III. Series.
D421.D5613   2007
909.82 — dc22   2007011770

To my father

ROBERT DINER

1907–1990

who endured the century

Contents

Cataclysms

Introduction

*Contingencies and Periodizations / Reestablished Spaces and
Revived Times / Peripheral Perspectives and Pivotal Events /
Continuous Narrations and Intentional Omissions*

⚜

This narrative unavoidably contains omissions; no historical
presentation located beyond mere chronological recollection can avoid the hazards of selection. For the historian, the abun-
dance of material that reality offers necessitates a reduction of
complexity. But these reductions are by no means employed arbitrarily; rather, they are implemented according to claims of historical importance and meaning. And while the constructed narrations follow the guiding hand of historical judgment, they aim
at a horizon of universal applicability.

Periodization is one of the prominent tools available for historical understanding. Considerations tied to an epoch's movement
from beginning to end catalyze further interpretation. Such temporal divisions apparently emerge from a distance, with hindsight, the distinction between time experienced and time reflected

having proverbial status. Nevertheless, there are exceptions—most manifestly those events earning the "real-time" qualification of being *historical*, which is to say events creating a strong impression that contemporary intuition will later be ratified by reflective historical judgment.

This impression was extremely widespread in 1989. Everywhere people were gripped by a certainty that an entire epoch was vanishing before their eyes. And everywhere 1917 was invoked, at least implicitly, as the epoch's beginning. In this manner, with the demise of Communism at the twentieth century's end, the events of the October Revolution were demoted to an opening act.

The following narration of the twentieth century's history will thus adhere to a periodization framed by the temporal icons of 1917 and 1989 and the historical meaning those two dates encapsulate. With the encapsulation rationalizing the omissions demanded by the historicization process, one of the narrative's focal points will be those events understood to highlight the profound antagonism between Communism and its opponents in a fundamental way. The antagonism unfolded as a political-social predicament that will be defined in these chapters as a universal civil war, a war articulated in terms of polarized semantic categories of "truth," political belief, and ethical value.

In the course of the twentieth century, this antagonism of values was played out in various, world-embracing conceptual modes: as freedom and equality, Bolshevism and anti-Bolshevism, Capitalism and Communism, East and West. For this reason, the clash between Communism and its adversaries could well be understood as one of the two basic interpretive axes for understanding the century. The axis is constructed vertically in that it cuts through nations, states, and societies. But its universal validity has been systematically confronted and called into question by validity claims located on the second, horizontally laid-out axis: by conflicts and oppositions based on primordial emblems of belonging, which is to say ethnicity, nationality, religion, and culture. This became explosively evident when the universal civil war of ideology and values came to its sudden end in 1989. It turned out that the massive weight of principles and ideas, the overwhelming rhetoric of opposing universalisms, had, as it were, merely temporarily neutralized a rhetoric grounded in highly particular legacies—a rhetoric of territory and ethnicity, distinctiveness and memory.

History is an open process. Although the significance of this observation may have been sometimes inflated, its basic validity remains unchallenged. The past's openness to future events is, to be sure, inscribed with paradox. Without any damage to facticity, the images of times gone by change in light of the living present. They become estranged, at times glaringly distinct. Hence the construction of history is marked by fundamental displacements in established narrations of continuity and causality. Contingencies pile up in place of such narrations. Temporal layers arrange themselves anew, endowing the epoch with an altered profile.

The perception has thus emerged that the cold-war era has slipped outside the continuities of historical time, that its presence has waned, its epistemic value evanesced. And yet this presumed evanescence has not resulted in an empty temporality. Rather, the fabric of a time that has waned has been replaced by reanimated memories of a past long believed buried—laid *ad acta*. In short, following the caesura of 1989, the apparent return to the Europe of older historical spaces has been accompanied by a return of traditional historical times.

Importantly, this sudden shift of temporal landscape did not just annul the ideological opposition between East and West; at the same time, the ideological, values-based interpretive axis for understanding the twentieth century also lost its interpretative monopoly. It was now obliged to share its hegemony with another interpretation—one that relied on ostensibly antiquated concepts such as ethnicity and geography. This new interpretive alignment would appear to reflect that of the nineteenth century while enhancing the possibilities for its historical assessment: through a fusion of seemingly clashing historical axes, the character of each emerges. In this book they are reassessed in terms of a complex intermeshing of long-term and short-term tendencies.

The perspective on twentieth-century events that will unfold here is somewhat unusual. Rather than proceeding from the European center, the book's narrative proceeds from its eastern perimeter—from the periphery inward. This spatial shift tends to create an effect of temporal estrangement, with spatial distance replacing its temporal counterpart, which is not yet present. In this way the twentieth century takes on a remoteness that—so the intention—will render it historical.

Our unfolding view will extend from beyond Europe's eastern edge. It will drift from the Baltic over and above the Black Sea to the Aegean. Such a vantage point, starting from the fringes of the continent, might be that of a virtual narrator situated on the legendary steps of Odessa, looking outward south and west. The horizon of ancient pasts that thus emerges consists of intermingling topographical metaphors and narrative images reducing the complexity of the historical past. The spatial view from north to south reflects a temporal shift from the present into emerging pasts—those of Constantinople, Byzantium, and Troy.[1] As with a palimpsest, this geography reveals a repetitiveness of events originating in a continuous struggle for control of the Straits—of the Bosporus and the Dardanelles. Wars fought in that region have had the quality of Trojan wars; the Crimean War fought between 1853 and 1856 and the battle of Gallipoli in 1915, one of the Great War's notorious episodes, were both campaigns for dominance in the Straits. One of the effects of the Crimean War was the initiation of modern archaeology at Troy: for the sake of military discipline, a historically informed British officer engaged his vexed troops in stand-by position at the Straits, ordering them to take up spades and pickaxes in order to dig for the ancient city's presumed ruins.[2] Approximately half a century earlier, the czarina Catherine II, in her effort to raise Russia to the rank of a great European power, reached back to the Odyssean myth by naming her newly founded Black Sea city "Odessa." The new city was thus announced as a spatially and temporally displaced counterpart to Troy, the same Troy that in ancient times had amassed immeasurable treasures by controlling the trade and shipping passing through the Straits. Russia's linkage to the West in fact depended on the passage through the Bosporus and the Dardanelles, which for centuries has been one of the main arteries of world trade.[3]

A century ago, Halford Mackinder identified southern Russia and the Black Sea region as the "pivot of history."[4] The judgment of this renowned geographer—later advisor to both the British delegation at the Paris Peace Conference and the Allied forces of intervention on the Black Sea's northern shore during the Russian Civil War—was inspired by the constellation of forces prevailing throughout the nineteenth century. During that period, England and Russia were opposing protagonists in a world embracing conflict, its epicenter situated in the Ottoman Empire, with further manifestations in the western Asian and central Asian perimeter of British India. Afghanistan was the perimeter's pivot—the scene of the "Great Game."

Challenged by Russia, and since the end of the eighteenth century on the verge of collapse, the Ottoman Empire was at the heart of the "Eastern Question." This was a term coined for a cluster of conflicts ensuing from Turkey's volatility and its menacing repercussions for the European balance of power—in other words, for a Continental peace and security menaced by ethnic strife in the Balkans and the Levant. In the nineteenth century, the Eastern Question was Europe's continuous calamity.[5] In June 1914 in Sarajevo, it became Europe's doom. And when at the end of the Great War, the Ottoman Empire, together with other dynastically legitimated multiethnic empires, fell apart, a world era had run its course.

In this account, the Eastern Question, especially its Greek ingredient, serves as a historical trope, as a metaphor for historical inquiry and narration.[6] There are good reasons for such a choice—and this independently of the fundamental importance archaic and classical Greece plays as an arsenal and sounding board for the Western tale. In the first place, it reflects the particularities of the spatial perspective introduced above. In the second place, the Greek nation-state, established around 1830, represents a unique fusion of geopolitical and ethnographical interpretive elements, so distinctive for one of our two historical axes.

The Eastern Question will thus organize the topographical dimension of our historical narrative. The narrative's temporal complement revolves around the year 1919—the year of the Paris peace conference, of revolutions and counterrevolutions, of the establishment of a multitude of ethnified nation-states, the drawing of borders, and the onset of endless conflict and strife on the Continent and beyond.[7] And the year 1919 symbolizes a unique merger of both interpretive axes: the axis of universal civil war and the axis of wars and conflicts centered on ethnicity and nationhood.

In 1919, the virtual observer at the legendary steps of Odessa turns his view westward—toward Central Europe.[8] With Moscow at his back, this observer gazes out upon Bucharest, Budapest, and Vienna. Further to the north, Berlin and Warsaw emerge on the horizon. London and Paris are rather remote. But this does not diminish their importance for the course of events on the Continent and in the colonial domain. Far in the West, beyond the line, America awaits its hour.

Witnessed from Odessa, however, history plays itself out in eastern Central Europe. In this region, the Polish national endeavor is particularly suited to a careful retrospective decoding of the epic's ciphers. This is the case for events of both the nineteenth and the twentieth century. For the Polish experience presents us with an exceptionally decisive fusion of the two axes of interpretation—to reiterate, a fusion of elements of national strife with elements of universal civil war. Crucially, both the Eastern Question, with its essential Greek component, and the notorious

Polish question would eventually become bound up closely with the emergence of Russia's power—just as European history in the modern era plays out *sous l'œil des Russes*.[9]

This account will attempt to "argue" history along the proposed double interpretive axes. The events chosen as essential to such an argument have achieved iconographic significance in contemporary European and Western memory. These events are the century's great catastrophes, with German history here occupying a central role. After all, both world wars, with their unprecedented horrors, were German wars, albeit in different ways. These wars brought about an end to American isolationism; they caused America to stretch its power toward Europe and Asia and from there into global supremacy. To a certain extent, it is because of America's involvement in world affairs that the twentieth century can be understood as divided in two: the first half as an epoch of catastrophes that would come to stamp the century's historical countenance; the second half, in sharp contrast, as an epoch of prosperity and welfare—at least for the West as the world's dominant culture.[10]

In any event, the century's dominant historical narration has been determined by its catastrophic first half for both contemporaries of the period and the generations that followed. The horror of the first half has obscured the second half—shrunk it to far less than its actual temporal duration. Awareness of this period has been recast by a collective memory permeated by cataclysm.

The debt owed this temporal dynamic explains the narrative's omissions. Entire continents are ignored—Africa, for instance. Latin America is absent not because it is considered somehow outside of history; but in the face of Europe's catastrophes, the Southern Hemisphere largely operated as an adjacent space. In the century's second half, in the Cold War epoch, history appeared to have been compressed: a frozen time. Its events will be likewise largely ignored in this account. Despite all apocalyptic drama generated by nuclear deterrence and a mutual capacity to destroy the world an indefinite number of times, the Cold War conflict produced forms of conduct tending toward repetition of the constantly same. It is well known that both the Berlin crises in the late fifties and early sixties and the Cuban missile crisis of 1962 pushed the world toward an abyss. A culmination of these crises in nuclear disaster would probably have meant the end of human-kind and with it the end of history. This may suggest a fundamental distinction from genocidal catastrophes: they do not imperil the future existence of the human race. However, their burden on posterity's memory is all the more ferocious.

1

Interpretations

Two Varieties of Universal Civil War

War and Civil War / America and Europe / Balance and Hegemony / Constitution and Nationality / Freedom and Equality / Warfaring Virtues and Mechanized Death / Two Kinds of Anti-Bolshevism / Race and Class / Sea Power and Land Power / Demos and Ethnos / Self-Government and Self-Determination / Fascism and Anti-Fascism / West and East

⁜

O n 10 November 1942, shortly after the landing of American troops on the shores of the North African coast, Ernst Jünger noted in his diary that through his entanglement in current events, he felt like someone caught less in a world war, more in a "universal *civil* war"—a *Weltbürgerkrieg*. The intensity of the struggle at work here was of an entirely different nature than what had been manifest in earlier wars fought by nation-states. In the face of America's involvement, such wars had been reduced to secondary affairs and were basically finished.[1]

The entry sounds rather odd: Nazi Germany had been at war with the detested Bolshevik Soviet Union for over a year. This war displayed all the signs of an ultimate conflict of planetary proportions. Its rules of engagement knew no mercy; indeed, in the East a veritable war of annihilation was unfolding. Nevertheless, Ernst Jünger assigned more historical importance to the arrival of American troops in the European theater. Why did he use the term *Weltbürgerkrieg*, with its strong overtones of the Continental philosophy of history? And just what was so important about America?

America's intervention in a European war is not just reminiscent of its decisive entry into the Great War in the spring of 1917. It also touches on something much more fundamental: on differences between Europe and America that Jünger viewed as scarcely irreconcilable. That author's presentiments regarding the onset of a "universal civil war" were soon confirmed.[2] At the Casablanca Conference in January 1943, Roosevelt and Churchill issued their demand for nothing less than unconditional surrender from the Axis powers. Negotiations were precluded. At the ensuing press conference, the two leaders offered an explanation of the concept of "unconditional surrender."[3] Especially Roosevelt was referring to Ulysses S. ("Unconditional Surrender") Grant, who of course imposed an unconditional capitulation on the southern states.[4]

Unconditional surrender is a principle of submission that usually follows civil war. It rules out any compromise that might allow for the continued existence of both parties. In fact, the co-existence of two governments in a single state is a logical self-contradiction. In an undivided polity, only one party can hold a monopoly on state and governmental use of force (or indeed violence); the vanquished party must be at least subdued and sometimes completely destroyed. For that reason, civil wars are the most brutal wars possible, intensifying animosities and the exercise of violence to a radical degree. The opposition of doctrines, worldviews, and values typically accompanying civil wars may contribute to their rationalization and justification, but their intensity derives from an uncompromising a priori inherent in the very opposition of either-or.

The goal of *political* destruction essential to civil wars generates an unlimited degree of radicalization. States may recognize each other as equal enemies on the basis of their institutional separateness, the mutual violence they exercise thus being limited and subject to the rules of war.[5] This violence does not strive for the enemy's destruction but is satisfied with a complaisance that preserves the existence of both body politics. Hence civil wars and wars between states are conceptual antipodes.

Although civil wars can take various forms, they are inevitably propelled by questions of religion and values, of ideology and principles.[6] Thus civil wars are always also wars of values. Correspondingly, a war of values fought between states will often approach the character of a civil war in its intensity. In this light, it would appear that Ernst Jünger's diary entry was less apocryphal than it seems at first glance. The United States represents a body politic completely different from its European counterparts. And in juxtaposition, yet in opposition, to traditional Continental states, the wars America fought were of a significantly different nature. Over the course of its history, the country has in fact been caught up mainly in conflicts that, as wars of values, have had the basic features of civil wars. This was the case with the War of Independence—an uprising against the English king. "No taxation without representation" was the battle cry of the rebels. The civil war between North and South continues to dominate American memory. America entered World War I with the intention of making the world "safe for democracy." And in turn, participation in World War II was perceived as a "crusade for freedom." Finally, the Cold War—a forty-year period of antagonism between East and West—was a war of values sui generis. Principles of freedom here stood opposed irreconcilably to an ideal of literal social equality.[7]

Hegel observes in passing that, in comparison with traditional polities, America represents a "civil [*bürgerlich*] society without a state."[8] From the Continental European perspective, there is indeed something supraterritorial, even boundless, about the United States, a quality accompanied by strong gravitation toward procedures, abstract values, and doctrines tending to confound traditional European ideas of state and nation. The genesis of the territorial European state rests especially on the neutralization of the political meaning of religious "truth" and therefore on the neutralization of "ideological" conflicts. America, founded on a plurality of denominations beyond power and politics, was remote from a societal order relying on the primacy of the state, as enshrined in Continental tradition. In line with the Hegelian understanding of America, this social construction tends to intervene in the affairs of others, in opposition to European practice. It does so, for example, by maintaining the convention of recognizing not states but only governments considered "lawful" according to its own understanding of legality.[9] At its very core, America's self-perception is revolutionary.

But such a revolutionary universalism differs significantly from both a universalism stemming from the French Revolution and, most markedly, the eudaemonistic experiments pioneered by the Bolsheviks. The American Revolution was blessed by a universalism of human and civil rights *not* confronted with a preexisting order that needed to be transformed. America's historical privilege consisted, as it were, of inventing a new world out of itself. American utopia established itself in the present; Continental revolutions projected their social visions into the future.[10] The exercise of violence in the French and, especially, Russian revolutions sprang from a desire to accelerate historical time. While America was establishing institutions offering a prospect of individual happiness in the here and now, the task of European revolutions was primarily overturning the past, toppling anciens régimes. The Continental traditions were driven by a philosophical-historical telos. America was more fortunate: it has known no *history*, even if it possesses a chronicle of past events.[11]

Beyond its philosophical claims and human pathos, the universalism of the French Revolution had particularistic parameters. Its universal values were dressed in distinctly French garb. This specific national coloring necessarily impeded the spread of freedom and equality; other nations' resistance to universalistic French form imposed through occupation turned increasingly against that form's universal content.[12] Indeed, through its political actions vis-à-vis others, the *république universelle* revealed itself as an imperialist manifestation of the traditional claim previously upheld by the kings of France, the *monarchie universelle*.[13] Napoleonic imperialism as a universalism in French colors consequently unleashed the nationalism of other peoples. For its part, America has persistently neutralized the ethnic and national affiliations of all those aspiring to join the New World commonweal: such aspirants can join only as *individuals*. All other emblems of belonging are relegated to the private sphere. That is the creed of American pluralism, transferred from the plain of denomination to that of ethnicity and culture. *History* in its Continental European meaning must be left behind.

Two contrasting temporal ciphers identify modern political history: 1815 and 1919. Each date stands for a major congress and the international orders resulting from it.[14] And each stands for a historical threshold from which ensuing history would be measured. The ciphers are opposing in that the main task of the Congress of Vienna was to bring a revolutionary epoch to a close,[15] while the outcome of the Paris Peace Conference contributed to a continuation of revolutionary tensions and political upheavals.[16] This tumult would persist through the entire interwar era and culminate in a new catastrophe.

The Congress of Vienna ended the Napoleonic Wars. The principle of balance between the great powers was restored.[17]

Also, the threat of revolution associated with France would be contained, that motherland of unrest placed under guard. In the domain of ideas, philosophy's intrusion into politics, climaxing in the year 1789, was exorcized. In the realm of domestic policies, the Restoration placed legitimist shackles on the principle of popular sovereignty, and it obstructed all popular intentions based on that principle's corollary—the principle of nationality. Moreover, wars were to be waged only *en forme*. For revolutionary *levée en masse*, the arming of citizens and calling up of mass formations, had undermined the absolutist state's strict divisions between military and civil, state and society, foreign and domestic, thus rendering war, as it were, into a boundlessly violent enterprise.[18] It was an event no longer subject to a strict regime and limited to a "theater of war." The use of force broke through all institutional limits. War and revolution fused together, forming a disastrous alliance for years to come. The Restoration had good reasons to tame this new type of warfare, dissolving the national guards and civilian militias that had emerged in the Napoleonic Wars and restricting an officer's career mainly to those deemed apt for it by birth—those belonging to the aristocracy.[19]

The effort to reestablish prerevolutionary conditions consigned the memory of recent "total warfare" to oblivion and resurrected the eighteenth-century *art* of warfare. Battles were to be fought according to the Old Regime's time-tested rules for "cabinet wars," confined to a circumscribed area, directed at limited and symbolically important objects, and pushed toward expeditious arrangements for peace. Strikingly, this continued to apply even in long, drawn-out military undertakings such as the Crimean War (1853–56), in which all sorts of modern war machinery entered into operation—railroads facilitating troop movements, telegraphs transmitting intelligence, trenches being prepared for positional warfare. In any event, the relatively high number of casualties in this war resulted less from the fighting proper than from disease and epidemics.[20]

The war that contained all the ingredients of World War I—Europe's "seminal catastrophe" (George Kennan)—was the American Civil War. The mobilizations by railroad, the massive armies sent into battle, the automatization of killing resulting from the invention of the machine gun, the ambushes carried out by lurking submarines, the involvement and suffering of the civilian population, above all the fusion of warfare and economic productivity, in short, the totalization of war—all these phenomena pointed toward a future still inconceivable in Europe.[21] The Old World certainly took note of the American Civil War, but the meaning of its horrors did not penetrate a European consciousness still shaped by the Restoration of 1815. For the war was unfolding in the New World, "beyond the line," in a civilization that Europe's aristocratic culture considered inferior. Following his brief comment about America as a civil society without a state, Hegel remarks in his *Philosophy of History* that the New World "will no longer concern us."

The taming of warfare in the post-Napoleonic era was the result of resolutions and measures introduced by the Restoration. The reestablished repression of popular demands based on the principle of nationality and popular sovereignty was meant to guarantee stability, order, and peace.[22] Revolution, rebellion, and unrest were to be ruthlessly confined. This was not astonishing. For the eastern powers, especially for the Hapsburg monarchy, considerable dangers inhered in the principle of popular sovereignty, not only for the political regime itself but also for the very integrity of the empire. In the end, such a principle threatened the fabric and existence of any multiethnic state.[23]

The conversion of the institutional principle of popular sovereignty into a series of metastasizing questions of nationalities marks one basic difference between the political cultures of Western and Eastern Europe. While revolutionary ferment in the West, more specifically in Paris in 1830 and 1848, expressed itself in the political language of "class," toward the East it had increasingly adapted the language of "nationality." And while social conflict in the West was embodied in the iconic urban barricade—class against class—in Europe's East such conflict took on ethnic colors. Barricades now became borders.[24]

In the classical West, popular sovereignty was mediated by political institutions. This culture of institutional mediation was modern in that it relied on the ideals and promises of the Enlightenment. For the narrative material of collective memory, it drew on those events that had contributed to the constitution of just those institutions. These events were mostly revolutions, hence political actions that had had an effect on the commonweal and had glorified the achieved freedoms of estate or class. Increasingly, these freedoms were being claimed on the basis of higher principles and in the name of all. In this manner, the freedoms pointed beyond their particular origins, consequently toward the universal.

There was also a demand for freedom and liberties in the East, in the premodern contexts of multinationally composed empires, where social stratification and ethnic fragmentation overlap. This resulted in a unique intermeshing of class-based social semantics with the emblematics of culture, religion, and ethnic belonging. Conflicts originally rooted in social structure and hierarchies of estate were increasingly rationalized in ethnic and national terms.[25] From this perspective, it is hardly surprising that the social revolution that broke out in Paris in July 1830 led in October to the national Polish uprising, or that France's February revolution of 1848 mutated further eastward into the "springtime of nations."[26]

One of the unsettling certainties of the Restoration order established in 1815 was that acceding to demands for popular sovereignty and the principle of nationality would have far-reaching consequences for a European peace based on the balance of power. It was particularly in the interest of the dynastically legitimated multinational Hapsburg and Romanov empires to thwart such demands and to challenge the peril of revolution that accompanied them. For Austria, the peril stemmed chiefly from the nationalities question; for Russia, it also stemmed from the increasingly apparent social question. England, although keeping its distance from the autocratic Eastern powers, was first and foremost concerned with questions of stability. Intervening only by proxy, the British avoided direct involvement in Continental affairs, upheavals, and popular unrest. For them, the power balance was a prerequisite for expanding beyond the seas. France in turn was eager to undermine the system established in Vienna in 1815. Especially in the wake of the 1848 revolution and the establishment of the Second Empire by Napoleon III, France was increasingly inclined to promote the nationality principle everywhere. Through its support of national movements, Paris did its outmost to remove the constrictions imposed on the motherland of revolution by the 1815 system. By promoting Italian unification, and to some extent facilitating the road to German unity as well, the Second Empire—to be sure, unintentionally—brought disaster on itself.[27]

The Vienna order would secure peace and stability for decades to come. Conflict, competition, and rivalry among the powers were moved from the center to the periphery of Europe, where measures were undertaken to calibrate the balance between them. This locus was the Orient and the Levant—the domain of the Ottoman Empire, the last universal Muslim power. It was, in fact, the traditional dumping ground of European politics. The term "Eastern Question" covered the empire's decay and its effects: the national awakening of peoples with long historical memories such as the Serbs and the Greeks; the great-power rivalry in the Straits, the Balkans, and the eastern Mediterranean—principally the long-term antagonism between England and Russia. These problems threatened not only to undermine the European system of order and stability but also to wash away the institutional and political pillars supporting the Vienna order.[28]

The Greek war of independence introduced the European powers to the potentially grim consequences of new states being established on the basis of ethnic affiliation and nationality.[29]

Greek independence involved a clear break with the principle of legitimacy so dear to the Eastern powers, especially the Hapsburg Empire. At the same time, such ethnically grounded states—carved from the soft fabric of multinational empires—generated endless conflicts, uprooting and eradicating those populations not seeming to belong to the titulary nation. The great powers thus demanded that the new Greek state grant its Catholic population, starting with the Franciscan order, the same rights as Hellenic Greeks. Accordingly, in the London Protocol of 1830 the Greek state committed itself to equal treatment of the non-Orthodox population. At the 1878 Congress of Berlin, this formal commitment would serve as a precedent for introducing minority protection in the newly independent Balkan states of Montenegro, Serbia, and Rumania.[30]

The concern of the great powers with protecting groups whose ethnicity or religion did not necessarily fit into the new, nationally conceived states reflected a sharpened awareness of problems that had become virulent under the sign of the national question. The Congress of Vienna had a general political mandate to disregard the claims of popular sovereignty in favor of dynastic legitimacy. But the Polish nation, although divided, was granted the exceptional privilege of preserving its language and culture.[31] In general the great powers took an active interest in national questions solely out of concern for broader political stability. Greece's independence as the first "ethnic" state was due to a compromise between Russia, England, and France aimed at newly adjusting the European balance of power. Even the czar—the "gendarme" of the Continental order of legitimacy restored in 1815 and the infatuated instigator of the value-rooted Holy Alliance—supported the establishment of the new "ethnic" state. That state was understood as a mere deviation, meant to increase his influence in the Straits and the Aegean. The deviation was in line with his policy of expansion at the cost of the Ottoman Empire, Russia's eternal foe in the region and key to the core conflict at work in the notorious

Eastern Question. However, the czar's anomalous decision ignored Austria's existential interest in thwarting any application of the nationality principle.[32]

During the revolutionary ferment of 1848–49, the czar intervened on behalf of the Hapsburg Empire. However, a short time later Austria chose to play a dubious role in the Crimean War, infuriating the czar by not siding with its old Russian ally but rather pursuing its own selfish interests in the strategically and economically important Danube principalities. The formerly close and intimate relationship between the two "black eagles" now permanently deteriorated. In the future Russia would no longer be prepared to stand by an Austria increasingly mired in imbroglios related to the nationalities question. Piedmont-Sardinia and Prussia seized the historical moment and fulfilled their national missions.[33] While Piedmont promoted the Risorgimento with French help, Prussia went to war against Austria in 1866 to force a military resolution to the lingering "dualism" between the two dominant German Confederation powers.

As a result of its defeat, Austria was ousted from the German domain and pushed toward the southeast—a development not without severe historical consequences.[34] After the "arrangement" with Hungary in 1867—an attempt to secure the monarchy by defusing if not resolving one of its most pressing nationality questions—the Austro-Hungarian Empire would persistently come up against the national demands of the southeastern Slavic peoples.[35] Their strivings threatened to erode the empire from within while simultaneously entangling it in future external military enterprises. The conflicts with Russia in the Balkans would become notorious, culminating in a confrontation that would destroy old Europe.[36]

The events in the Balkans preceding the First World War bore all the hallmarks of ethnically based territorial conflicts. The decline of the Ottoman Empire and the emergence of future nation-states based on language and autocephalous churches pushed the newly awakened peoples into military conflicts with their former imperial masters as well as one another. And while the new states claimed national or religious homogeneity, the extraordinary intensity of their disputes over borders and populations took the shape of military confrontations stamped with the horrors of "ethnic cleansing," as the phenomenon would eventually be called.[37] Thus the Balkan Wars of 1912–13, fought mainly over the Ottoman province of Macedonia, were notorious for an intensity and ferocity alien to wars between established European states that were still being conducted in the traditional way. While the latter wars were primarily military affairs, the former were carried out as ethnic civil wars.[38] The so-called Balkan atrocities were inflicted not just on opposing armies but to a large extent on civilian populations. Those groups not fulfilling the requirement of belonging to the dominant ethnic group became targets of merciless violence. This unrestrained use of force was referred to at the time as "demographic warfare." It was anything but European war *en forme*.[39]

Although the Great War was sparked by events in the Balkans, the circumstances leading up to it suggest a much wider range of causes, both short-term and long-term.[40] For some time now, the European balance had been shaken, the traditional nineteenth-century constellations supplanted by a rather paradoxical dualism of alliances. The so-called revolution of alliances that finally evolved in the 1890s had brought an end to the long-term rivalry between England and France and the enduring antagonism between England and Russia. This was especially the case in two realms: that of the Eastern Question in the Balkans and the Levant and that of the Great Game in Asia; the revolution's result was a transformation of the European power system. At the same time, military technology was being revolutionized; armies and fleets had been expanded enormously. The political and logistical mechanics of mobilization were now extremely sophisticated, intermeshing with intangibles linked to the Continent's network of alliances.

Everything seemed to have changed deeply, with a single exception: Austro-Hungary continued to wrestle with its nationalities problem and constantly threatened to come into conflict with Russia in the Balkans. Events in 1908 thus already prefigured the constellation of 1914. In response to the Young Turk revolution in Constantinople, the Hapsburg monarchy risked annexing the provinces of Bosnia and Herzogovina, which it was administering as a result of the Berlin Congress of 1878.[41] This development sparked a vehement protest by Serbia and denunciation by Russia. But the czarist empire was too weakened by its defeat in the Russo-Japanese War of 1904–5 and the ensuing revolution in 1905 to be taken seriously as a military threat. Humiliated by Germany, which sided with the Austro-Hungarian monarchy, Russia backed off. In July 1914, the situation was different. Mobilizing its army, Russia finally interceded for Serbia. For its part, a modernized Germany, which in Prussian form had managed to push Austria out of the German confederation in the direction of the Balkans in 1866, now found itself allied with a rather traditional Hapsburg Empire, an entity that had transferred its unresolved nationalities problem into the arena of great power politics, hence from the Continent's periphery into the heart of Europe. And since Austro-Hungary had become the "pivot" of German foreign policy,[42] its problems were passed on to Germany. The events unleashing the world war were in any case the expression of a failing tied to the retrograde elements in nineteenth-century politics. In 1914 it seemed that just what the Congress of Vienna had sought to prevent had come to pass: a linkage of tensions created by issues of nationality with the imponderables of great-power politics.

Initially, the intention was to wage a war *en forme;* a brief campaign was envisioned. But the war's character soon changed, in a manner allowing none of the restraint in the application of military force manifest in the wars of the nineteenth century.[43] All previous limits were surpassed. And as long as unlimited resources could be sacrificed to the Moloch of war, nothing seemed to stand in the way of its lasting forever.[44] In the end, the entire economy of the warring states was marshaled in its service. And the more it became a total war, the more it resembled a civil war.[45]

But can the Great War really be described as a "civil war"? This in fact appears doubtful. Despite the magnitude of its violent dynamism, it was not marked by any clash between two camps laying a global claim to truth[46]—the sort of clash between opposing value systems, ideas, and worldviews figuring so prominently in Europe's wars of religion, the French Revolution, even the American War of Independence. This is the case despite the propaganda emanating from both sides to the effect that this was a war of ideas.[47] The labor and sacrifices being demanded of everyone required justification, and appropriate words were easily found. "Heroes" thus confronted "shopkeepers," French superficiality German profundity, German socialism Russian despotism, culture civilization.[48]

A cultural-historical interpretation of political mentalities might approach the Great War as a struggle of ideas, but this corresponds less to reality than to the exalted self-understanding of nations bludgeoning one another on the field of battle.[49] Above all, the enmity between Germany and England produced opulent portraits composed of hate-filled motifs. The German Empire saw itself as an exceptionally modern European state that was attempting to alter the existing power relations. It felt that England, a conservative empire committed to the status quo, was an obstacle in the path of its destiny. Patronized as "English," rational, utilitarian, and empirical values were both dismissed as mere externalities and invested with attributes such as hypocrisy, self-delusion, and fraud—in short, scorned as "bourgeois liberalism," whose exponents had to be brought low.[50] In the face of this exultant Germany, England saw itself as a citadel of steadfastness, its proud mission lying in bringing others "the law": the norms and values of the status quo Britain represented, emerging from the nineteenth-century power arrangement and with a canon of virtue consisting of duty, honor, dependability, and social stability symbolized in both sport and the conventions of chivalry. As the British perceived it, these public values were thrown into question by the importune German *Machtstaat* with its noisy modernity.[51] And further, the German Reich was now granted the role of troublemaker previously assigned to France as the motherland of revolution. In fact, especially in its conduct of war Germany was considerably less squeamish about using means destined to transform old Europe from the ground up. Reason of war trumped customs of war.[52] In fighting the war, the German high command not only concerned itself with the imperial cohesion of its eastern adversary, aiming to chop it into national morsels. It also struck at its very social order by helping Lenin and the Bolsheviks. The decomposition of the Russian Empire and the outbreak of revolution corresponded to the German inclination to break up the constellation of the two-front war.[53]

For Germany the world war became a struggle to break free from conventions identified with the archenemy England: a banally experienced world, a materialism averse to everything metaphysical, a despicable reality of exchange, trade, and money earning. Germany wanted to change the world; England was straining to preserve it. In the end, a struggle was being played out here between hierarchal orders bound up with two different epochs, one past, the other future:[54] England was the dominant power in a waning century; Germany hoped to lead the coming century. From this perspective, the Great War can indeed be viewed as a war between cultures—in the words of Franz Marc, a "European civil war."[55]

Nonetheless, the concept of civil war—and certainly of universal civil war—can hardly be applied to World War I. The concept of universal civil war presumes a secular schism in which state loyalties and national distinctions are undermined by an opposition of classes or values. Nevertheless, within the divergent sociocultural awareness of contemporaries, this power struggle may well have taken on the meaning of a civil war; in any event, it intensified the ideological enthusiasm of the warring parties,[56] even if the violence raging in the European slaughterhouse did not adhere to any antithesis of basic values.[57] At best, this war might be considered a "European civil war" in which exalted middle classes faced off in the trenches with the differently, nationally colored values of their bourgeois constituencies.[58] And yet, such an overextended notion of civil war does little to illuminate the violent cataclysms that brought down old Europe. The Great War can be described as a civil war only insofar as each side aimed at the total defeat of the other. But it was not a war of antipodal, socially anchored worldviews, a war splitting the configuration of nations along fault lines of class and values.

Until the sudden onset of the Great War, the menace of catastrophe had remained hidden. Nothing comparable had loomed on the prewar era's perceptual horizon. Only a few dared imagine the war of the future.[59] The potency of the destructive forces lay dormant, encoded in a mechanization of weaponry that would shatter all established conventions of European warfare.[60] It would have a devastating impact on the consciousness of a fading world numbed and narcotized by the virtues of predictability. The blessings of technology and progress, until then celebrated as an inexhaustible source of social wealth, as liberation from hardship and misery, were now inverted, mercilessly revealing their destructive side.[61]

From the right distance, the catastrophe of the Great War can be understood as a collision between the forces of industrialization and technical progress and a premodern sensibility, largely agrarian in its conception of the world and its values.[62] This premodern sensibility was by no means universal. But it managed to find a niche precisely in that locus where destructive potential has always been sheltered: in the ranks of the military. The officer's career was pursued mainly by members of the nobility and by bourgeois individuals oriented toward aristocratic norms and ways of life.[63] Bound to the traditions and values of the past, the military acted as a brake on the otherwise overwhelming tide of modernization. Indeed, it prided itself on preserving more of tradition than any other socially and politically relevant institution or class, even if this was primarily a matter of forms, conventions, and mentality. At the same time, the technological innovations of an industrial society were pouring into the ever-expanding military apparatus, transforming its armies and fleets. This heralded a fateful fusion of modern weaponry and the traditional conduct of war, though the military remained unaware of its dire potential. Europe's civilization was hurled blindly into a cosmos of destruction—a trauma that would permanently stamp the twentieth century.[64]

The actual gravedigger of the European century was less the political will to destruction than the conduct of the war, which slipped from the control of those meant to direct it. In retrospect, the breach in the body and the spirit of the nineteenth century is clearly visible. At the Battle of the Somme in 1916, British troops marched toward the German lines in formation to the sound of bagpipes without seeking cover, kicking a rugby ball ahead of them as they marched. They seemed stoically unfazed by the prospect of death in a hail of machine-gun fire.[65] For their part, the German gunners merely had to reload their machine guns. They could not believe their eyes: the British were marching to their doom like lemmings, their officers at the fore.

In his "patriotic reflections," Werner Sombart mocked the British mode of combat. He was repelled by their idea of transferring "fair play" from the rugby pitch to the battlefield. In his view, the idea stemmed from their being a nation of traders. Nothing was really existential; everything was a game.[66] The German military may well have considered the British assault on the Somme as having a sharply unreal quality, as bizarrely ritualized, compared with the practice of other armies. But in fact, the British conduct was not so fundamentally different, for soldiers from other countries also repeatedly ran toward the enemy's machine-gun positions, as if they hoped to convince the mechanical devices of the enduring superiority of human resources. Beyond the clash of armies was another between man and machine.[67] It was as if the premodern virtues of daring, courage, and self-sacrifice were futilely rising one last time against the automatized efficiency of the world of machines. David Jones has called the Somme offensive the last great exploit of the Old World. After the offensive, nothing was the same; the conventions of warfare had been fundamentally transformed.[68] In Ernst Jünger's view, war and life itself had assumed a new *Gestalt:* the machines had taken command.[69]

The machine gun's impact on the battlefields of the Great War was staggering.[70] It enhanced the already-privileged position of defense in relation to attack to a degree that had been inconceivable. A single machine-gun nest could break many assault waves, and when combined with barbed wire, the defensive positions were virtually impenetrable. Only tanks would allow a renewed mobilization of offense. But before they arrived on the scene, an entire generation would expire on Europe's killing fields. In any event, the armies' command staffs, spatially distant and perceptually estranged from the war front, made no efforts to abandon the strategy of attrition, the bleeding to death of the adversary.[71] In a Sisyphean effort, they pinned their hopes on even more firepower, more massed men, and a fresh, perhaps decisive offensive that would finally lead to the long hoped-for breakthrough.[72]

The war, which had long since mobilized the home front with all its resources, became total when the machine gun rendered defense impregnable. Some 80 percent of all the Great War's casualties were a result of this weapon. The horrific effects of gas and automatic artillery also spread a great deal of terror,[73] but the machine gun acquired a special status on the European battlefields. Although it had been around before 1914, there was little awareness of what it meant.

This mental blindness had various causes. One was the romantic-aristocratic image of the battlefield, despite all technological advances still oriented toward a rapid campaign. The generals believed that the key to victory was rigorous training, audacity, and the resolve of the foot soldier, trained in the offensive use of the rifle and bayonet. Years of exacting instruction were required for a British rifleman to fire his weapon in rapid succession.[74] French infantry soldiers were themselves drilled exclusively in offensive tactics. In 1913, General Joseph Joffre insisted that the sole precept the French army knew was attack, even at the expense of heavy losses; any other approach was contrary to the nature of warfare and hence to be spurned. The tactical assault, he observed, culminated in the élan of the bayonet thrust.[75] Astonishingly, despite developments in long-range weaponry, the *arme blanche* was still held in huge esteem by the commanders in chief. The same was true for the cavalry, embodying the classic aristocratic form of warfare. Despite the broad devastation caused by the machine gun and the gruesome hindrance posed by barbed wire, there were repeated cavalry attacks—and this despite the fact that the Russo-Japanese War had already made clear to anyone who could see that the machine gun had voided their efficacy. An observer of the battles in the Far East had noted wryly that in view of the machine gun's frightful firepower, the cavalry now had no function other than to cook rice for the infantry.[76]

Even as late as 1926, the former commander of the British Expeditionary Forces in France, General Sir Douglas Haig, was not prepared to give up his romantic image of warfare. He was convinced that aircraft and tanks had only a supporting role in any decisive operation; the final blow would still be delivered by the infantry's bayonet charge and the charge of the cavalry, wielding bared sabers like outstretched lances.[77] The cult of the horse and the naked blade was apparently the last attempt on the part of the traditional warrior caste to escape the increasing depersonalization of warfare.

The resistance before World War I among the higher eche-lons of the British (and not only British) officer corps to accept-ing the machine gun for what it was—namely, an indiscriminate weapon exponentially increasing defensive capacities—was thus in part a consequence of the proverbial antimodernism of officer-gentlemen. Motivated by romantic conceit, their traditionally self-reproducing warrior caste did indeed work to discredit this envoy of the industrial age as an "unfair weapon." Hence instead of en-trusting the flat-firing machine gun to the infantry, it was shunted off to the artillery, with its ballistic ordnance. In France automatic weapons were first incorporated into the approved arsenal in 1910. The Germans were far more open-minded on this score. As early as the Franco-Prussian War (1870–71), Prussian forces had used machine guns in the battle at Wissembourg, although only sporadically and while advancing. The weapon's enormous po-tential as a defensive asset thus remained unrecognized.[78]

In any event, traditions and mentalities alone were not re-sponsible for virtually expelling the machine gun from the Euro-pean imagination before the Great War. In the first place, there was the Gatling gun, a weapon that had been developed outside Europe, in the New World during the American Civil War,[79] where, in an alarming but potent dialectic, the mobilizing of mass armies had led to the invention of a weapon of mass destruction. Even in the United States, however, the memory of the machine gun and its destructive power was steadily fading. It was barely used in the Indian wars. General Custer did not have one at the Battle of the Little Bighorn in 1876.[80] In the second place, it was primarily used *outside* the military's perimeters, as a police weapon in quelling strikes and other forms of labor unrest.[81] The weapon's superiority in this context was due to its mechanical advantages: automatic fire reversed the unfavorable relation between the few custodians of the law and their many opponents. This was especially the case in a situation where few stood against many by definition: in the colonies. Long before the Great War, the machine gun was used to enhance the power of the "white man" over the "native" population. Strictly speaking, it was an instrument of colonial subjugation. Indeed, the domination of Africa in the age of imperialism around the turn of the century would have been inconceivable without the machine gun's intimidating powers.[82]

In the European battle theater, the machine gun, an essentially colonial weapon, would prove to be a Trojan horse for precisely those power relations taken for granted in the overseas colonies, but whose significance had remained hidden to the increasingly racist European consciousness. It transferred the violence exercised unceremoniously on the colonial periphery to the heart of old Europe, contributing substantially to its destruction. Once again, the secret of this destruction was the denial of a dramatic reversal: the weapon's automatic mechanism had nurtured the white man's illusion that when the few defeated the many, this was due to natural superiority rather than the instrument at his disposal.

Like the comparable images of slaughter from Langemark, Ypres, Verdun, Isonzo, and other Continental battlefields, the stoic readiness of the British troops on the Somme again and again to storm German positions defended by machine guns and surrounded by barbed wire barriers, despite murderous repulse,[83] may have elicited a bewilderment in outside observers similar to that sparked in the typical scenarios of colonial warfare—indeed, a similar sense of "magic." In 1898 in the Battle of Omdurman, the British army, assisted by indigenous auxiliary troops led by Kitchener and including young Winston Churchill among its officers, employed six Maxim machine guns to mow down the proud warriors of the Mahdi by the thousands. This was, in fact, no battle but a massacre,[84] for the charging Mahdi warriors refused to understand the machine gun's enormous firepower.

In light of later events on the Great War battlefields, it seems doubtful that the white man really understood his own weapon. How could the nature of his superiority in the colonies have escaped him? Was he unable to recognize that it was the automatic weapon that permitted the few to rule over so many, and not the natural blessings of race? Actually the colonial masters were not so simpleminded. Among the British military forces in Africa, only officers, hence white men, were allowed to handle machine guns. The native troops were not to gain any knowledge of their mechanics—of the precondition for white rule. Such caution reveals a self-reflective insight captured ironically in an anti-imperialist couplet: "Whatever happens, we have got / The Maxim Gun, and they have not."[85] And yet, there was no great desire to renounce the racist illusion of a superiority that was God-given, not simply the result of the machine gun's firepower.

The subjection of those who were colonized would not last for ever. Paradoxically, the Great War pushed things forward: for the first time nonwhite colonial troops appeared on Europe's battlefields; for the sake of military efficacy, they were not only *allowed* to kill white soldiers but were ordered to do so. By participating in the carnage, they achieved an equality that, although precarious, nevertheless contrasted with their usual colonial subjugation.[86] Many of the early nonwhite anticolonialist leaders thus emerged from the emancipatory trenches of World War I.[87]

The equality issuing from Europe's killing fields was universal. In the face of the machine gun, everyone could serve the apparatus of death—workers, peasants, the nobility, the bourgeoisie. The machine gun simply cancelled attributes and capabilities, whether inherited or acquired, mental or physical. The finger on the trigger made everyone lord of the battlefield. In the Great War's struggle for survival, the barriers of class and estate were transcended, their value having plunged into an abyss.

Machines make people equal. Already in the nineteenth century, civil equality had advanced together with the industrialization process. But the equality had been circumscribed, shackled politically in the traditional legitimacies. Now, however, equality achieved a breakthrough precisely at the point where it had become existential: in the indiscriminate slaughter of the battle-field; in the trenches defended by machine-gun emplacements.[88] Such an experience of equality could not be easily forgotten. Once the Great War came to an end, it demanded its political tribute.

But the equality ratified on the battlefields soon provoked a re-action: ideological objections to the leveling experience of auto-matic equality. Those objecting were inclined toward a staging of martial individuality and exclusivity. They wished to reawaken aristocratic values and virtues. During the war, few men could participate in action in the skies. In that realm, through the air duel, the dogfight, it was tempting to nurture the illusion of a long-gone world, one sunk into ruins. But the exhausted duel of the flyers could not revive mentalities refuted by the machinery of war.[89] Those upholding status, class, and estate had to go else-where to voice their protest against equality and the machine.

Increasingly, the disillusioned German veterans of trench warfare found a substitute for the world of experience lost in the war in one particular location: that where, following the decline of the old world, social equality tried to acquire a revolutionary hear-ing. This equality was mercilessly repressed by a force hardened in the experience of the front: "praetorians against proletarians";[90] counterrevolutionary in the face of the domestic enemy, national-ist or even racist in the face of the external enemy. The Freikorps were executors of such a force—not least in service to the Weimar Republic.[91] They were deployed against the Spartacists and rebel-lious workers in the suppression of the republic of councils in Mu-nich and to smother the violence that flared up in the Ruhr in the spring of 1920. These "wanderers into the void" were also sent into action on the now-fluid eastern frontier,[92] where they were used to brutally quell strikes as well as Polish nationalist stirrings.[93] This counterrevolutionary violence surfaced most sharply in the Baltic, where the struggle against Reds, Latvians, and Estonians was ethnically and socially charged to the same degree.[94] The

Freikorps here revealed itself as a civil war's racist army. The so-called Baltics cultivated a form of fighting attributed with special cruelty and recklessness.[95] In view of the executed horrors and devastation, Ernst von Salomon, a machine gunner in the Lieber-mann Freikorps, spoke of a burning of "the bourgeois tablets, laws, and values of the civilized world."[96] The historic borderland of the Baltic had become a special battle zone in the Russian Civil War. Various social and ethnic conflicts mingled in a ferment of political mentalities later distilled into Nazism. A special variety of anti-Bolshevism was taking shape.

Truly unusual protagonists, only inadequately described by the distinction between red and white, confronted each other in the Baltic region. The confrontation reflected both the fronts formed in the civil war and the complex circumstances behind the genesis of the Baltic states, especially Estonia and Latvia. The equivocal attitude of the Allied powers confused the situation even more. France and the United States supported the counterrevolutionary Russian Whites in the civil war in the Baltic, committing themselves to preserving "the only and indivisible Russia." In contrast, England stood by the Baltic states in their quest for independence,[97] for instance, dispatching a squadron into the Baltic Sea to assist the governments of Estonia and Latvia. This situation, baffling enough to begin with, was further complicated by the presence of German formations, mobilized as part of the anti-Bolshevik intervention on orders from the Allies and on the basis of Article 12 of the Compiègne armistice. These formations had been sent to the Baltic by the Reich government to prevent a Bolshevik advance into East Prussia, as well as to provide cover for the withdrawal of regular German units no longer willing to serve in combat. They comprised German-Baltic units of the so-called Landeswehr, in addition to Freikorps forces. Together with the first Guard Reserve Division, transferred from East Prussia to Cour-land, they were combined into the Iron Division under the command of Major Bischoff. The German Legion under Otto

Wagener, later Hitler's Reich economy commissar, also deserves mention. Count Rüdiger von der Goltz was appointed commander in chief over all the German troops.[98]

Although the German units had been sent to the Baltic for defensive purposes and to fight the Bolsheviks, they were viewed with suspicion by the Estonians and especially the Latvians. The not unjustified feeling was that under the pretext of anti-Bolshevik intervention, the units had been sent to reinforce the German Balts and, if possible, to undermine the hard-earned independence of the Baltic republics with the help of the counterrevolutionary White Russian warlords. In April 1919, units of the German-Baltic Landwehr overthrew the Latvian government in Liepāja, which sparked opposition from the Entente. The British issued an ultimatum calling for the withdrawal of the German units or their subordination under Latvian command. There were similar clashes between such units and the Estonian military.[99]

However the conflicts between Reds, Whites, Latvians, Estonians, Germans, Russians, and Allied intervention forces evolved, the battles on the Baltic frontier revealed a special potential for violence. This stemmed from the unusual blend of civil war on national disputes, already enflamed during the world war by plans of the German Reich to annex and settle the region.[100] After the war, the German government dropped such plans. But with rumors spreading in the Reich that the Latvian government was willing to reward mercenaries with both citizenship and land for settlement, soldiers proved increasingly willing to serve on the Baltic front of the Russian Civil War. Disillusioned with the situation at home, many Freikorps fighters were ready to move elsewhere. These "last Germans" (Ernst von Salomon's term for them) enriched the already confusing situation tied to the Baltic civil war with an additional, colonial dimension.

In this way, the Baltic conflict was marked by a merger of national, colonial, and counterrevolutionary motives. In Courland, Livonia, and Estonia, the merger led to support for the

German-Baltic element by *reichsdeutsch* irregulars. The measures taken in the February 1917 revolution had already stripped these people of their privileges, hence of their historically embedded social position. As a result of that position, they had become a paramount, visible object of both nationalistic and social revolutionary violence: a double threat deriving from the overlapping of ethnic origin and social status typical of the Baltic territories. To be a German meant to be a merchant, a landowner, the lord of a manor—in short, a baron. "Latvian," on the other hand, signified a dependent farmer who performed menial tasks. In the end, this overlapping of ethnicity and social standing led to a fusion of the struggle of classes and estates with "national" conflicts into one and the same event. This was especially the case when, filled with social hatred, the peasants began to ransack and set aflame the nobility's estates. Such an explosion took place in Riga in 1905, and the unrest there soon spread to the countryside in Courland and Livonia, where above all the German-Baltic landowners were targeted. In circumstances resembling a civil war, there were dozens of deaths; over five hundred manor houses were plundered and destroyed.[101] These events functioned as a social and political alarm signal—one prompting the creation of a nationalistically colored German self-defense association.

The fact that many of the first prominent Nazis stemmed from the Baltic-German milieu does not necessarily imply a general tendency among the German populace there. Nevertheless, the specific experience of the Baltic conflict, with its distinctive fusion of "race" and "class," may have influenced the diverse political orientations entering into Nazism. Alfred Rosenberg is here a good example, Estonia-born and raised and eventually finding his vocation as "Reich minister for the occupied eastern territories." Another is Max Erwin von Scheubner-Richter; already active in 1905 in Baltic-German self-defense, he marched at Hitler's side to the Feldherrnhalle during the beer hall putsch in November 1923, where he was shot down by the police in a hail of bullets, an early "martyr of the movement." Nazi artist Otto von Kursell and the virulent anti-Semitic propagandist and Nazi diplomat Arno Schickedanz had belonged to the same student fraternity in Riga.[102] The Balts were conspicuous in the Nazi Party. In fact, they were so numerous among the party journalists that Hitler joked about the *Völkischer Beobachter* being a Baltic paper. As it was, Hitler's anti-Bolshevism was deeply influenced by the German Balts.[103] A considerable number of the irregulars transferred from the Reich to the Baltic in the "year of decision," 1918–19, would later join the ranks of the Nazi party, especially the SA. Most of the SA leaders assassinated in June 1934 in the "Night of the Long Knives" (the so-called Röhm putsch) had been Freikorps fighters, and many had seen combat in the Baltic.[104]

The unbridled violence of the Baltic battles was directed against the Bolsheviks *and* the eastern peoples, deemed socially and ethnically inferior.[105] Indeed, it was this violence that lent the Freikorps a certain allure. In their clashes on the "frontier"— against Poles in Upper Silesia, Latvians and Estonians in the Baltic—the Freikorps and other irregulars experienced highly violent conditions approximating those found in the colonies. Indeed, a surprisingly large number of the older Freikorps officers had served in Africa and were apparently accustomed to the unrestrained use of force.[106] Also, the Freikorps indulged in a kind of aestheticizing of violence, expressed in an array of rituals and symbols that would later be assimilated into insignia of the Nazi elite: the silver death's head on the cockade of the Iron Division or the white swastika of the Ehrhardt Brigade. The praetorians of the civil war harbored a deep hatred of the Weimar Republic, and their commanders even toyed with the idea of forging a military and settler state in the Baltic–East Prussian domain. The idea was to use such a state as a base from which to assault and destroy the loathed democratic regime in Berlin. The Ehrhardt Brigade, active mostly in the Reich and providing the main counterrevolutionary storm troops in the Lüttwitz-Kapp putsch of March 1920, embarked on such a venture.[107] After being disbanded, some of its former members belonging to the "Organization Consul" helped murder Republican politicians such as Matthias Erzberger and Walther Rathenau, prompting Reich Chancellor Wirth's famous outcry, "This enemy is on the right!"

Not all Freikorps members went on to join the Nazi movement. But wherever they were active—from the civil war against the Reds within the Reich to the ethnic struggles in the Baltic borderland—mentalities emerged that nurtured *völkisch* and Nazi tendencies. These mentalities coalesced into a racist anti-Bolshevik weltanschauung that differed fundamentally from Western-style, liberal-democratic anti-Bolshevism. While the latter was based on a concern with forms of society and modes of social encoding, as manifest in the real world, the Nazis transformed Bolshevism into a biological phenomenon. In other words, their distinctions were centered not on a *political*, socially grounded opposition of classes and values but rather on a racist conception of ethnicity. In short, for Nazism, Bolshevism was less a political than a racial attribute fusing the "Slavic sub-race" with the "Jewish intelligentsia."[108]

In the twentieth century, when it came to interpreting reality in social terms, a pair of concepts associated with the Enlightenment and deriving from the late eighteenth-century revolutions stood opposed to each other: freedom and equality.[109] The concept of freedom basically denoted liberation from the traditional ties of an estate-based, corporative nature. It was grounded in the principle of the free individual whose obligations to society were construed as an expression of free will. Such contractualism is, of course, pivotal to Western political philosophy, especially its Anglo-American variety. For its part, the concept of equality, originally understood as equality before the law, increasingly evolved into a concept antithetical to freedom, the two concepts having acquired contrary social meanings in the first third of the nineteenth century, as an outcome of the French Revolution's radical tendencies.[110] Within the socialist tradition and in Marxism, this opposition was expressed as that between the bourgeoisie and the proletariat. The great powers themselves gravitated toward one or another of these dominant concepts, value decisions here being tied to both geographical constants and traditions reaching far behind the century's temporal horizon. In turn, spatially anchored modes of life and the resulting political cultures left their mark on the internal constitution of the various polities.[111]

In this respect, the difference between maritime and continental political cultures would have lasting significance.[112] Maritime civilizations such as England tended to limit monarchic rule, institute a separation of powers, and create a more civic society. The insularity conferred by nature protected the community from various tribulations suffered by the continental powers. Having emerged from the older empires, these powers were beset by territorial conflicts and standing armies that shaped their inner circumstances and ways of life, allowing scant scope for individual rights.[113] In contrast, the constitutions of maritime polities reflected their civil societies; at the same time, the external use of force by these polities was distinctive. Simply by deploying their navies and the destructive power they wielded from a distance, they were able to protect their political cultures from contamination by the direct use of force. Although their use of such force was total, it was well beyond their shores. This was the case with both economic blockades and the indiscriminate use of force connected with long-range weaponry.[114] In this way, the threat of strategic aerial warfare with intercontinental missiles continues to reflect the basic approach of the maritime powers.[115]

During World War II, the weapons turned to by the Anglo-Saxon powers for use against Germany and Japan manifestly reflected the same strategy. The reduction to ash of German cities from the air and the dropping of atomic bombs on Hiroshima and Nagasaki reflected a policy of using unlimited air space to crush the adversary,[116] very much the policy of insular sea powers operating from a great distance. The atomic bomb averted a lengthy land war, much feared by maritime powers. In this way, civil society's political culture was shielded inside the country from any mental fallout that might have arisen from the application of total force abroad.

Compared with the sea powers and the force at their disposal, deployable from a safe distance, continental states are at a great disadvantage. Their largely terrestrial force makes physical proximity more or less unavoidable, with lasting consequences for their domestic conditions. As suggested, continental powers must maintain standing armies, and in states of emergency, the soldiers are assigned a domestic policing function. In such emergency circumstances, the differences between maritime and continental traditions become evident, as shown by a comparison of English *martial law*, which remains subject to judicial power, with the French *état de siège*, steered by the executive.[117] These differing traditions form canons of values and are embedded in the corresponding political institutions.

In the twentieth century, the waves of an "Atlantic revolution" swept over the political cultures of the Continent, especially in the wake of the world wars.[118] It mainly consisted of Anglo-Saxon political forms and values that spread ever further east: liberal-democratic attitudes, constitutions, concepts, political ciphers, penetrating the Continental civilizations. The successive adoption, from west to east, of Atlantic constitutional forms and modes of interaction was readily apparent in Germany after 1918 and 1945, and in East Central and Eastern Europe after 1989.

The Atlantic penetration of continental Europe took place in two movements of varying speed. Cultural change drifted eastward more slowly, whereas political change followed the faster historical vicissitudes. The long-term, culturally encoded changes emerged from the tension between maritime and continental factors. By contrast, the shorter political changes emerged from the tension between freedom and its absence, self-determination and autocracy, democracy and despotism. In the nineteenth century's cultural-geographical dynamics, either England and Russia or France and Russia confronted each other. In the twentieth century, this dualism shifted into the sharper, politically and ideologically charged confrontation between the powers representing freedom, on the one hand, literal equality, on the other hand. The United States followed in the footsteps of England, while Russia transformed itself into the Soviet Union. The demise of relatively short-lived ideological antagonisms in 1989 has simply served to highlight the likely endurance of these two deep-seated cultural-geographical traditions.

Historically, the mergers between cultural-geographical constants and ideological surges have been highly diverse.[119] The antagonism between two power blocs after 1945 was an extreme example of such a merger—the ideological dimension being, in any case, the sole focus of contemporary attention. Already in the nineteenth century, state powers had emerged as bearers of differing values, ideas, and sociopolitical missions, even if the conflicting values took second place to the cultural-geographic encodings of both politics and the balance of power.[120] In any case, it is striking that in one way or another, the great powers of the nineteenth century were forced to both foster and hinder value-related factors. France was considered a nest of revolutionary ferment, if only because it used every opportunity to alter the status quo established in 1815. Russia represented reaction. England viewed its own role mainly as guaranteeing stability and security, only secondarily as championing the liberal freedoms.[121]

The October Revolution in 1917 transformed the political landscape of Europe and its major powers. There was a basic reversal of the nineteenth century's classic constellation of states, with France and Russia switching roles. The formerly autocratic Russia, now Bolshevik, espoused a radical variant of literal equality: the proletarian revolution. France, to the contrary, assumed the vanguard of the anti-Bolshevik intervention. Britain, albeit the financier and arms supplier of the Russian counterrevolutionaries, remained largely committed to its traditional balancing role on the Continent. In America, Woodrow Wilson, representing a liberal-democratic codex of values now also spreading eastward across the old Continent, did not have a clear position regarding the Bolsheviks. He ascribed the Russian Revolution to dreadful socioeconomic conditions, seeing parallels with the French Revolution. As a republican-minded American, he was distrustful of the counterrevolutionary Whites, above all for their monarchist leanings. All told, despite their ideological reservations about the rule of the soviets (the councils of workers and peasants) in Russia, the Great Powers assembled in Paris in 1919 seemed less interested in determining *who* should rule in Russia than that there simply be a functioning government there.[122]

For the Americans, the democratic revolutionary events in early 1917 in Petrograd were opportune. They made it easier to enter the Great War, although this would probably have happened in any case.[123] In the end, Berlin's resumption of unlimited submarine warfare was a great provocation, as was its effort to threaten the United States from Mexico. Nevertheless, entering the conflict before February 1917 would not have suited Washington, which, sunning itself in liberal pathos, considered the pact between the democratic Entente and the despotic czardom a misalliance. America cultivated the self-image of a freedom-championing power remote from Europe's quarrels, which is why Washington chose to join the conflict as an "associated" rather than "allied" power.

Russia's February Revolution thus offered America its long-awaited chance to combine realpolitik with the idea of democratic mission. When in April 1917 in a speech before a joint session of Congress, Wilson announced America's entry into the war against the kaiser's German Reich, he was able to combine a celebration of the fall of the czar with words of scorn for the "Prussian autocracy." Wilson's credo of a liberal order, which culminated in the famous dictum of making the world safe for democracy, was soon challenged by the October coup and the Bolshevik procla-mations.[124] In actuality, the programs espoused by Wilson and Lenin were both similar and contradictory.[125] On the one hand, each program raised a universal claim based on a social interpre-tation of the social environment;[126] on the other hand, the two programs espoused diametrically opposite notions of freedom: in the words of Thomas Masaryk, world democracy versus world revolution.[127] Wilson's "Program for World Peace," announced to Congress on 8 January 1918 and known as his Fourteen Points, was conceived as a response to the Soviet government's "Prin-ciples of Freedom" of December 1917, which along with stipulat-ing that there be no annexations or indemnities, called for the "right of peoples to self-determination." Aside from a mention of Poland's independence, a right to "self-determination" was not included in Wilson's Fourteen Points.[128] But a month later, in a February 1918 speech to Congress, he used precisely that term.[129] His appeal to the national consciousness of Europe's peoples had an impact equal to the threat of social revolution.

The principle of self-determination tore through the structures of old Europe like a projectile, although the collapse of the multina-tional empires did not require Wilson's speech. The demand for democracy and popular sovereignty, echoing through the previ-ous century, was itself undermining the cohesion of these multi-ethnic aggregates. They finally broke apart as a result of war and increasingly acute tensions between both the various nationalities (and the populace) and imperial authorities.

Democracy, popular sovereignty, and the principle of nation-ality had become the gravediggers of the dynastic, multiethnic empires. These components of the new era could be subsumed under the rubric of self-determination. In the process, a major dif-ference emerged between the Anglo-Saxon, especially American, political theory of self-determination and the traditional Continental self-understanding. The Anglo-American theory viewed self-determination as the right of a "people" in the sense of a *population* to provide itself with sovereign institutions and choose its government. For its part, the continental tradition emphasized the right of a *nation* to self-constitution independent of other nations, whereby *nation* was construed as an ethnically determined and historically grounded community. Within this conceptual framework, being affiliated with a nation was less an expression of political will and subjective decision than an "objectively" existing affiliation. Hence where Western political cultures tended to understand self-determination as involving a principle of *self-government*, this to a large extent institutional concept shifted as it moved eastward into a concept of *national self-determination*. This shift would be reflected in the formation of states based on ethnicity. More concretely, it led to demands that ethnic groups be incorporated into already existing, nationally kindred, and territorially adjacent polities—in short to irredentism.

Western principles tied to the concept of self-determination as self-government were difficult to realize in the cultural-geographical and political contexts of Central and East Central Europe. The long historical memories on the Continent rendered it virtually impossible to form institutions aimed at neutralizing ethnicity. What remained was a compromise between the Western, Anglo-American notion of institutional self-government and the more Eastern and Continental understanding of national self-determination. In the treaties signed in the Paris suburbs, the compromise was reflected in the stipulations concerning the protection of minorities, and it was further incorporated into the constitutions of the new or expanded states.[130] Self-determination and minority protection thus turned out to be complementary; while the principle of self-determination gave the titulary nation priority, minority protection limited the hegemonial effect of self-determination on domestic affairs. The newly created polities, for example, the restored Polish republic, perceived this as a restriction placed on their hard-won sovereignty.[131] The entire interwar period was ridden with conflicts arising from the tension between titulary nations and minorities. The former sought to cast off the obligations of minority protection imposed on them in 1919, while the latter struggled to assure that the principle was enforced.[132] The Western powers had in any event not reached any consensus regarding the very survival of ethnic minorities. Rather, they presumed a process of step-by-step assimilation into the state or titular nation. Minority protection was meant to advance this process, not impede it.[133]

Both during the Second World War and especially in the postwar era, the principle of self-determination and the Western demand for self-government would lead to some tension between the United States, which was traditionally anticolonial, and Great Britain, which hoped to preserve its empire. Before America's entry into the war, in the Atlantic Charter of August 1941, Roosevelt (similarly to Wilson before him) sought not only to proclaim the precepts of a new liberal-democratic world order and of free trade but also to initiate a process of decolonization.[134] The dissolution of the colonial empires was an implicit motive in the shaping of America's war policy. Thus Article 3 of the charter recognized "the right of all peoples to choose the form of government under which they will live" and the desirability that "sovereign rights and self government [be] restored to those who have been forcibly deprived of them."[135] The peoples living under colonial rule understood this article as a commitment to their imminent independence; Churchill rejected such an interpretation. In his view, the article only applied to those peoples subjugated by the Nazis, certainly not to the British Empire.[136] This disagreement between Washington and London over self-determination for colonial peoples, especially in Asia and India, would persist until the end of the war. Only Churchill's replacement by Clement Attlee ushered in a policy of decolonization. In any event, England had been totally exhausted by World War II, and a new conflict loomed, the Cold War, which demanded enormous energy.

The Soviet Union also expressed reservations regarding self-determination. Allied since the summer of 1941 with Britain and (indirectly) with the United States in the struggle against Nazi Germany, it felt obliged not to reject the Atlantic Charter outright. But Moscow was determined to retain those territories, especially the Baltic states, that had been absorbed into the Soviet Union on the basis of the 1939 accord with Hitler. It was also suspicious of those points in the charter enunciating the framework of an "indivisible world market" based on liberal, democratic values of free trade.[137] These points had in fact been developed fully in the spirit of the American doctrine of freedom. Already at the turn of the century, Washington had proclaimed its open door principle, whereby all nations would have equal trading and development rights in China (as opposed to the emergence of separate spheres of interest and economic dominance by particular nations). The idea of an indivisible world market and multilateralism in foreign trade was directed against the Axis powers, whose policies promoted autarky and the creation of closed economic areas. But its thrust also worked against the closed economic system of Soviet socialism and, though in attenuated form, the protectionism of the colonial empires.

Both the Soviet Union and Great Britain thus had misgivings about the principles of a liberal world economy and the absolute right of self-determination.[138] Although Roosevelt ended up diluting much of the Atlantic Charter's binding force for the sake of preserving Allied harmony, differences and tensions would still form around these principles, foreshadowing postwar realignments among the victorious powers.

The clash between a West stamped by Anglo-American attitudes and Soviet Russia ran through the entire century, although it did not fully unfold ideologically and power-politically until after

1945. Two phases can be distinguished in this struggle between West and East, freedom and equality. The first phase involved the various interventions by the Allied and associated powers and the "border states" associated with them in the Russian Civil War (1918–20). This phase continued in milder form in the interwar period, in policies aimed at isolating Soviet Russia (later, the Soviet Union).[139] But with Washington's formal recognition of the Soviet Union in 1933 and Moscow's admittance into the League of Nations the following year, the antagonism abated, only to emerge again with the Hitler-Stalin pact of 1939. With the German attack on the Soviet Union in June 1941 and the formation of the anti-Hitler coalition, the Western-Soviet relation then again changed, this time abruptly (albeit once more temporarily). The second phase of the conflict would set in with the end of World War II. From that point onward, the clash between freedom-centered and equality-centered values would traverse several stages. During the Cold War it would appear as a great confrontation between East and West—a bipolarity of fear based on what George Kennan would term a "mathematics of destructive forces."

Taking various historical shapes as it unfolded, the decisive stages of this confrontation of values marked most of the twentieth century, beginning with the October Revolution of 1917 and more or less finishing in 1989. "Universal civil war" in fact seems the appropriate metaphor for describing this global political confrontation, which was itself informed by clashing philosophies of history.[140] On a vertical plain, the confrontation cut through previous state and national loyalties, corresponding in this way to the nineteenth-century antinomies of freedom and equality, bourgeoisie and proletariat, revolution and counterrevolution. Decolonization also appropriated the political terminology of 1789: in the second half of the twentieth century, entire continents were raised to the status of revolutionary subjects, with commentators now beginning to speak of a *tiers monde* in analogy to the *tiers état*.

Much speaks for the confrontation between freedom and equality as the central interpretive axis for understanding the twentieth century. When applied, this axis does justice to the tense reality embedded in the century's warp and woof of events, with one exception: the years 1941 to 1945. But despite their brevity when measured against the steady confrontation between freedom and equality, these years have left imperishable traces on the consciousness of posterity. In the face of these years, the impression emerges of an incriminated event producing a kind of temporal compaction, one drawing both preceding and ensuing epochs into its vortex. That these few years lay claim to such a huge region of memory is doubtless due to the affectively and cognitively unendurable nature of contemplating mass murder—contemplating "Auschwitz." The years collide violently with the civilized world's expectations of rationality, from now on placing a burden on historical memory. The memory of this event inscribes itself into the epoch as its actual emblem.

An interpretation of the twentieth century in terms of the clash between freedom and equality is thus incapable of assimilating two events. Neither the wartime alliance against Hitler's Germany of those earlier and later adversaries, the Anglo-Americans and the Soviets, nor Nazism's biologistically based mass annihilation of human beings, can be reconciled with an understanding of the century as a universal civil war of values and ideologies. In this regard, it is striking that although no causal connection exists between the wartime alliance and the Nazi mass murder, such a connection, endowing coherence, has been created in historical memory. In retrospect, things seem to suggest that the 1941 pact between the Western powers and Moscow came about because of the mass murder—as if the Anglo-Americans and the Soviets had reached an agreement to oppose the *biologism* of German Nazism on the basis of a shared *societal* interpretation of their social realities. It is as if the biologizing of the social emanating from Nazi Germany prompted the protagonists in the century's defining confrontation to call a truce, in order to confront a phenomenon radically incompatible with the Enlightenment's defining ideas. For a short period of less than four years, two fundamentally opposing interpretations of the world faced each other on the battlefield. There was no shared secular reality between them. In contrast, the powers espousing a societal interpretation of the world, the Anglo-American proponents of freedom, on the one hand, the Soviet proponents of radical equality, on the other, could draw together on the basis of historically transmitted and geopolitically shaped premises. This rapprochement led to a formation of fronts resembling the original constellation of the Great War, Even the designation of the post-1941 events as the "Second World War" presumes a continued unfolding of past events. From the perspective of the Anglo-American West, it seemed appropriate to view biologizing Nazism as a direct extension of the Prussian power-state; from that of the East, to view it in familiar images of a heroic war to defend the motherland. Between these allied forces, a tacit agreement prevailed to suspend potentially disruptive confirmations of the continued opposition between freedom and equality. In 1943, the agreement was reflected in Stalin's symbolic decision, so gratifying to his Anglo-American allies, to dissolve the Comintern. Nevertheless, measured against the universal civil war waged since 1917 between proponents of liberal-democratic freedom and an ideal of literal equality, the anti-Hitler coalition constituted a manifest, dramatic exception. Following Germany's defeat, the enduring conflict between the liberal West and the Communist East returned with an intensity that seemed meant to efface memory of the years 1941 to 1945.

It may seem startling to locate Nazism outside the conventional boundaries set by the universal civil war between Bolshevism and anti-Bolshevism. For was not anti-Bolshevism an integral, even decisive, component in the Nazi negative canon of values? Did the Nazi regime not consider the Communists and Soviet power its foremost enemies? Were the two antagonists not pitted against each other across Europe, for instance, in the Spanish arena, where all the signs of a universal civil war were manifest in the second half of the 1930s? The attack on the Soviet Union, bound up with a ruthless war of annihilation in the East, together with its rationalizations, seemed to provide ample evidence of the Nazis' extreme anti-Bolshevism.

It would be incorrect to contend that National Socialism was not radical in its anti-Bolshevism. Yet its anti-Bolshevism differed fundamentally from that of the interventionist powers in the Russian Civil War of 1918–20. Nor can it be equated with the antagonism that kept the world in suspense for decades after the collapse of the anti-Hitler coalition. Indeed, the huge divide separating Western, liberal-democratic anti-Bolshevism from that of the Nazis is obvious. The former was political; it was fought out in the arena of differing views of social reality. The conflict between West and East was a confrontation between political systems that both espoused values rooted in the Enlightenment. As a conflict between factions on a global scale, their antagonism took on the trappings of a civil war. Thus it transcended traditional demarcations based on loyalty to a state or a nation. This is reinforced by the figures of the defector, the agent, the traitor, and later the dissident. Within his or her polity, the dissident represents the universal canon of values of the opposite side.[141]

National Socialist anti-Bolshevism was of a completely different nature. Its racializing, biologistic character contradicts the concept of civil war. Thus, the Nazi worldview had no interest in defectors from the racially inferior opposition. The fiction of racial immutability prevented the Nazis from admitting supporters from beyond the perimeter of the German racial community and peoples regarded as *artgleich* (racially similar). They had no interest in political "proselytizing." The racially defined folk was absolute; all *Artfremde* (those alien to the race) were excluded. With its categories of race and space *(Raum)*, National Socialism exceeded and destroyed concepts such as territory, state, and nation.[142] It more closely resembled an extreme form of integral nationalism than a warring faction in the universal civil war over values. As such, it was similar to Italian Fascism, albeit distinct in its biologistic worldview.

At the beginning of their alliance, Fascist Italy and Nazi Germany were brought together to a large extent by their respective interests in foreign policy rather than by their common ideology. This accord culminated in the Spanish Civil War. The rapprochement of the two powers had been initiated by Italy's attack on Ethiopia in October 1935. This imperialistic colonial war on the Horn of Africa had isolated Italy internationally, while alienating the Western powers of England and France. In the spring of that year, Rome was still allied with London and Paris in the short-lived "Stresa Front" against Germany.[143] The League of Nations issued sanctions against Italy in response to its aggression against a member state. The German Reich, which had quit the League of Nations in the autumn of 1933, came to Italy's aid with urgently needed supplies of coal. It was not alone in this, another league member, the Soviet Union, furnished Fascist Italy with crude oil: even the "fatherland of all toilers" had to be realistic and protect its foreign interests.[144] When the Berlin-Rome Axis was proclaimed in the fall of 1936, concurrent with their joint intervention in the Spanish Civil War, only two years had passed since Italy, in reaction to the attempted National Socialist putsch in Vienna and the murder of the Austro-Fascist Chancellor Dollfuss, had massed troops at the Brenner Pass with the aim of thwarting an attack by Hitler on Austria and countering German desires for expansion in Central Europe.

The Spanish Civil War is officially regarded as the classic, indeed archetypal, confrontation between the powers of Fascism and anti-Fascism in Europe. In the self-image of anti-Fascism, the

Spanish Republic soon acquired an iconic status, Nazi Germany and Mussolini's Italy standing behind the Falangist rebels on the Iberian Peninsula, the republican forces being aided by volunteers from all over the world organized into special "international brigades." Moreover, the Spanish Republic was supplied with arms and matériel by Moscow and assisted by Russian military advisors. The extent of that aid, which the Republic paid for dearly from its gold reserves, would not become known until the late 1950s. Recent revelations indicate that the Soviet shipments involved deception if not treachery toward the republic.[145]

The confrontation in Spain thus seemed to have all the characteristics of a major front in the universal civil war of ideologies. Those wedded to the "anti-Fascist" viewpoint had a clear interest in this representation, especially once Germany and Italy intervened. The political rhetoric of the republican camp had itself contributed substantially toward stylizing the war into a decisive clash with European Fascism. The Nazis themselves cultivated this image of the events in Spain. In Goebbels' propaganda, the fighting there was consistently presented as an ideological battle in a universal conflict between Fascism and Bolshevism.[146]

In fact, the romantic image of the "poet's war" drawn by volunteers in the International Brigade was a deception.[147] The deception is reflected in the reactions of the Western powers and in the conduct of France and especially England. London and Paris tried to avoid entanglement in the Spanish imbroglio and persuade other states to do likewise. The aim of this effort was to preserve peace in Europe—a lofty goal of the Western powers, notably Britain, which felt obliged to stay out of Continental squabbles for the sake of maintaining the balance of power. And the states that openly intervened, Nazi Germany and Fascist Italy, were themselves motivated by calculations tied more to foreign policy and strategic alliance than to ideology. Hitler wished to harness General Franco's rebellion against the Spanish Republic to further Germany's strategic aims and undermine the European system of collective security. Also, it seemed likely that following a victory by Franco, Spain would stand alongside Germany in the event of a great European war. In any event, a German intervention would have the effect of estranging Spain from London, Paris, and Moscow, powers that needed to be kept from exercising any future influence on Spain in the framework of alliance policies.[148] Other factors were less significant. For example, the often-repeated observation that modern instruments of warfare were tested in Spain and that particularly the Luftwaffe had found a testing ground for its bombers derives from a statement by Göring at Nuremberg that later research has shown to be unfounded.[149] Moreover, Germany was less interested in an expeditious victory by Franco than in a drawn-out civil war.

It is thus clear that the alliance between Germany and Italy emerging from the Spanish Civil War was largely prompted by complex foreign-policy calculations tied to Italy's Ethiopian adventure.[150] Berlin's foreign ministry was pleased to keep Italy occupied in Africa and the Mediterranean; in this way, Rome's unfavorable stance toward German interests in Central Europe could be effectively neutralized, an approach vindicated in the *Anschluß* with Austria in March 1938. Also, Mussolini's actions in Ethiopia aggravated differences with London, impelling Italy to move ever closer to Berlin.[151] All these proceedings unfolded under the primacy of an alliance policy revolving around the fundamental European conflict of the 1930s: the coalition of the Versailles status quo versus the powers wishing to revise that treaty's order.

Italy's intervention in the Spanish Civil War reflected its expansionist policy, the program of *mare nostro* meant to further its power-political and strategic aims. There was an anti-French component to these ambitions. The traditional Franco-Italian rivalry in the western Mediterranean and North Africa would endure throughout the war, with Italy and Vichy France pursuing their conflicting aims under the aegis of German hegemony. Rome's Ethiopian adventure and intervention in Spain had cast doubt on Mussolini's role as "Europe's mediator."[152] Nonetheless, in Munich in 1938 Il Duce succeeded in refurbishing his faded image as an intermediary. Relations in Europe were not yet as polarized as they would seem from a wartime perspective. We thus find London and Rome reaching an understanding in the Mediterranean in January 1937, in the middle of the Spanish Civil War.

England was committed to preserving peace in Europe—and indeed at any price. Its paramount concern was maintaining stability. The Spanish conflict could not be allowed to expand into a general European war. If the Conservative government had any sympathies, they were with the rebels surrounding Franco. But in principle London was indifferent to Spain's internal situation. Given such ideological agnosticism, the British found it relatively easy to foster adequate relations with both sides. Economic interests encouraging precaution in both directions were also at play. But the decisive factor was Spain's allegiance in a future European conflict. Should the expected greater war finally erupt, Germany wanted a Francoist Spain on its side, whereas England was intent on securing the good will of whichever party proved victorious.[153] Importantly, the Baldwin government's nonintervention policy was approved by most of the British populace and, to large extent, by the British trade unions.

To further its aim of confining the Spanish Civil War to the Iberian Peninsula and assuring nonintervention by the major powers, England exerted pressure on France. Unhappy with the Franco-Soviet agreement of May 1935, London cautioned Paris against any measures that might help trigger a European war. If France intervened in Spain, it could not expect British support in a conflict with Italy. But in fact there was no need for such pressure. Although Léon Blum's Popular Front had now and then furnished the Spanish government with clandestine aid, it was constrained on this issue by domestic politics.[154] The socialists themselves were split between interventionists and pacifists, a schism hardly conducive to swift political decision making. Finally, the Popular Front was chiefly interested in realizing its social programs and wished to avoid hurling itself into a Spanish adventure.[155]

Initially, the Soviet Union also hesitated to become involved in the Spanish Civil War. During the 1930s, it had sought to preserve peace in the framework of the League of Nations and the system of collective security. This strategy was neither unselfish nor unproblematic. Peace abroad made it possible for Stalin to wage war at home, to carry out his relentless program of accelerated "social development." In helping protect the Soviet Union from foreign turbulence and military challenges, the principle of collective security thus had a dubious function: allowing Stalin to focus on "building socialism in a single country." But in the West, Nazi Germany loomed as a danger; in the East, Japan had launched its campaign of conquest in Manchuria in 1931, thus itself threatening a direct confrontation with the Soviet Union. For these reasons, there was no real alternative to Moscow's participation in the Western policy of collective security.[156]

Because the British strategy of containing the Spanish Civil War was in the Soviet interest, Moscow decided to join the international Nonintervention Committee. But when the Soviets urged its fellow committee members to intercede in response to the German and Italian intervention in Spain, relations with London deteriorated. The British were distrustful, and fears were voiced that in a mode of ideological relapse, the Soviets were about to inaugurate a new round of Bolshevik intrigues on the international stage.[157] Old tensions between England and Russia flared again at the Montreux Conference in July 1936, when the Soviets advanced the traditional Russian demand that the Black Sea be opened only to warships from countries adjoining its shores. The British, who wished to preserve a hard-won balance of naval power, felt threatened by the Soviet initiative. They feared that Moscow was trying to plunge its overstretched empire into the imponderables of a continental war in Europe.

In their turn, the Soviets were displeased with the Western powers' military restraint in the face of the German and Italian actions. Their distrust was intensified by the fact that Japan's aggression against China in 1937 had gone unpunished. The ultimate result of such European and Asian developments would be that seemingly paradoxical volte-face of August 1939, the Hitler-Stalin pact. Perceived as initiated with Madrid, the unfolding scenario was confirmed for the Soviets in 1938 in Munich, where they were excluded from the meeting between Hitler and the Western powers, with Mussolini in attendance. At the same time, Moscow feared a possible understanding between London and Berlin at Poland's expense, which would draw Nazi Germany's frontiers even closer to the Soviet Union. This was in any case the Soviet perspective regarding its turn toward Nazi Germany and away from the status quo. The British were concerned with other problems. They considered the military action on behalf of Spain that Moscow was urging to be a dangerous proposition. They preferred to work out a compromise with Italy in the Mediterranean rather than risk a major war to gratify the Soviets.

As an iconographic event, the Spanish Civil War has contributed greatly to an enduring narrative of global struggle between classes and ideologies. But the romantic effects of this narrative have far exceeded the significance of the material that it recounts. This narrative bypasses an entire crucial dimension of the Spanish events: the policies regarding alliance and security as developed by the various European powers. It bypasses the important opposition between those powers wishing to maintain the status quo and other powers bent on either demolishing it or, like the Soviet Union, partaking of the results of the demolition. It bypasses the crisis in Asia, Japan's invasion of China, which, however one tries, cannot be subsumed under the dualistic schema of Fascism versus anti-Fascism, Bolshevism versus anti-Bolshevism. And it bypasses the civil war conducted by the Soviet regime itself, as played out, for instance, in Stalin's conviction that he had to settle accounts with the party's old Bolsheviks, reflected in his bloody purging of the Red Army officer corps in 1938. Nazi Germany's intervention in Spain does not necessarily define that country as the open battlefield in an enduring universal civil war over values. Nor can the crushing of Czechoslovakia and the subsequent extinction of Poland be construed as further stages in an ideological war between Bolshevism and anti-Bolshevism. Rather, these acts were the outcome of an ultrarevisionist German expansionism and nationalism propelled by a fanatic integralist impulse. The fact that the mainly Central European internationalists who fought in the trenches of the Spanish Civil War may have understood their activities differently belongs to another story. Or in any case, that different, widely held perspective has given an ideological cast to a complex of motives with, in reality, a power-political core.

Within the power-political constellation emerging with the Spanish Civil War, it is difficult to discern the sharp demarcating lines of an ideological opposition.[158] Spain was not the arena for a decisive round in a civil war over values spreading over the globe, as retrospective accounts of the events there would often have us believe. Rather, within this conflict players jostled for trumps and positions in a westward-directed European war of revision. Only later, beginning in 1941, was this transformed into an eastward-directed racist-ideological war of annihilation. For decades, the opulent revolutionary portrait of the Spanish Civil War would help mask one of Nazism's most characteristic features: the biologism of its weltanschauung, located outside the horizon of all usual social interpretations of reality.

German Nazism was as fundamentally different from liberal universalism of Western provenance as it was from and Bolshevik internationalism. In its hermetics of biologism and racial theory, it cannot be reconciled with the conceptual structure of a civil war. The racist Slavophobia of the Nazis functioned as a self-imposed obstacle precisely at those moments when they might well have enjoyed success as one faction in a universal civil war over values, for instance, by inciting the various ethnic populations in the Soviet Union against the Stalinist regime.[159] But the anti-Bolshevik civil war waged by Nazi Germany was not about conflicting values. It was a race-ideological war of subjugation and annihilation. As a civil war, it was inauthentic.

The biologistic elements of Nazi anti-Bolshevism grew from a *völkisch* matrix injected with racial ideology. These elements surmounted and smothered the political substance inherent in a civil war. It is thus not surprising that otherwise classical antagonists in a universal civil war of values, vehemently opposed as proponents of either freedom or radical equality, could come together on the basis of what they had in common: things originating, as suggested, in a societal interpretation of history, hence in the Enlightenment. This rapprochement took place in the exceptional historical situation prevailing between 1941 and 1945, when what was at stake was the confrontation and defeat of the biologistic threat. Once this had been accomplished, freedom and equality abandoned their ceasefire in order to resume their interrupted struggle of values with even greater intensity—for over forty years. The principle of freedom won when the social blueprint for material equality foundered on its own inadequacies. The principle of literal equality ultimately failed because of a fundamental discrepancy recognized by Marx. In the idiom of the critique of political economy, the forces of production were shackled by politically determined relations of production. Freedom, formerly considered a dispensable diversion of the privileged classes, had meanwhile matured into a force of production, adopting itself to new technologies. With nothing of equal value to offer in opposition, the system of equality expired without ceremony in 1989 and 1990.

2

Conversions

Nation and Revolution

War and Revolution / Society and Ethnicity / Expansion and Intervention / Red Nations and White Nations / Patriotic Wars / Borders and Minorities / Hungary and Rumania / Greeks in Odessa / Poles and Soviets / Stalin and Tukhachevsky / Germany and Russia / Revision and the Status Quo / Hitler's Wars / Poland's Frontiers / Germany's Unity

⁜

From the war had sprung revolution, and not just the Russian insurgency. The Great War was the progenitor of all those rebellions that followed Red October. In 1919, Central Europe looked as if it were hurtling toward radical transformation. In Berlin, the Spartacus League staged an uprising. In Vienna, all signs pointed to storm. In Bavaria, the Munich Soviet Republic was proclaimed. Bolsheviks were in power in Hungary. They were able to open a path for the Russian Revolution straight to the center of Europe. The prevailing anxieties and conjured-up prognoses suggested it was only a question of time until the Red Army was at the gates.[1]

No revolution without a world war.[2] After decades of dormancy, the idea of radical change had reawakened. Because of the previous calm, the reawakening was quite unexpected. Since the quashing of the Paris Commune in 1871, revolution had withdrawn from Europe's urban centers. Encircled by social reformism in the West, it had disappeared from the strategic arsenals of the workers' movement. Social democracy had duly distanced itself from revolution. The homage it paid at the altar of high socialist principle was, to be sure, all the more profuse, a ritual performed in the shadows of historical-philosophical discourse. But all speculation to the contrary, revolution did not spring from any societal telos. Its return in 1917 was triggered more by the imponderabilities of the war than the afflictions of oppression.[3] Insurgency erupted where military defeat loomed or decrees handed down by the victorious powers at the Paris peace conference were perceived as draconian. In this situation, the Russian Revolution played a unique role.[4] It preceded the postwar arrangements and had a lasting impact on them. Red October broke into the war as a result of Russia's military and social exhaustion in face of the Central Powers, themselves to be vanquished by the Allies. In the eastern theater, the Central Powers manifestly maintained the upper hand until the European conflagration's end. The trophy of this superiority was the enormous amount of territory ceded to Germany by czarist Russia—actually the defeated front of the Allied coalition. The March 1918 Treaty of Brest-Litovsk reflected the actual power relations on the eastern battlefields. Even the revolutionary government had to accept its stipulations.[5]

Along with exhaustion, despair, and social deprivation, the nature of the war's conduct on the eastern front hastened the uprising. Compared with the relentless corset of trench warfare in the West, combatants in the eastern theater were far less restricted. Moreover, the closeness of the front brought troops into the capital. The dissatisfaction and despair of the troops, who were being repeatedly thrown into battle, soon turned against their own regime. The February revolution, a mutiny by peasants in uniform,[6] had already been sparked by the insurgency of the Petrograd garrison. And the Bolshevist October Revolution would have been hard to imagine without Russia's epidemic of war-weariness and demoralization, spreading in the wake of an offensive in July that had soon turned into a catastrophic rout.[7]

After the October Revolution, the Allies and associated powers were guided by the exigencies of war in their approach to their former ally Russia. Their motive for intervention was less the revolution and more the fear that Russia would withdraw from the war. Such an eventuality, it was recognized, would have dramatic repercussions.[8] The elimination of the eastern front could only be a boon to Germany, which was exhausting itself in a two-front war.[9] The Allied and associated powers were under pressure. It had become clear that the Bolshevik government would be neither able nor willing to prevent German troops from advancing across territories they already occupied, to the east and southeast of the Russian land mass. Great Britain in particular saw the approaches to its Asian and Indian possessions threatened by a potential German thrust.[10] Also, rapprochement between Germany and Russia would have brought the release and return of war prisoners, replenishing the ranks of the Central Powers. A final concern was preventing German access to the stores of weapons and munitions that had been shipped to Russia to supply Allied units.[11] Even before the October Revolution, steps had been taken to strengthen the wobbly Russian front by bringing in troop reinforcements from the Entente powers. After Russia's de facto removal from the war and the voicing of fears that the Germans would now have free access to the inexhaustible natural resources of Siberia, the Allied War Council also asked Japan to send troops to Russian territory.[12]

The early Allied intervention in Russia was clearly part of the overall effort to defeat the Central Powers. The political aim of overthrowing the Soviet power was secondary to military concerns. Initially, overtures had even been made to the new regime with the aim of maintaining the wartime coalition. However, the Bolshevik government was not favorably disposed toward the Allies.[13] Thus already in November 1917, the Bolsheviks released documents concerning secret agreements between Russia's former allies and the czarist regime to divide up territory after a victory.[14] Moreover, the revolutionary government made no bones about its desire to carry the revolution to Asia in a struggle against imperialism.[15] Yet no matter how radical the Bolshevik pronouncements, the Allies' main concern was Germany. In the top political echelons of the Entente, the mood oscillated between hope and anxiety: hope that the new Russian regime would eventually resume the military struggle against the Central Powers; anxiety that it might even ally itself with Germany.[16]

The intervening Allies only turned to containing or combating the revolution after victory over the Central Powers had been assured. The intervention itself had very mixed consequences. As a foreign intervention on behalf of the counterrevolutionary Whites, it bolstered the Bolsheviks' claim to be the true trustees of the nation, elevating them to the rank of a patriotic party. The national question in the civil war provided further paradoxes. The representatives of old Russia not only were bent on restoring the ancien régime; they also wished to reestablish the shattered territorial unity of the czarist empire. They here clashed with those peoples that had left the empire as a result of the German policy of dismemberment and the onset of the 1917 revolution.[17] In this way, civil war, intervention, and national quarrels had coalesced into an impenetrable muddle. These events unfolded in the broad cultural-geographic border area stretching from the Baltic Sea to eastern Poland and White Russia and beyond to the Ukraine and the Black Sea. A similar fusion of civil war and national uprising was taking place in the Caucasus and the Central Asian parts of the former empire.[18]

The October Revolution was thus not so much a social-revolutionary uprising as the outcome of an endless and debilitating power struggle. It was the expression of military and social exhaustion; above all, it was the outcome of Russia's weakness in face of the Central Powers. The situation was similar to the revolutionary uprisings that soon broke out in the territory of the former Central Powers. They too were a reaction to war and defeat.[19]

In view of the previous constellation of allies and adversaries, the situation evolving in the crisis period 1918–19 had a paradoxical tenor. Together with Germany, Austria, Hungary, the Ottoman Empire, and, to a limited extent, the Italian kingdom, Russia belonged to the losing side in the Great War. For all their differences, these countries shared a common problem: war, defeat, postwar developments, and the imminent results of the peace deliberations in Paris produced revolutionary shock waves.[20] In Germany and Austria (more specifically Vienna), events took on an unmistakable social-revolutionary cast, appropriating the language of class warfare. In Hungary, the events emerging from defeat and decisions taken at the Paris peace conference were of a more complex nature. Although at first glance social-revolutionary, the Hungarian Soviet Republic's basic impetus was in reality highly nation-centered. The chief concern in Budapest was prophylactic: to forestall a massive loss of territory and population by activating revolutionary energies. On the other hand, the new Turkey emerging under Kemal Pasha was steered by obvious national-revolutionary and anti-imperialist principles. In Italy, nationalistic expectations for expansion had been thwarted by the results in Paris. This led to the notorious *vittoria mutilata*, tied to an outbreak of social-revolutionary and counterrevolutionary violence.

These various situations in which military defeat combined with hunger blockades, social misery, territorial losses, and national humiliations were crucial for both the social rebellions and the ensuing counterrevolutionary reactions. The internal confrontations in West Central Europe reflected a sharp social divide, class against class. As one moved further east, conflicts took on a more national tint. Political discourse underwent a veritable conversion, from class conflict to national struggle. A distinct arc of conflict emerged from this general meshing of military defeat, social revolution, and national battles on the frontier. It spanned Central and East Central Europe, from the Baltic to northern Italy and the Adriatic. In a conspicuous manner, it overlapped with the cultural-geographical area previously under the control of dynastic supranational empires.

The nation-states that succeeded the collapsing empires looked to a troubled future. Fledgling in their independence, they were mired in bloody border battles without and festering conflicts between nationalities within. The polities born from the breakup of the multinational empires were not intent on becoming civic states in the Western model, nor was their territory particularly homogenous in ethnic terms. The region's titular nations in any case diverged from its ethnic minorities. These nations had emerged from the world war with indeterminate borders and provisional governments.[21]

A central objective of the Paris peace conference was to regulate the complex processes involved in the formation of new nation-states. The conference's foremost task was demarcating borders and determining the area comprised by restored, expanded, and new states such as Poland, Rumania, and Czechoslovakia. This highly problematic mission assumed by the Great War's victors was all the more weighed down by events unfolding in these same areas during the course of the Paris negotiations.[22]

The factors shaping the territorial decisions taken at the conference were not just theoretical. The original intention of the Allies had been to base resolutions on the principle of self-determination and the potential economic viability of the new states. But due to swiftly changing circumstances, the deliberations, unfolding over some eighteen months, often left no choice but ratifying faits accomplis on the ground. The Allies looked on with apprehension as the complex process of territorial reconfiguration was compounded by revolutionary uprisings and civil wars. This ferment interacted with the procedures for determining territorial borders, since the Allies often favored those nations hoping to partake of neighbors weakened by revolutionary upheaval.[23]

The front lines in an emerging universal civil war would thus have far-reaching consequences for the territorial makeup of the new nation-states in Central and East Central Europe. German Austria, for example, was able not only to forestall revolutionary trouble at home but also to exploit the calamities of neighboring Hungary for the benefit of its territorial ambitions in Burgenland.[24] In Germany, revolutionary activity was massively repressed by the provisional government of the Council of People's Deputies, in part because of the threat generated by the territorial questions raised in Paris. The government was in any case not prepared to encourage France's exorbitant demands on the Reich by tolerating the revolutionary unrest inside Germany. At the same time, by pointing to the Bolshevik danger at its doorstep, the provisional government could hope for greater leniency from the victorious powers. Hence by playing up the dangers emanating from a sovietized Russia, the German negotiators at the armistice talks in the forest near Compiègne managed to postpone the imminent demobilization of the German armies in the East.[25] Article 12 of the armistice agreement of 11 November 1918 contained a corresponding proviso. From a historical perspective, it can be considered an early building block in an evolving strategy, pursued primarily by the French, of erecting a cordon sanitaire as a bulwark against Bolshevik Russia.

The ambitious food-supply operations for starving populations carried out by Allied relief organizations, especially the American Relief Organization headed by Herbert Hoover, were also meant to forestall a spread of desperation encouraging revolutionary activity.[26] In the spring of 1919, Otto Bauer, the eminent Socialist state secretary in German Austria's foreign office, rejected an appeal for aid from the Hungarian Soviet government, indicating that Austria, and especially Vienna, was totally dependent on American aid. Lenin in turn made a—tactically transparent— offer to the German Council of People's Deputies: the Soviets would send trains loaded with wheat to Berlin for its hungry population.

In general, one pattern was quite conspicuous in the peace conference's territorial decisions: states that seemed about to slide into Bolshevism could expect disadvantages, while governments acting along counterrevolutionary lines could anticipate territorial gains.[27] Given this fact, it is hardly surprising that the territorial conflicts shifted into interstate civil wars between "white" and "red" nations. The territorial conflict between Soviet Hungary and its enemies Rumania, Czechoslovakia, and Serbia revealed just such a shift, and a similar situation crystallized in the Baltic between 1918 and 1920. The circumstances that led to the 1919–20 Polish-Soviet war were analogous.

Germany and Russia had not been invited to officially participate in the Paris deliberations, although their presence hovered over the negotiations table. The shadow of the excluded, of *Russia and Prussia* as the Anglo-Americans liked to call them, was constantly present.[28] The negotiators hoped that by means of territorial arrangements in the area between Germany and Russia— *Zwischeneuropa*—they could prevent a possible blending of Soviet-inspired social-revolutionary tendencies and a German appetite for revenge and revision. The most extreme and frightening scenario was the spread of Bolshevism to Germany.[29] The Council of People's Deputies took on the task of nipping such an eventuality, with all its internal and external repercussions, in the bud. It did so not just to please the powers assembled in Paris, but very much for its own reasons. Friedrich Ebert was well known for abhorring revolution. And in 1918–19, Ebert's so-called Majority Socialists had the results of Russia's Red October right before their eyes.

They had no intention of letting anything even remotely similar come to pass in Germany.[30]

French policy was aimed at weakening Germany over the long term while effectively containing the Soviet Russian regime, if not abetting its overthrow. For different reasons, both Germany and Russia had become outcasts; any ties between them were to be prevented. The arsenal of resolutions incorporated to this end in the Versailles Treaty included a prohibition of the annexation of German Austria by Germany and other, quite well-known resolutions regarding territorial boundaries, security policy, and the economy. And in another turn of the screw, possible Hapsburg inclinations as well as Hungarian revisionist intentions were frustrated in East Central Europe by the security system of the Little Entente, which comprised Czechoslovakia, Yugoslavia, and Rumania and was promoted by the French.[31]

Parallel with its efforts to establish a *barrière de l'est,* France overtaxed its abilities and resources in the Russian Civil War in its bid to support the counterrevolutionary Whites. In December 1917, England and France had already agreed on their separate zones of intervention, though they had not yet taken action in the field. France was assigned Bessarabia, the Ukraine, and the Crimea; England was still entangled in the lingering Transcaucasian hostilities. But at the end of the year, after the armistice in the East and especially after the German-Soviet "dictated peace" of Brest-Litovsk, the intervention could finally be launched. The combat-weary Armée d'Orient, commanded by General Franchet d'Esperey and stationed in Salonika, was charged with a costly and exhausting intervention effort in the northern area of the Black Sea and southern Russia.[32] The effort far exceeded the moral and material resources of the French polity itself, heavily drained and exhausted by the war. It is thus no surprise that the intervention policy soon foundered. After a series of military humiliations, as well as a mutiny among the French troops, the Allied commanders in southern Russia felt obliged to change course, opting now for precisely the less-direct strategy of the cordon sanitaire. Two pillars supported this approach to containing Soviet Russia: Rumania and Poland, the "Thermopylae of Western civilization," as an article in the French press put it in the spring of 1919.[33]

The merger of the two above-described objectives, the power-political encirclement of Germany and the counterrevolutionary containment of Soviet Russia, itself an undertaking of Napoleonic dimensions, produced a blend composed of traditional forms of power and elements of ideologically motivated civil war. The climax of the blending process took place on 21 March 1919, when the Hungarian Soviet Republic was proclaimed in the very heart of Central Europe. This event coincided with France's decision to break off its intervention in southern Russia.[34] The proclamation of the republic involved a highly distinctive conversion of national into social semantics. Indeed, the events in Budapest had paradigmatic importance for the fusion of nation and revolution. They alarmed the Allies; France, in particular, saw a challenge to its role of securing order in the Balkans. All sorts of danger to the structure of French stability in Central Europe could emerge from Hungary. A glance at the map was enough to understand what calamities a regime like the Hungarian Soviet Republic, located in such a strategic position, could produce if unchecked. Hungary appeared fully capable of forming that feared revolutionary access route from Soviet Russia to Central Europe. Moreover, the new regime represented a highly volatile mixture of social-revolutionary and national motives. This augured ill for the stability desired by the Allies.

The Hungarian Soviet Republic drew its strength from this mixture. Yet its prospects looked extremely bleak. Without support from the outside, namely, from Soviet Russia, and without a revolutionizing of the immediate region, the republic was doomed, above all because the internal support it was offered simply provoked counterrevolutionary intervention from the outside. The temptation of further radicalization also contributed to the revolutionary regime's downfall. Over time, ever-larger segments of the population felt alienated from it, eventually falling into the open arms of the Hungarian counterrevolution, entrenched in Rumanian-occupied territory. Also, the creation of the revolutionary regime in Budapest furnished Hungary's neighbors Rumania, Czechoslovakia, and Yugoslavia, states that in any case had ambitions on Hungarian territory, with handy arguments. France, present throughout the region through the military missions of the Armée du Danube, encouraged these states to intervene. It appeared as though an international rape of Hungary was in the offing.[35]

The intervention by Hungary's neighbors was driven less by counterrevolutionary motives than by territorial greediness.[36] The latter blended well with the French policy of counterrevolutionary intervention and a securing of Central and East Central Europe through a cordon sanitaire—a policy that went far beyond the intervention in Hungary. France wished to exploit the national aspirations of the new and expanding states for its own needs. In this respect, it is important to note that the Allied intervention in the southern Russian Civil War had not been an exclusively French affair. The interventionist forces included contingents from other states pursuing their national agendas. The most significant of these was Greece, which provided a large troop contingent to reinforce the White volunteer army under Denikin.[37] Greece had entered the Great War at a late point and had suffered relatively minor losses. The Allies believed it had to earn the right to its territorial claims. In return for participation by Greek troops, French prime minister Clemenceau, chairman of the peace conference, promised his Greek counterpart Venizelos that France would support Greek territorial demands in eastern Thrace and might take a favorable view of extensive Greek claims on Smyrna.[38]

Such a problematic tradeoff was nothing unusual, especially since it was accompanied by expectations in keeping with the nineteenth century's irredentist nationalisms. Mythicized images of history pointed the way. The new and expanded states emerging from World War I had expansive dreams—of a Greater Greece, a Greater Rumania, a Greater Poland. The participation of Greek troops in the Allied intervention in the northern area of the Black Sea should be interpreted in the framework of a nineteenth-century idea of nation-building, an interpretation in fact widespread in Greek historiography.[39] The participation of Greek troops in the Allied intervention in southern Russia was thus seen as analogous to the role played by Piedmont-Sardinia's troops in the Crimean War. At that time, Cavour had hoped that by fighting alongside England and France, he could gain the support of these powers for Italian unificatory aspirations.

The presence of Greek troops as part of an interventionist force in southern Russia and the Ukraine was consequently motivated by *national* concerns. Moreover, the motives were not based exclusively on the agreement haggled out between Clemenceau and Venizelos. Rather, Greek involvement was also motivated by a desire to protect the interests of the ethnic Greek population in southern Russia. There were Greek communities all along the Black Sea coast—at the Pontus, in the Caucasus, Crimea, and the Ukraine. The southern Russian-Ukrainian city of Odessa had a sizable Greek community that had played a key role in the "invention" of a Greek national consciousness at the beginning of the nineteenth century. There had been Greek colonies in the area long before Catherine II, and these had been significantly expanded during her reign, which saw the founding of Odessa on the ruins of a Tartar village. In the course of World War I and the subsequent civil war, the Greek population swelled as a result of a massive flight of ethnic Greeks from the Caucasus. The Greek population in the Pontus region was also affected by the war's calamities. The Pontus Greeks were tempted to establish their own state in agreement with the local Armenian population—or to join an expanded Greece.[40] With the collapse of the Ottoman Empire and the Russian revolutionary upheaval, it seemed possible to realize such Greater Hellenic aspirations, the Megali Idea of the restoration of a new Greek nation-state with Constantinople at its center, Byzantium redux. In their struggle against godless Bolshevism, Greeks also contributed to the defense of the imperiled Greek Orthodox Church while standing by Holy Russia, a nation with which the Greeks, all intra-Orthodox squabbling notwithstanding, felt a close inner bond. Consequently, the idea of the Greek intervention in Russia's civil war being spurred by strong national motives is far less odd than it might first appear. The dedication with which Greek troops carried out their duties for the Allied interventionist force itself seems a clear sign of such motives.[41]

In contrast, the French troops displayed little enthusiasm for the enterprise. One reason for this was that the French contingent was composed largely of colonial troops from Algeria and Senegal. The North and West Africans were disinclined to subject themselves to decimation in a military venture with all the marks of a colonial intervention and in an area beset by a hostile climate and a galloping flu epidemic. Another factor was their battle-weariness. After the armistice, these troops had hoped for demobilization and discharge from service. Instead the Paris government had dispatched them to a civil war far from home, a war whose end was nowhere in sight. The eminently imperialist character of the entire enterprise was not lost on these soldiers and sailors, who had been heavily politicized by war and revolution. Aside from intervening on behalf of the Whites, Clemenceau was intent on gaining compensation for French credits to czarist Russia, now lost in the aftermath of the Bolshevik revolution, by winning access to the rich resources of southern Russia. The landing there of the interventionary forces was carried out with one eye on the coal-rich Donets Basin and the opulent breadbasket of the Ukraine.[42]

From the start, the French contingent's reluctance hampered the operation; ultimately, the reluctance led to the operation's termination. In general it stood under an unfavorable star. The indigenous Russian-Ukrainian population had little love for Denikin's volunteer army. There was constant friction with the French-led intervention troops. Military defeats, such as that at Kherson, were not long in coming, which led to a further decline in morale among the ranks. Mutinies flared, and there was repeated insubordination among the French troops. In Sevastopol, some French soldiers even declared their solidarity with rebellious workers.[43] Greek troops, reputed to be especially reliable, were called in to suppress the rebellion. But the French commanders treated their Greek counterparts with marked disdain, keeping the Greek commanders in the dark about decisive events and confronting them with faits accomplis.[44] Acting on its own, the French expeditionary leadership decided to scrap the whole undertaking and prepared to withdraw; given the sorry state of the French forces, the move seemed prudent. Yet for the local Russian-Greek population, the withdrawal of the Allied forces from Odessa and Sevastopol spelled potential disaster, including the loss of its ancestral homeland in southern Russia.[45] The French saw the pullback as a mere logistical operation. But the indigenous Greeks feared that the Ukrainian population would equate them with the hated Hellenic soldiers. In panic, they swarmed onto the quays, clamoring to be transported away by the Allies—a scene that was a dark prelude to the Greek mass tragedy in Asia Minor in 1922. After their withdrawal from southern Russia in the spring of 1919, the Greek troops were transported to Bessarabia, and then shipped in July to Smyrna, embarking for the Hellenic adventure in Anatolia.

With the end of the French intervention in southern Russia, the policy of direct involvement in the civil war between Whites and Reds came to a close. Instead, smoldering and flaring territorial conflicts between the new and expanding states in Central and

East Central Europe would be supported by the Allies, with the aim of containing any revolutionary peril. The participation of Greeks and smaller national contingents of Poles and Rumanians in the southern Russian effort had already revealed this tendency to exploit the national aspirations of other states. The same can be said for the crossing of the Transylvanian line of demarcation by Rumanian troops; the Hungarian-Rumanian war it provoked contributed to the downfall of the Bolshevik regime of Béla Kun in Budapest. The presence of Rumanian troops in Budapest from August to November 1919 brought an end to one stage in the universal civil war. At the same time, it resolved the territorial conflict between Hungary and its neighbors, with Hungarian losses being ratified by the peace treaty of Trianon (1920). For Bucharest, World War I ended with the realization of its ambitions regarding Transylvania. The Rumanians were jubilant in their final victory over the Hungarian archenemy.[46]

In his military foray into Hungarian territory, the Rumanian prime minister Bratianu was only tangentially interested in overthrowing the Bolshevist regime in Hungary. The Rumanians viewed the conflict with the Bolshevists for what it really was, namely, a national and territorial conflict. Nevertheless the anti-Bolshevist rhetoric proved useful. For the Rumanians wished to justify their actions in the eyes of the peace conference in Paris, their aim being to realize the territorial claims laid down in the secret wartime agreement of Bucharest in 1916. In the face of a Bolshevist Hungary, their claims to Transylvania were easier to push through — just as Bessarabia had been wrested from a Soviet Russia now labeled an outlaw state.[47]

The events that led to the founding of the Hungarian Soviet Republic themselves raise doubts as to whether the revolution of 21 March 1919 had actually been driven by social-revolutionary motives. Immediately after the new state was declared, there was talk everywhere that its emergence reflected no real revolution but rather a national-Bolshevist, national-revolutionary, indeed straightforwardly nationalist venture, its purpose being to wrest concessions from the Allies in the troublesome question of territorial claims. This image of a national rebellion in revolutionary guise seemed to impress others as well. Mussolini, for instance, believed the March events in Budapest represented a linkage of nationalism with socialism worthy of imitation.[48] Likewise, representatives of the American Coolidge mission on hand in Budapest repeatedly noted in their reports that the territorial question was an insult to Hungarian national pride: despite all the revolutionary rhetoric, they indicated, the revolution was in fact a *national* rebellion against the imminent territorial dismemberment of Hungary.[49] There was no question of any Bolshevist sentiment among the populace, nor even of any socialist sentiment. In reality, things were quite simple. Hungary had been one of the Central Powers. Its neighbors derived certain advantages from their status as wartime associates of the Allies. Denied the role of keepers of the counterrevolutionary grail, the Hungarians were left with only one option: reversing the usual approach in East Central Europe and embracing Bolshevism. A conservative Hungarian newspaper expressed it as follows: in order to present a credible threat to the powers convening in Paris, Hungary had no choice but to set fire to its own house.[50]

Budapest in fact experienced no social-revolutionary upheaval. Rather, power was simply handed to Béla Kun and his Bolshevik followers. The Hungarian government under the liberal prime minister (and later president) Mihály Károly had come under massive pressure.[51] The representative of the French military mission in Budapest, Lieutenant Colonel Fernand Vix, had issued an ultimatum in the name of the Paris peace conference: Hungary had thirty-six hours to withdraw far behind the line of demarcation laid down in the Belgrade military convention in order to permit Rumanian troops to move into the evacuated zone.[52] The Allied order appeared to have authorized the Rumanians to advance their troops into Hungarian territory, which would necessarily

have prejudiced any final territorial decision. In any case, the ultimatum made it clear to the Hungarians that they had little to expect from a future final resolution in Paris; huge losses of territory
and population were imminent. Also, the economic unity of the
country had been shattered. Important agricultural regions were
in danger of being lost but above all those areas that constituted
the industrial backbone of the Hungarian economy. There could
be no compensation for the loss of the coal mines, already a reality.[53] The resulting energy deficit led to a surge in unemployment,
exacerbated by punctual demobilizations. The continuing blockade by the Allies could only lead to catastrophe. In short, the
national question, made pressing by the looming territorial dismemberment of Hungary, mutated into a social question as the
economy spun out of control. The main stratum behind the national resistance was thus the hard-hit working class.

Otto Bauer dubbed the constellation that emerged in Hungary
a "dictatorship of desperation."[54] Initially, there had been no
effort to install a Communist regime, Károlyi's plan being rather
to form a government made up solely of Social Democrats in
order to mobilize sister parties in the Western nations to oppose a
Carthaginian peace against Hungary. The Communists were to
be given the task of supporting the government from outside, with
one eye toward Soviet Russia. But events soon took their own
course. The Social Democrats decided to join the Communists
in a new socialist party. Communist leaders were released from
prison, where they had been in detention since February on
charges of incitement to rebellion. And instead of orienting itself
toward the West, the new Hungarian Soviet government turned
to the Russian Bolsheviks and the October Revolution.[55]

The readiness of the peace conference to give Rumania a
green light to march into Hungarian territory crystallized in an-
ticipation of the decision to evacuate Odessa and to hand over all
supplies, armaments, and equipment provided for the Whites in
southern Russia to the Rumanians—this to help them stabilize the

Dniester front.[56] Wilson and Lloyd George, who otherwise had misgivings about the French policy of intervention, also came out in favor of strengthening the "Rumanian fortress" against Bolshevism.[57] And Rumania made itself ready to realize its territorial claims in Hungary by overthrowing its Soviet government. This decision was all the easier since the French scheme of a *barrière de l'est* and a cordon sanitaire foresaw no role for Hungary. It was not difficult to hand Hungary over to nationally motivated dismemberment by its neighbors.[58]

The fact that Hungary let itself be bullied this way was not simply the result of France's grand design for Central European politics. The problems lay deeper, in the country's ethnic diversity and an unresolved agrarian question. With the military collapse in 1918, a problem that had long plagued the Hungarian half of the Hapsburg monarchy became even more apparent: Hungary's substantial ethnic diversity was fundamentally incompatible with the more modern, unitary territoriality of a nation-state. Traditionally, Hungary had been a confederation of the lands under St. Stephan's crown, dominated by Magyar magnates, a nation ruled by nobility whose Magyarization policies could only provoke the nationalism of other ethnic groups.[59]

For decades, this notorious combination of a dominant agrarian aristocracy with festering issues of nationality had hampered every effort to reform and modernize the country's institutions.[60] This was the case for both problems of political legitimacy and land reform. Ultimately, Hungary's social admixture stood in the way of every demand for the introduction of universal suffrage.[61] It was thus no surprise that the non-Magyar ethnic groups— Slovaks, Croats, Rumanians, to name only the most important— wished for a way out of Hungary. Also, they came under the gravitational pull of the new nationally minded neighbor states. Indeed, the staggering territorial losses that Hungary had to cope with after the war, as laid out in the Vix ultimatum and ratified at

Trianon, were largely due to the country's explosive mix of unresolved agrarian and multiethnic questions. But even Hungary's
dismemberment was no solution to the accumulated problems.
The losses placed an enormous number of ethnic Hungarians—
Magyars—outside the new borders. Overnight they found themselves in foreign states. Quite apart from the territorial exactions
of its neighbors, Hungary thus faced a difficult question: what
form of Hungary did it wish to be?

In view of the country's multinational makeup, the Soviet
government in Budapest proposed a federative approach, both
national and internationalist. The approach was national in that it
preserved the territorial integrity and economic unity of the ancient crown lands and sought to defend its borders in a patriotic
war.[62] The Hungarian Soviet government could be sure of popular support, especially from the army, which had promptly transformed itself into a revolutionary army for these patriotic reasons.[63] The fact that most of the officers in the Hungarian Red
Army came from areas forcibly occupied by neighboring states
strengthened its the patriotic mood.[64] And the approach was
international insofar as the government's proposed solution to
the nationalities problem was to promote a de-Magyarization of
Hungary, with autonomous institutions and self-government for
the non-Hungarian segments of the population.[65] With such
often contradictory promises, it hoped to persuade these non-
Hungarians to remain within the Hungarian state. A blueprint
for a potential revolutionary Danube federation encompassing a
number of states beyond Hungary proper was meant to neutralize the country's nationalities question. In any case, a federation
would preserve economic unity, the chief concern of the workers
in the spring of 1919.

Béla Kun's popularity thus rested largely on his commitment
to preserve Hungary's territorial unity; his constituencies were not
at all annoyed by a defense of Hungarian integrity against the
"Entente imperialists" through the use of slogans of class struggle

and universal civil war.[66] At the same time, the Hungarian Communists were increasingly disliked because of the harsh measures they took against the counterrevolution at home. The position of the Commissariat of the Interior, for example, seemed bizarre: it retaliated against the actions of the Rumanians, labeled as counterrevolutionary Whites, by punishing Hungary's own political reactionaries, as though what was unfolding were class warfare proper.[67] The upshot of this Red terror was a desire on the part of the aristocracy and upper bourgeoisie for both its quick termination and the imminent arrival of the "counterrevolutionary" Rumanians; even the middle classes viewed the approaching foreign troops as saviors.

At the beginning of August 1919, the experiment of the Hungarian Soviet Republic came to an end. The 133 days of Béla Kun were over. The Hungarian Bolsheviks and members of the left-wing segment of the Social Democrats fled across the frontier, most into nearby Austria. Some one hundred thousand refugees crossed the border, which proved a wise decision. After the withdrawal of the Rumanians, the White Hungarian exile government—headed by prime minister Pál Teleki von Szék and with the former commanding admiral of the Austro-Hungarian navy, Miklós Horthy, as war minister—unleashed a wave of terror whose excesses dwarfed the horrors of the Red regime. The anti-Semitism surfacing in this new cataclysm was notorious.[68]

From its outset, the Hungarian revolution, as a national "anti-imperialist" revolt against the policies of the Entente, had no real prospect of preserving the country's territorial integrity. The reasons for this were manifold: its excessive social radicalization; Béla Kun's error in mistaking the nationalistically motivated support of the population for a pro-Communist attitude; the revolution's international and regional isolation. The plan to link up strategically with the Russian Red Army, thus realizing a threat initially meant to deter the draconian conditions set by the peace conference, had failed. This projected pathway of revolution into Central Europe had been, in the end, the only serious pressure the Kun government could exert to preserve Hungary's territorial integrity.[69]

The plan had been based on false calculations—more on wishful thinking than on reality. Károlyi had been informed by his military advisers Aurel Stromfeld and Jenö Tombar that the Red Army was less than 250 kilometers from the Carpathian Mountains. They suggested it would be a few weeks at the most before the army broke through the Rumanian lines and reached the Hungarian frontier.[70] This assessment was based on an error that would be cleared up only slowly. The forces referred to by Stromfeld and Tombar were in fact the Red Ukrainian army. At the time Béla Kun took power, it was involved in fighting the Ukrainian Whites under Semyon Petlyura, in a far more distant region than Budapest assumed. For its part, the Red Ukrainian army under Antonov-Ovseyenko—basically a partisan force little inclined to deployment beyond homeland borders[71]—faced a clash with powerful Polish forces concentrated around L'vov.

Budapest could not expect any help from the Russian Bolsheviks, whose hands were tied. This involved dramatic events in a theater of the Russian Civil War further to the east. After the Allied loss of Odessa in April, the Whites under Denikin had been able to advance to Kharkov in the eastern Ukraine. At stake were the indispensable Donets Basin and the Danube region.[72] To win this strategically decisive battle, the Soviet high command had dispatched all available troops to this front, including the Ukrainians now integrated into the Red Army. In so doing, the Soviets left open their western front. Polish units moved into the breach, taking control of the strategic railway line between Budapest and Kiev. That decided the fate of the sole remaining connection between the Russian and the Hungarian revolution. It was sealed by the so-called White Poles under Marshall Piłsudski and Denikin's White troops.[73]

The decision by the Russian Bolsheviks to give priority to the struggle against Denikin and thus to the civil war at home was a crucial factor in the isolation and downfall of the Hungarian Soviet Republic. A similar constellation emerged in August 1920 as the Polish-Soviet war was reaching its climax. Here Moscow gave priority to the fight against the Whites under Wrangel in southern Russia over support for Tukhachevsky's advance on Warsaw. At that point at the latest, it became clear that the revolution in Russia was geared mainly to Russian concerns. Aspirations for world revolution, if a consideration at all, were clearly secondary.

In the cases of both Hungary and Poland, the Bolshevik decision to favor the needs of the Russian Civil War over a world-revolutionary effort may have been guided by a wish to avoid excessively challenging the Entente and the Allies. An attempt to forge links with the Hungarian Soviet Republic would have prompted an Allied intervention going well beyond involvement of the republic's neighboring states. The Russian and Hungarian revolutions thus had different fates. In historical perspective, there is symbolic resonance in the fact that the Red Army's August 1919 offensive against Denikin in the Ukraine coincided with the end of Béla Kun's rule in Budapest.

Rumania was one pillar of the "Thermopylae of Western civilization." The other pillar was Poland. The Bolshevik revolution's wave broke over Poland, in a war that, despite all its world-revolutionary pathos, had all the features of a national conflict. Viscount d'Abernon, British ambassador in Berlin and head of the Anglo-French military mission dispatched to Warsaw, would judge the Polish-Soviet war of 1920 to be one of the most fateful battles in world history.[74] However this now largely forgotten war is ultimately assessed, its consequences were substantial.[75] It can be understood superficially as having led to a regulation of borders between Poland and Soviet Russia, the March 1921 Peace of Riga. It can be understood less superficially as having spelled the end of the Russian Revolution's world-revolutionary orientation.

Boundary arrangements are more than just a few lines on a map. They are the expression of deeper changes, in this case the transformation of the Russian Revolution into the Soviet state. To constitute a state means distinguishing between internal and external—a distinction that could be ignored in the earlier revolutionary élan. Following the Polish-Soviet war, the Soviets were in any case forced to accommodate their world-revolutionary leanings to accepted modes of diplomacy, an accommodation leading inevitably to a step-by-step decline in importance for the world revolution's central command, the Comintern. The contours of Soviet state power emerged with corresponding sharpness. Particularly striking is the concentration of basic Soviet policy decisions in the period following the war's end. One good example is Trotsky's brutal suppression of the March 1921 sailors' mutiny at Kronstadt—a decision made in a quasi-civil war, demonstrating statehood on an interior level. The New Economic Policy, marking the end of wartime Communism, was introduced right after the mutiny's suppression.[76] By 1922, the Soviet Union's founding process—a process initiated as a "turn to socialism in one country" in the aftermath of the Polish-Russian war[77]—had finally been formally completed.

For Soviet foreign policy and its formation, the end of the war in Poland was of constitutive importance.[78] Along with the trade agreements signed with England and Germany in the spring of 1921—overtures to the West—relations with the Weimar Republic were given special weight.[79] Despite all the ideological differences between Germany and Russia, the two outcasts of the Paris peace conference, there was a distinctive geopolitical convergence between the two states, something like a continuation of the "negative Poland policy" long pursued by Prussia and Russia.[80] The rapprochement between Germany and Moscow was in fact anchored in the Polish question. Already apparent in the 1922 Treaty of Rapallo, the rapprochement was furthered in the 1926 Berlin Treaty—a confirmation of German-Soviet cooperation even after Germany's entry into the League of Nations. Then in 1939 the Hitler-Stalin pact extinguished Poland as a state.[81]

The 1920 Polish-Soviet war strengthened the Polish national identity developed over the course of the nineteenth century to the same extent that it determined Poland's territorial perimeters as set down in Riga in March 1921.[82] To a certain extent, that war can be viewed as a belated Polish war of independence against imperial Russia. It was characterized by a remarkable fusion of nationalistically colored traditional antagonisms with an ideological war of values that had begun in 1917. Correspondingly, the war has been interpreted in markedly different ways. From the Polish perspective, the war was mainly a successful defensive war against the traditional Russian enemy, who once again had designs on Warsaw—this time decked out in red. On the one hand, for Poles the "miracle on the Vistula" took on a downright metaphysical significance. It seemed as if the national telos of Polish history had finally been realized. The August 1920 assault on Warsaw by the Russian Revolutionary general Mikhail Tukhachevsky reawakened all the Polish memories of partition and nineteenth-century uprisings brutally suppressed by czarist Russia. On the other hand, for the Bolsheviks the war was mainly a defensive struggle against a second front, opened up by White Poles, in the counterrevolutionary wars of intervention imposed on them by the imperialist Entente and its allies.[83]

Both interpretations of the event are accurate; but both situations were more complicated than either interpretation suggests. While the Poles, in their national exuberance, had almost lost sight of the interventionist character of their military move, the Soviets sought to reinforce the pathos of class with the pathos of nation. In defending themselves against an intervention by the White Poles that stemmed ostensibly from the imperialist machinations by the Entente, the Soviets proclaimed a war on behalf of Mother Russia. Such a war was endowed with an intense iconic significance derived from its connection with earlier great patriotic events: the Polish occupation of Moscow in 1610, the Napoleonic invasion in 1812, the outbreak of World War I in 1914.[84] In the context of a semantics of civil war and interventionist aggression, couched in terms of class struggle, recourse to such patriotically calibrated discourse was a novelty. But this shift of political semantics can be explained by the historical significance of Poland in Russian memory. The fact that the Polish "lords" had once more attacked the Russian motherland had astonishing consequences. Thousands of former czarist officers rushed to defend the red flag. Deserters from the Red Army flocked to reenlist. Aleksei Brusilov, whose name was indelibly associated with the Great War's only successful Russian offensive, called on his compatriots to defend the homeland.[85]

In the battle cry "war against the Polish *panowie*," homage was being paid to an early form of Soviet patriotism, marked by a fusion of the categories of class and nation. The slogan articulated the traditional animosity of White Russian and Ukrainian peasants in the eastern borderlands toward their mainly Polish landowning masters.[86] In a period of a power vacuum, the latter group had coalesced into a Committee for the Defense of the Frontier, meant to preserve both Polish-national and class interests. Throughout the borderlands, there was a striking merger of social, ethnic, and cultural affiliations. Poles thus preferably executed Bolshevik commissars; Soviets liquidated Roman Catholic priests.[87]

At the same time that Soviet slogans centered on class struggle were taking on a national coloring, internal differences among the Bolsheviks were becoming increasingly apparent. There was a tension between two Soviet fronts in the Polish war: the western front under Mikhail Tukhachevsky and the southwestern front under Alexander Yegorov. As a member of the war council of the southwestern front, Stalin was subordinate to Yegorov. In his thrust to the west and Warsaw, Tukhachevsky seemed to be pursuing thoroughly independent world-revolutionary goals of his own.[88] Stalin, on the other hand, gave priority to fighting the Whites under Wrangel in southern Russia, and thus to Russia's civil war, over any export of the revolution to the West. An internal Soviet conflict thus emerged within the war between "aristocratic" Poland and "patriotic" Soviet Russia, a conflict between the principles of world revolution and "socialism in one country" that seemingly decided a favorable outcome for Poland in advance.

In any case, the Polish war also had profound effects on Poland. At the end of the Great War, the nature of the future Polish state had still been open to question. There was no clarity regarding its territorial perimeters or ethnic composition. Its population included not only Polish Catholics, but also Ukrainians, White Russians, Jews, Lithuanians, and Germans. The territorial yardstick for the new state was the federal monarchic Polish-Lithuanian Commonwealth and its successor body politic dismembered by partition in the last third of the eighteenth century.[89] To this extent, Poland saw itself as a restored rather than new nation. The tension between a past-focused vision of a Polish commonwealth controlling substantial territory and the changed social circumstances of the present produced structural discrepancies hardly amenable to political solution. When it came to ethnic and religious coexistence, what may have functioned in a premodern, corporate state and social order generated enormous tensions in the context of modern principles of popular sovereignty and democratic participation.[90] During the entire interwar period, the nominally Polish yet factually multiethnic Second Republic suffered from insoluble minority problems; more than a third of all Polish citizens were not ethnic Poles.[91] These problems were in turn the expression of an unresolved political identity, wavering between a unitarian nation-state and a state defined by its various nationalities.

So which Poland would it be? There were two competing conceptions. The Polish National Democrats under Roman Dmovski espoused a central state that would seek to Polonize the non-ethnic Poles. This position was challenged by the Second Republic's founder, Józef Piłsudski, whose goal was the creation of a federated multiethnic state of the Polish nation. One aim of such a federated structure would have been to incorporate both the Jagiellonian empire's medieval–early modern borders and the non-Polish ethnic populations living within them. This visionary federation under Polish leadership was ultimately to encompass the entire area from Finland to the Black Sea, including at least Lithuania, White Russia, and the western Ukraine. Such a concept was based on an institutionally or culturally based notion of Polish statehood, rather than one that was ethnically constituted; its realization would have made it possible to integrate populations in the eastern borderlands that defined themselves primarily in term of language and religion rather than nation. In the end, such a notion was more imperial than national in its aspirations. To be sure, the two opposing concepts in the Polish-Soviet war were likewise imperially oriented: on the one hand, a Polish concept, itself harking back to early modern configurations, that sought to subsume different ethnic populations beneath an aegis of Polish national hegemony; on the other hand, an imperial Russian concept that had been further universalized by way of proletarian internationalism.

The territorial arrangement made at the end of the Polish-Soviet war extended the Polish frontiers far beyond the "ethnographic border," known as the Curzon Line, that had been proposed by the Allies.[92] The result of the arrangement was a territorially overextended Polish national state that had no interest in a federal structure. Rather, the new Polish state was bent on Polonizing its non-Polish ethnic groups.[93] Moreover, the extension of Poland's boundaries beyond its ethnic frontiers meant that identical ethnic populations lived on both sides of the new borders: in the East, Ukrainians, White Russians, and Lithuanians; in the West, Germans. In the context of ongoing state centralization and Polonization of the population, Poland's problematic ethnic composition was bound to place a double burden on the Second Republic: an unresolved minorities problem within, a festering border question without. As a result of the questions of borders and minorities, Poland's relations with its neighbor states were extremely difficult; effectively this meant a political isolation of the restored Polish Republic in Central and East Central Europe.[94] Its relations with Lithuania, Czechoslovakia, and the German Reich were strained. Despite the Riga treaty, Polish-Soviet relations themselves would be overshadowed by contentions when Warsaw responded to the Soviet Union's entry into the League of Nations in 1934 by renouncing its obligations for minority protection. The intent was to thwart the possibility of Soviet intervention in Geneva on behalf of the Ukrainians and White Russians living in Poland.[95]

The personality of head of state Piłsudski has significance for understanding the dilemma of Poland as a restored nation. His biography reads like a narrative of the distillation of Polish national self-understanding from a broad imperial substrate. Józef Piłsudski was born in 1867 in the environs of Vilna, at the time a city largely inhabited by Poles and Jews. His background was the Polish-Lithuanian minor nobility.[96] In the czar's autocratic empire, he became involved in revolutionary activity and was banned to Siberia. In 1892, he helped found the Polish Socialist Party. His brother Bronislav, likewise an active revolutionary, was implicated in an attempt on the life of Alexander III, the same assassination plot that cost Lenin's brother his life. Felix Dzerzhinsky, a revolutionary and Bolshevik, and like Piłsudski from a minor noble background, attended the same school in Vilna, though a decade later.[97] In contrast to Piłsudski, who would foreswear revolution and embrace Polish nationalism, Dzerzhinsky remained attached to imperial conceptions, even if in an internationalist, Bolshevik form. In World War I, Piłsudski commanded the "Polish legions" he had formed within the Austro-Hungarian army.[98] From December 1917 onward, Dzerzhinsky headed the Cheka, the Bolshevik "extraordinary commission," or secret political police, he had helped establish and that was known as the party's "sword and shield."[99]

The 1920 Polish-Soviet war was a war of national separation and imperial co-optation. The military confrontation meant a renegotiation of who belonged to the Polish nation and who did not. Historical residue reemerged everywhere. Even the Polish contingents on the battlefield reflected the history of partition, with Prussian, Russian, and Austrian traditions colliding. Polish units that had fought on the side of the victorious Entente in the Great War refused to obey Poles who had sided with the defeated Central Powers. Many soldiers were still uncertain about their ethnic affiliation. For example, Russian Ulans were among the units under Polish general Zeligovsky, who had fought in the civil war on the side of the intervention forces under French command and against the Ukrainian Reds near Odessa. Likewise, Polish riflemen could be found in the ranks on the Soviet western front.[100]

Social and ethnic markers of national belonging were reconfigured not only on the battlefield but also in Warsaw. There were doubts about whether certain professional groups in the working class, such as the trade union members among the weavers and the metalworkers, actually belonged to the Polish nation. In July 1920 entire working-class neighborhoods were temporarily cordoned off. Also, the war between national Poland and imperial Russia exacerbated relations between ethnic Poles and Polish Jews, which had become increasingly tense since the 1880s. Doubts were raised about whether Polish Jews belonged to the Polish nation. They were suspected of espousing the tradition of the supranational empire. Representatives of the Jewish workers' movement were taken into custody, Jewish soldiers were sent back from the front, and Jewish nurses were removed from field hospitals. A sizable number of Polish Jews were imprisoned—interned, rather tellingly, in a camp originally meant for Soviet POWs.[101]

Poland constituted itself as a "white" nation in face of its "red" military adversary, the Russian empire. This was to have dramatic consequences for the Polish Communists.[102] In any case, they and their predecessor organization, the Social Democratic Party of the Kingdom of Poland and Lithuania, founded by Rosa Luxemburg, represented a tradition deprecated in Poland. It was alleged that they had placed the exigencies of class struggle above the nation's desire for independence. The stigma of national treachery clung to them and would continue to do so. Reservations about the Communists were intensified by their sense of loyalty to Soviet Russia, a state nationally minded Poles saw as simply a newer version of the hated empire. In this way the Polish Communist effort to gain a solid foothold in Polish society was doomed to failure from the start.[103]

While national Polish contours were sharpened by a clear demarcation from imperial Russia, Communists familiar with the situation in the eastern border area tried to dissuade the Soviets from an offensive strategy vis-à-vis Poland. Karl Radek, secretary of the Comintern and a native of L'vov, warned Lenin not to harbor any illusions that the Polish workers were impatiently awaiting the Red Army's onslaught in order to cast off their chains.[104] And in fact, Warsaw's workers formed battalions to defend the nation; poorly armed, they threw themselves against Tukhachevsky's army. After the Soviet failure on the Vistula, Lenin could not avoid conceding that Radek had been right all along.[105]

The Polish-Soviet war had begun in 1919 with seemingly insignificant skirmishes, after the German Ober-Ost command began pulling back troops that had been kept mobilized on Allied instruction. The vacuum formed by the German withdrawal drew both Poles and Soviets into its vortex.[106] The actual war began in May 1920 with the march of Piłsudski's troops on Kiev, the Polish marshal thus trying to put his plans for a federation into action. The move proved a failure, provoking a Soviet counterattack that brought the Red Army to the gates of Warsaw in August. The counterattack's director, Tukhachevsky, was a twenty-seven-year-old Russian nobleman who enjoyed boasting that he was no older than Bonaparte had been when he was entrusted with the Italian campaign.[107] However inflated this sense of self-esteem, as a convert to Marxism Tukhachevsky appears to have taken the idea of world revolution very seriously. He did not hide his objectives, proclaiming in daily commands that the operation's final goal was Warsaw.[108] It seemed that nothing could stop the general in his westward advance.

Precisely what the Soviet leadership thought about Tukhachevsky's offensive tactics and world-revolutionary enthusiasm can hardly be reconstructed. But the evidence seems to point to the party, the Comintern, and the Red Army leaving the question of the assault on Warsaw open, waiting to see how the situation evolved and evading a strategic decision.[109] The responsible authorities were thus inclined, it seems, to keep things hovering in the balance. From their vantage point, with Denikin having been defeated at Novorossysk, the civil war was nearing its end. Negotiations with England had been initiated for a trade agreement ending the Allied economic blockade and paving the way for Russia's return to the world economy.[110] On the Entente's side, such an agreement was a pet project of British prime minister Lloyd George, who hoped to revive the flagging postwar British economy through trade with Russia while simultaneously "taming" the Bolsheviks. For the community of nations, Russia was to become a predictable quantity once again.[111] Such intentions were incompatible with visions of world revolution.

For the Bolsheviks, negotiations with London were important in another way. It had long been understood that France and

Britain, little liked as imperialist interventionists, were not pursuing common goals vis-à-vis Russia. France was intent on the overthrow of the Bolshevik regime. It recognized White general Wrangel, who had established himself in southern Russia, as the legitimate representative of the Russian state. The British were more wary. The anti-Bolshevist hardliner Churchill even suspected Lloyd George of harboring certain sympathies for the Soviets.[112]

Hence Tukhachevsky's advance on Warsaw threatened Soviet Russia's movement from a revolutionary condition to one of statehood. It threatened the negotiations with the British, raising the possibility of the renewal of the interventionist Entente coalition, now drifting apart, for a second anti-Bolshevik crusade. Lloyd George had already dispatched the Anglo-French military mission under Viscount Lord D'Abernon and French general Maxime Weygand to Warsaw. Their task was to stand by the hard-pressed Polish state in face of the red onslaught.

As indicated, Tukhachevsky failed. Warsaw's defenders held their ground, and the Soviets were forced to pull back. The end of hostilities led to peace negotiations and, in March 1921, to the Treaty of Riga. In the view of contemporaries, this extraordinary turn of events, was due to the help of French general Weygand, an analogy thus being drawn to the "miracle on the Marne." But the Poles had fought the battle basically on their own and kept the Entente mission at arm's length.[113] It is in any case unclear if the confrontation between the Poles and the Soviets on the Vistula was an actual battle, the expected clash between enemy armies. Even Piłsudski was startled by the course of events. Tukhachevsky's troops apparently had lacked sufficient striking force as they approached Warsaw, having become overextended. On the long march west, their lines had become increasingly stretched. It thus actually seemed that the Soviets had withdrawn before any real showdown. They had probably sought to avoid the showdown because their left flank had unexpectedly been left exposed. The armies from the southwestern front Tukhachevsky had demanded for cover had not been dispatched—this included the elite units of the First Red Cavalry under Semyon Budyonny, the *konarmiya* so richly described by Isaak Babel.[114]

The "miracle on the Vistula" was largely the result of internal Soviet differences. In retrospect, these can be easily rationalized as reflecting a basic conflict between the ideas of world revolution and "socialism in one country." But a closer look reveals something more trivial. Stalin does not appear to have given any thought to releasing the *konarmiya* from his control. Rather, he used the indecisiveness of the Moscow leadership to withhold the cavalry and other troops from Tukhachevsky and thus from the western front—even though officially they had been placed under Tukhachevsky's command. Instead, Stalin sent them against L'vov—in order, some have suggested, to keep them occupied there.[115] For his part, Lenin shared Stalin's view that a military operation against Wrangel in the south was far more important than a relatively hopeless thrust to the west.[116] In the final analysis, the leadership in Moscow was simply not prepared to link up the western and southwestern fronts. The southwestern front was meant to bring the civil war in southern Russia to an end, which was achieved with the victory over Wrangel in November.

The internal Soviet wrangling during the Polish-Soviet war strengthened Stalin's hand. The war's results worked to the future general secretary's advantage, the end of impassioned world-revolutionary internationalism and the decline of the Comintern coming at the expense of Western-oriented intellectuals like Trotsky, furthering the party's nationalization and Russification.[117] Stalin also knew how to put the Polish-Soviet war to good use institutionally. In taking control of the armies on the southwestern front, he was able to establish a subservient political power base. Voroshilov, Timoshenko, Rokossovsky, Zhukov, and others were connected with the First Cavalry and later belonged to Stalin's political clique.[118] Tukhachevsky would eventually be accused of Bonapartism; along with other high-ranking Red

Army officers, he would be liquidated in the 1936–38 Great Purge. His June 1937 death sentence, as well as that of other commanding generals and corps commanders, would be signed by the former commanding echelon of the southwestern front in the Polish-Soviet war: Voroshilov, Budyonny, and Yegorov.[119]

Mainly as a result of the corrosive problem of borders and nationalities, Poland's international isolation intensified in the 1920s and 1930s. Relations with Czechoslovakia—a state that relied, like Poland, on France and its Central European policies—were extremely strained, since Prague had exploited the chance offered by the Polish-Soviet war to take possession of the disputed Olsa region around the Silesian city of Teschen (Cieszyn and Těšín), an important industrial and transport center. In October 1938, Poland, though not a revisionist power like Germany or Hungary (which both wished to cast off the peace conditions set in Versailles and Trianon), would itself use the opportunity presented by the September Munich Agreement and Germany's subsequent takeover of the Sudetenland to annex the Olsa region.[120]

The ominous military and economic ties between Germany and the Soviet Union during the interwar period can be traced back to the Polish-Soviet war.[121] Germany and Russia had been extremely reluctant to accept the existence of a Polish state; their border and nationalities conflicts with that state and the exclusion of these two powers from the evolving European security system were reason enough for a rapprochement. The 1920–21 plebiscites aimed at demarcating the German-Polish border were accompanied by pronounced hostility toward Poland on the German side. The Russian march on Warsaw was greeted by Germans with great glee. In Gleiwitz (Gliwice) in August 1920, German demonstrators were exhilarated by rumors of a Soviet victory. They waved images of Lenin and Trotsky—though, of course, for reasons of nationalism, not class. The subsequent clashes between Germans and Poles, at the time Poles and Soviets were confronting each other at the Vistula, led to the second Silesian uprising.[122]

In their wish for an end to Poland, the German borderland population felt an inner bond with the Russians.[123]

The rapprochement between Germany and Russia, so important for the Weimar Republic, was thus largely due to their common animosity toward Poland. The first steps toward secret cooperation were initiated during the Polish-Soviet war.[124] The Soviets requested intelligence from the Germans on Polish troop concentrations in the West. They also asked for military aid, which the Germans were unable to provide due to the international situation and their declared neutrality. The German authorities did agree, however, to impede the transport of armaments for Poland through the North Sea–Baltic Canal.[125] And after the Soviet defeat, arrangements had to be made for returning the Soviet soldiers who had opted for German internment in East Prussia during the hasty withdrawal from Poland.

In the interwar period, two competing attitudes toward Germany were politically dominant in Soviet Russia. One, revolutionary, was espoused by the Comintern. The other, grounded in realpolitik, represented the state and was expressed through Soviet diplomacy. With the waning of revolutionary expectations, the second attitude gained the upper hand, especially since such expectations had always been illusory when it came to Germany. The prospect of a linkage between the Russian Revolution and a possible German revolution had evaporated with the end of the Polish-Soviet war at the latest. The idea of a revolutionized Poland functioning as a "red bridge" had foundered on the banks of the Vistula. In a detailed memorandum, Soviet special envoy Victor Kopp—a close associate of Trotsky sent to Berlin to arrange for the release of Soviet soldiers in German internment camps—cautioned against any revolutionary activity in Germany.[126] Rather, Soviet policy was best oriented toward cooperation with Germany's conservative forces, an assessment shared by Karl Radek, an established expert on the German situation.[127] The reckless Communist uprising in central Germany and Hamburg in March 1921, which was sanctioned by the Comintern, and the activities of the German Communist Party in Saxony and Thuringia, are best seen as late reflexes of a revolutionary hope long since eviscerated. In this context, there was a powerful symbolic dimension to the fact that army commander Hans von Seeckt, an outstanding proponent of close German-Soviet cooperation against Poland and Versailles, had been responsible for smothering Germany's last revolutionary flames. But whether it took the path of revolution or reaction, a German-Soviet community of shared interests was inevitably emerging, just as Radek had predicted.[128]

In this period, such commonality of interests was grounded mainly in a shared opposition to the order of peace and security laid down in Paris. While Germany was seeking, with Soviet help, to circumvent the Versailles provisos regarding armaments technology and the military, the Soviet Union was chiefly interested in breaking through an isolation inflicted by the cordon sanitaire. The political vector of this German-Soviet bond was shared enmity toward Poland, an enmity at work in the question of borders, of the German minority, and of the very existence of the Polish state. The intensity of this "companionship in misfortune" (to paraphrase Churchill) was inversely proportional to the closeness of the ties one or the other state assumed with the West, in other words with France and Great Britain, pillars of the League of Nations. For example, after the signing of the Treaty of Locarno in 1925, marking the onset of genuine peace between Germany and France, the German Reich had joined the League of Nations in 1926; but it would retain a certain balance between East and West through the Berlin Treaty concluded with Russia that same year. The latter treaty's signing, together with German misgivings about the paragraph on sanctions in Article 16 of the League of Nations statutes, were signals to the Soviet Union that despite Germany's co-optation into the system of collective security, it would not act against Russia.[129] It had proved impossible to negotiate an

"Eastern Locarno" providing international guarantees for Poland's and Czechoslovakia's western borders with Germany (in the same way the eastern borders of France and Belgium had been guaranteed). For this reason, German political parties and governments, especially those on the right, could nurture the prospect of a revision of the eastern frontier.[130] Any realization of such a prospect naturally required good relations with the Soviet Union.

In May 1933, Reich Chancellor Hitler renewed the Berlin Treaty, despite his notorious anti-Bolshevism. He may have done so in acknowledgment of the Reichswehr's desire to continue cooperating with the Red Army. To be sure, that cooperation would come to an end the following autumn. Arrangements to terminate the Rapallo policies had already been made under Hitler's predecessor, Brüning; with his pro-French tilt, Papen had introduced an anti-Soviet tendency into German foreign policy. In contrast, the Schleicher government, on notoriously intimate terms with the Reichswehr, hoped to change course once again and intensify relations with Moscow. Such a strictly realpolitik-based orientation, driven by anti-Polish considerations, seemed self-evident to the Soviets. Realpolitik was apparent. In discussions with Schleicher, the Soviet foreign minister Litvinov could thus voice the view that it was only natural for Communists in Germany to be treated the same way as Russia treated enemies of the state.[131] In any case, cooperation between the Red Army and the Reichswehr lost its raison d'être once Hitler decided to restore unrestricted German sovereignty in matters of defense and armaments.[132] But despite constant tensions during the 1930s, economic exchange between Germany and Russia continued basically undiminished. The Soviet Union went on importing about half of its metal-processing machinery from Germany, while the Reich covered a sizable portion of its needs for oil, manganese, and wheat through Soviet imports.[133]

In 1934, a year after Germany's departure from the League of Nations (and two years after the departure of Japan), the Soviet

Union joined the organization. In their rapprochement with the Western powers, the Soviets endorsed the system of collective security; in May 1935 they signed a treaty of mutual assistance with France. To bolster this turn in foreign policy, which went hand in hand with increasing internal repressions that culminated in the Great Purge, Stalin made use of the almost-forgotten Comintern, an institution for which he had shown little liking. At its seventh "Brussels conference" in the summer of 1935, Stalin proclaimed the "popular front" strategy as binding Soviet policy for the Communist parties in the West. One motivation for this move was a particular desire to influence the French political scene. Although Stalin's belated recognition of the need to cooperate with Social Democracy, previously denounced as the archenemy, helped to bolster the struggle against Fascism, this about-face also resembled a castling move in an international power-political game of chess. Within this game, Stalin would end up downplaying the ideological anti-Fascist antagonism with Hitler, instead placing weight on the more durable notion of an incompatibility between "imperialism" and the Soviet Union. In this respect, Moscow's balanced relations with Fascist Italy during the 1930s undermined the notion of the centrality of ideological constants in Soviet foreign policy.[134]

After Chamberlain, Daladier, Mussolini, and Hitler came to an understanding about the Sudetenland in Munich in September 1938, thus consigning Czechoslovakia to its fate, Stalin believed any alliance was conceivable. Germany and the Western powers had worked out an agreement on a quandary of European politics, while leaving the Soviet Union—a Continental power actually allied with Czechoslovakia—outside in the cold. The policy of collective security had finally collapsed. Also, there were rumors that Britain and France intended to direct Hitler's attention eastward. In Moscow, Hitler's purported appetite for the Ukraine had become notorious; perhaps, it was felt, the Western powers were prepared to allow him a free hand in Central and East

Central Europe.[135] In light of such considerations, any difference in Stalin's eyes between the "imperialist" regimes of the Western democracies and Fascist Germany was bound to evaporate. As an orientation point, what remained was the unshakable truth of history's geopolitical constants. Coalitions were to be forged and alliances weighed according to traditional patterns of power management and diplomacy.[136] The main concern was to exploit antagonisms in the "imperialist camp" to one's own benefit. The end of the Polish state was one possible scenario. A shift in the European system of alliances involving a rapprochement between Germany and Russia would necessarily entail a renewed partition of Poland. Poland would thus turn out to have been a "seasonal state" within the fading Versailles order.

In terms of geopolitical givens and historical affinities, it seemed easier for Russia to forge a rapprochement with Germany than with the Western democracies. For in their autocratic decision making, dictatorships were not impeded by superfluous institutional rituals of legitimation and public support. Hence while in the democracies the August 1939 Hitler-Stalin pact may have taken faithful Communists by surprise, against the backdrop of such reasoning, despite initial consternation over the pact's power-political consequences, its signing could only confirm liberal, anti-totalitarian certitudes.

Nevertheless, Nazi German–Soviet cooperation could itself not manage without some legitimatizing embellishment or ideological underpinning. The Soviets thus halted their anti-Fascist propaganda; and in Germany, Soviet virtues were now praised profusely, even going so far as talk of a spiritual affinity between the two peoples. In a March 1940 communiqué to Mussolini, Hitler referred to the long path the Soviet regime had traveled from international Bolshevism to Russian nationalism.[137] In April 1941, Stalin suggested to Georgi Dimitrov, chairman of the Comintern, that his organization be dissolved for the benefit of the national autonomy of the various Communist parties—for the sake of a kind of "national Communism." The customary May Day slogans of class struggle needed to be replaced, Stalin indicated, by others extolling the value of nationalism and national liberation.[138]

The first intimations of possible Soviet rapprochement with Nazi Germany had surfaced in the spring of 1939. In March, speaking at the eighteenth party congress, Stalin informed the Western powers that in the event of a conflict he would not be the one to "pull the chestnuts out of the fire." As early as May, Maksim Litvinov, the People's Commissar for Foreign Affairs, a man of bourgeois Jewish origin—in the 1930s his name had been a byword for collective security and rapprochement with the West—was suddenly removed from power. Units of the secret police stormed into his offices, his private phone line was cut, and Stalin ordered his successor, Vyacheslav Molotov, to cleanse the bureaucracy, removing all Jews from office.[139]

The German-Soviet rapprochement had initially been driven by the Polish question. A historic fourth Polish partition would help align both regimes with their national destinies. Molotov's October 1939 speech about the "bastard of Versailles" stood in the tradition of one approach to potential German-Russian relations. Even after Hitler had placed a damper on military cooperation, the common ground between both peoples had been repeatedly stressed by leading cadres in the Red Army. On all possible occasions, top-ranking Soviet military men had expressed their esteem for the Wehrmacht. Tukhachevsky, now vice-chairman of the Soviet War Council and a long-time admirer of the German military tradition, had praised the Red Army for emulating the example of the Reichswehr. At a reception at the Italian embassy in Moscow on 7 March 1936, he had seen nothing dishonorable in uncorking a bottle of champagne and drinking a toast with the German military attaché to the Wehrmacht's successful occupation of the demilitarized zone in the Rhineland.[140] In September 1939, during joint parades and processions by German and Soviet troops on the soil of a freshly conquered Poland, there had been unanticipated reunions between a number of old buddies from the days of cooperation on military matters and arms technology.[141]

In light of the approaching war, Stalin saw the pact with Nazi Germany in basically strategic terms. His stance was rooted in two indelible experiences, the Great War and the civil war. The constellation of the looming world war suggested that the "imperialist" powers would once again tear each other apart. And just as earlier on Bolshevik Russia had withdrawn from the great-power struggle, now it was imperative to keep the Soviet Union out of the war between Germany and its traditional adversaries, England and France. As a neutral party, Russia would derive certain benefits from such an "imperialist" war. At the very least, it would regain control of those territories the Russian empire had temporarily forfeited.[142] It seemed to be only a matter of time or opportunity until Russia, now in the form of the Soviet Union, could turn back to traditionally salient concerns linked with the old Eastern Question: the Balkans, the Straits, access to the Persian Gulf. In that region, it could only collide with Britain.

The Soviet distrust of Britain and France thus stemmed from memories of the Russian Civil War and Western intervention. It was intensified when London and Paris rallied in support of the beleaguered Finns in the Winter War of 1939–40. After attacking Finland on 30 November, the USSR was duly expelled from the Anglo-French–dominated League of Nations. Germany, on the other hand, had declared its disinterest in the Baltic and Finland, thus indirectly handing this area to the Soviet Union. When Moscow asked for German help in connection with the blockade of Finland, Germany agreed, and the Soviets then failed to further pressure the Reich to fulfill its promise.[143] Aired in 1940, the French proposal to open an Allied front in the Black Sea and Caucasus regions, thus hindering German-Soviet cooperation and preventing armed hostilities from erupting in the west, was itself highly reminiscent of the civil war and Western intervention.[144]

Also, in March 1940 the British and the French were making preparations to bomb the strategic backbone of German-Soviet cooperation: the oil fields and refineries in Baku, which would involve flying from Iraq over Turkish and Iranian air space. After the fall of France, the plan was leaked by the Germans to further intensify Soviet suspicions of Britain.[145]

In the wake of Germany's blitzkrieg against France in May–June 1940, Stalin's expectations that the "imperialist" war would take a course similar to the Great War vanished. In the interwar period, France had gained the reputation of a formidable Continental military power. This same France had been crushed in a few weeks by the German war machine. Consequently, Stalin's idea that the war would drag on endlessly as it had in World War I had turned out to be mistaken. The warm congratulations Molotov conveyed to Berlin on the occasion of the German victory probably corresponded little to the actual mood in Moscow. The hasty incorporation of the Baltic States into the USSR and the realization of German pledges regarding Bessarabia were palpable signs of a profound uneasiness.[146]

The changed assessment of the situation after the French capitulation left the Soviets with two options. The alliance with Germany could be strengthened and a long-term policy of spheres of influences could be pursued at the expense of the British Empire, an orientation in keeping with traditional Russian policy from the nineteenth century. Or the Soviets could look ahead to an unavoidable head-on confrontation with Germany. Of course, to emerge victorious from that collision would require enormous effort and sacrifice; what the Soviets would most need was time. According to a later statement by Molotov, the USSR could not have been prepared for war until 1943.[147] A postponement by Hitler was unlikely. It was well known that he was in a hurry—a human life span racing against historical time.[148]

Hitler's decision to attack the Soviet Union in the summer of 1941 was based on several factors. First, it was in harmony with his worldview and the notion that Germany had a right to lebens-raum in the East at the expense of the Slavic peoples. This racial-ideological viewpoint merged with a political anti-Bolshevism itself infused with racist elements. Even if the philosophical and ideological proclivities of the German dictator cannot be understood in a narrow, programmatic sense, they clearly embraced and radicalized certain circumstances and situations, thus influencing the conduct of the war in the East. In the first place, from the outset this war was waged as a racial-ideological war of annihilation and not, as on the western front and in North Africa, as a conventional power struggle in keeping with the rules of war.[149] Second, Hitler's decision to attack Russia emerged from the previous power constellation. Hitler's campaigns before Operation Barbarossa can be seen as campaigns of revenge and hegemony. He could thus convince those around him that only a swift victory over the Soviet Union could shatter British hopes for a strategic alliance with the other Continental power on the eastern flank of Europe. From this perspective, the decision was something like a strategic chess move based on Napoleonic patterns.[150] Third, the decision may have reflected the deterioration of German-Soviet relations in the wake of the Reich's unexpected blitzkrieg victory over France. Beforehand, the Soviet grab of the Baltic and Bessarabia, Soviet claims to northern Bukovina, and the stationing of Soviet troops in Lithuania had already led to a certain ill will between the coalition allies. There were also disagreements regarding trade and the supply of goods. Shipments were irregular, doubtless the result of bottlenecks and technical problems, yet these repeatedly engendered doubts on each side about whether the other side was trustworthy.[151]

At the same time, an exceptionally explosive situation had emerged as Germany and Russia threatened to clash in the Balkans, following the classic pattern of European great-power rivalry in this region.[152] Germany had entered the old trajectory of Hapsburg monarchy expansion, collecting the fragments of

France's collapsed southeast European interwar alliances. Under the Reich's aegis, the territorial disputes between Hungary and Rumania had been resolved. When the Soviets, in consultation with the German Reich, requested a Bulgarian-Soviet agreement on the transit of Soviet troops for the "defense of the entrance to the Black Sea," the request was promptly rejected.[153] In November 1940, Molotov conveyed Stalin's demands regarding Soviet air and naval bases in the Bosporus and the Dardanelles and Soviet territorial claims "south of Baku and Batumi." The German response was a blunt no.[154] When Bulgaria then granted transit rights to German troops in February 1941, relations between Germany and the Soviet Union reached a nadir. Germany had made the Balkans part of its sphere of influence, to Russia's detriment. On 6 April, following a 27 March coup d'état in Belgrade and the conclusion of a friendship treaty between the new Yugoslav government and the USSR, Germany launched a two-pronged attack on Yugoslavia and Greece from Bulgaria.[155] The step was inevitable, especially since Hitler was firm in his eminently ideological resolve to attack the Soviet Union. Nonetheless, such a dramatic decision required an acceptable form of rationalization, if only to satisfy his military and diplomatic entourage.[156] This is not meant to suggest that Hitler followed a consistent ideological-philosophical program—that the elements of realpolitik were mere material for play. But in the fusion of extreme ideological components with a situation growing increasingly radical, the ideology came into play *as if* what was unfolding reflected a rigorous and consistent blueprint.

Stalin had not taken the Nazi worldview at face value. It did not correspond to his view of politics, in which political rule rested less on ideological consistency than on caprice: principles counted for little, and everything was subordinate to the overriding aim of preserving power. Given the primacy of geopolitics and historical lines of conflict, "imperialist" England was a far more serious adversary for the Soviet Union than Nazi Germany—and this even when developments in the Greek theater in the spring of 1941 offered hints of potential Anglo-Soviet convergence. On 13 April, the same day Belgrade fell to the Germans, Stalin demonstratively embraced German ambassador Schulenburg as they both saw off Japanese foreign minister Matsuoka at the White Russian train station in Moscow, thus seemingly putting the lie to all rumors of an imminent German-Russian confrontation.[157] The fact that Hitler ultimately left no option but coming to an arrangement with England, in accord with the Great War's constellation, was beyond Stalin's control. But the alienation between the anti-Hitler coalition's partners, surfacing after Stalingrad and becoming acute after the defeat of Germany and the military exorcism of Nazism, reveals the durability of those conflicting lines of tradition to which Stalin and Churchill were *both* firmly attached.[158]

A historical continuum was not only apparent in the transition from World War II to the Cold War. It also strongly informed relations between postwar Poland and its neighbor states. Since 1920, hostility to Poland had been the starting point and practical foundation for German-Soviet rapprochement. In Polish memory, this juncture pointed to an even more distant past: to the end of the eighteenth century and the era that followed. In various configurations, a link emerges between Poland's national independence and Europe's freedom. In the aftermath of the January 1863 uprising in Poland, Karl Marx commented on this reality rooted in Poland's fateful political geography, its location between Prussia and Russia.[159] The Polish nation constituted itself against both Germany and Russia. It only developed its pronouncedly freedom-centered, antitotalitarian tradition because of the autocratic character of the two neighboring states in the nineteenth century and their dictatorial character in the twentieth century. Freedom from German and Russian subjugation was converted into one of the Polish nation's defining features. German-Soviet agreement on the Polish question was thus always more than a mere correspondence of regimes. In this manner, the independence of the Polish nation was in confluence with the preservation of Europe's freedom. This historical line leads straight to 1989.

Polish resistance was always equally directed against both totalitarian successor states of the partitioning powers, Nazi Germany and Soviet Russia. Hopeless from the onset, the Warsaw uprising of August 1944 is emblematic for Polish history: aimed militarily at Nazi Germany, it was directed politically at Soviet Russia. The westward shift of the country's frontiers after 1945 had done away with its notorious minority problem: the Jews had been in any case exterminated, the Germans expelled, and the White Russians and Ukrainians were now beyond the new eastern frontier, which in its basic demarcation corresponded to the ethnographic Curzon Line drawn by the Allies in 1919. But precisely this shift westward now bonded the new Poland to the Soviet Union. Understating themselves as the "United Workers' Party," the Polish Communists sought to link the national question as a territorial question with political and social values: equality versus freedom. No security for Poland, no territorial integrity, except in alliance with the Soviet Union on the basis of a common social order—that at least was the dictum. In 1955, as a response to West Germany's entry into NATO, the Warsaw Pact was baptized in the capital of a Poland still considered territorially insecure; this fact did not lack symbolic resonance. In 1965, the 1945 Polish-Soviet Friendship and Mutual Assistance Treaty was reaffirmed with explicit recognition of the "inviolability of the national border" on the Oder and Neisse rivers. In this manner, as long as the territorial question in the West remained unresolved, the position of the Polish Communists would remain by and large unchallenged. Against the backdrop of such a close intertwining of domestic and foreign, social and national concerns, any opposition to the Communist rulers could be considered akin to treason.

When the Bonn government under Willi Brandt signed the Eastern Treaties, thus recognizing the Oder-Neisse line and the inviolability of the Polish state, the intertwining strands of this structure, so significant for Polish history, could finally come undone. In the face of "normalization," the Communist Party thus gradually lost the power monopoly in Polish society it had claimed—a monopoly based on its role as guardian of Poland's national integrity, in fraternal alliance with the Soviet Union. To this extent, the increasing success of the Polish protest movement—ranging from the Committee for the Defense of Workers' Rights (KOR) to Solidarity, which appeared on the scene not only as a trade union but also as a champion of Polish freedom—can be understood as a result of Brandt's *Ostpolitik*. As a last step in the process Brandt had initiated, Poland's western borders were recognized by a united Germany in 1990, the belated fulfillment of what could have been achieved in the interwar period with an "Eastern Locarno." With German unification and the border treaty with Poland, Germany now had definite borders, recognized for the first time in its history both at home and by its neighboring states.

3

Regimes

Democracy and Dictatorship

Weimar Lessons / Hermann Müller and Ramsay MacDonald / Tradition and Contingency / Stability and Crisis / England and France / Social Democracy and Radical Republicanism / Parliamentarianism and Authoritarianism / Cabals and Intrigues / Papen and Schleicher / Hitler and Hindenburg / Access to the Ruler / Emblematics of Contingency / Dictatorship and Dictatorship

⁜

The twenty-seventh of March 1930 is a fateful date in modern German history. It marks the resignation of the last parliamentary cabinet of the Great Coalition—a cabinet led by Chancellor Hermann Müller, a Social Democrat—hence the fall of the Weimar Republic's last parliamentary government. This decisive turn preceded another date, now become a negative temporal icon: 30 January 1933, the date Hitler was sworn in as chancellor. Even contemporaries regarded the latter date as a momentous shift of epochs. The former date takes on crucial meaning in historical hindsight and in the framework of historiographical interpretation. Müller's resignation did not provide a hint of the coming catastrophe. This only became generally visible once Hitler took the reins of power. In the interim, one presidentially appointed cabinet succeeded another as the carousel of the Weimar crisis spun gradually out of control. So what justifies stressing the downfall of the Müller government in 1930?

The answer to this question lies in a distinctive quality of the historiography of Weimar, where a disciplined, empirical reconstruction of the past is inevitably shadowed by an urgent issue: that of possible alternatives, not only to Hitler but to the broader course of events, dramatized in retrospect as a crossroads in German history.[1] These events, then, are constantly reexamined in a search for conceivable escapes, historians of Weimar thus repeatedly, explicitly and implicitly, asking: did things have to turn out the way they did?

The question of possible alternatives to what transpired defines Weimar historiography as political to a high degree. This is already manifest during the Weimar Republic's time span. Its history unfolded in a temporally compacted space; at its end, weeks, days, even hours are of urgent interest.[2] The steadily contracting arena for constitutional and political action was occupied by steadily fewer persons. Increasingly, what counted were their inclinations, obsessions, idiosyncrasies, in situations changing at an ever faster pace. The observer is thus drawn into the orbit of a reality reminiscent of court intrigue. Both witnesses to the events looking backward and a horrified posterity have been fascinated by the period's economic, financial, and social policies, the pace of inflation and the rate of unemployment, and the legal and intellectual reflections on unfolding events. All this has been oriented toward that subliminal epistemological question: did it have to turn out the way it did? And beyond this, Weimar historiography took on special political significance in offering the West German polity an arsenal of experience for constitutional formulations, political action, and the formation of a postwar political culture. By 1949 at the latest, the Weimar period had become the Federal Republic's permanent point of reference: Bonn was to become what Weimar had been denied. In this way, in its encapsulation of historical experience, the Weimar Republic emerged as a constitutive storehouse of memory and experience for the second German republic. It was imperative to learn from Weimar's mistakes and avoid its aporias. Finally, what happened then was never to happen again.

An entire torrent of secondary conclusions has issued from Weimar historiography's primary political lessons. Real and imagined certainties about the past have been reflected in findings engraved into Germany's institutional self-awareness.[3] One such certainty about Weimar revolves around the calamities of its democracy—or, more precisely, around the paradigmatic opposition and strict dichotomy manifest in this period between democracy and dictatorship. This dichotomy has emerged as a kind of emblem of the interwar years—and this far beyond Germany. It amounts to one of the fundamental insights into the epoch's experience. If only for the sake of civic education, after World War II a sharp demarcation line between democracy and dictatorship had to be established in Europe's "post-Fascist" societies, especially West Germany. But in fact, under close scrutiny, insights into both the Nazi dictatorship's rise and the horrors it perpetrated that emerge from this conceptual schema hardly prove adequate.[4] In this context, in the face of the catastrophe following the erosion of Weimar's republican and parliamentary options between 1930 and 1933, rather than juxtaposing democracy and dictatorship, it might prove more productive to juxtapose dictatorship with dictatorship.[5]

One advantage of this shift of perspective is its potential for closing a yawning gap in the approaches taken to reconstruct political causalities: the gap between, on the one hand, the theoretically highly unified structural discourse regarding a German "special path," a *Sonderweg* emerging from the nineteenth century and, on the other hand, those various approaches beginning with the facts and circumstances of Weimar's demise. The question of the validity of the notion of a special German path would be posed in a less-dramatic manner if it did not involve a constant groping into a very distant past in search of preconditions for much later events.[6] Nevertheless, questions regarding continuity and contingency and the circumstances leading to the worst of all conceivable scenarios continue to be disturbing, their potency undiminished. Even after we shift our perspective from democracy versus dictatorship to dictatorship versus dictatorship—in view of Nazism's drastic consummation, probably a kind of volte-face—the question still needs to be asked: did it have to turn out the way it did?[7]

In historical retrospect and in view of the emerging catastrophe, the path from the fall of the Müller government, by way of various presidential cabinets, to an increasingly authoritarian regime began with an apparent trifle. Social Democratic Reichstag deputies indebted to trade-union interests refused to support the government headed by Social Democratic chancellor Hermann Müller in a fierce cabinet debate over a particular social-political issue. The German People's Party (DVP), a coalition partner increasingly oriented to the interests of heavy industry, had plans to reduce unemployment benefits for workers; precipitating the government's fall, the SPD faction's move was meant to stymie these plans.[8] Rising joblessness had made reform of Weimar's unemployment insurance program unavoidable. Since reform required a national law, it was a task for the parliamentary majority, thus for the parties in government.[9] Within the cabinet, the conflict might have been postponed for a while, but it was not amenable to resolution. The measures submitted by the two parties at the opposite extremes of the coalition, the SPD and the DVP, were at loggerheads. The restructuring program proposed by the SPD was designed to preserve the obligations of local and state authorities along with the national government by raising the monthly wage deduction to 4 percent and instituting a special emergency levy for unemployment insurance on all workers receiving a regular wage. The DVP, to the contrary, categorically refused to sanction any increase in the monthly compulsory deduction, pressing instead for a reduction in benefits.[10] The SPD parliamentary faction also rejected a procedural compromise negotiated at the last minute by the Center Party and approved by the DVP. Given this situation, the government had no alternative but to resign. Müller was replaced by Heinrich Brüning, who was appointed by President Hindenburg. Brüning's presidential cabinet by no means guaranteed that Hitler would come to power. But the Weimar Republic had been shunted onto a precipitous track, one leading toward increasingly authoritarian rule.

On 27 March, dramatic proceedings took place in the SPD faction, which had been granted fifteen minutes to discuss a possible decision before the ministers convened their cabinet meeting. Labor minister Wissell stood opposed to interior minister Severing. Wissell was able to rely on the support of the national executive of the General German Trade Union Federation (the ADGB). Hermann Müller-Lichtenberg (the chancellor's namesake), a member of the ADGB and its most outspoken advocate within the SPD faction, threatened the party with ADGB opposition should it opt for the proposed compromise. There was probably no need for such verbal threats. The SPD faction was already convinced that the party could not distance itself unduly from the unions, and the compromise was rejected with few dissenting votes. In the cabinet, the DVP proclaimed the coalition dissolved. This parting of the ways was all the easier since collaboration between the parties had in any case lapsed with ratification of the Young Plan for reparations payments. Choked with tears, luckless Hermann Müller thanked his cabinet members for their loyal cooperation.[11]

Even contemporaries realized that the fall of the Müller government was a dark day for Weimar, an evil omen for the republic and democracy. Some were astonished at the insignificance of the issue at stake: a mere 0.25 percent increase in the payment for unemployment insurance, a sum of some 70 million marks, to be divided equally between employers and employees. Was that sufficient cause to sweep the Social Democrats from power and imperil the republic? The need to restructure the ailing unemployment insurance system had haunted the Great Coalition for some time. It had been a constant stumbling block between the two wings of the cabinet, the SPD and the DVP, with the Center Party repeatedly trying to forge a compromise between the workers' party and the party of heavy industry.[12] Still, the unemployment issue was only one factor in the deterioration of relations between these parties in the wake of Germany's economic downturn in 1928. For the SPD and even more so for the trade unions, this tension involved a symbolic conflict over the all-important preservation of Germany's social-political achievements—the real success of the November 1918 revolution. Since these achievements meant more to the Social Democrats, especially to its trade-union wing, than rallying to the republic's defense, the SPD faction's decision on 27 March 1930 seemed far less momentous to the protagonists than it now appears in retrospect.

The faction's stance, which in light of its consequences seems excessively rigid, was a reaction to an ongoing offensive by employers wishing to abrogate the terms of a November 1918 agreement with the trade unions, negotiated and signed in Weimar. This agreement had formed the basis of a compromise between the forces of the ancien régime and those of the German revolution.[13] Facing the threat of insurrection, management had granted seemingly unavoidable concessions to the workers: social policy instead of nationalizations; an eight-hour workday at full wages; collective wage agreements.[14] But as the republic sailed into smoother waters, these arrangements seemed increasingly open to revision. For years, the employers had considered the level of social benefits and wages too high. Given the general profit levels in German business, wages were indeed excessive, and they limited the capacity of German firms to compete in the international market.[15] Still, there was a huge difference between trying to rein in social benefits and wages and a readiness to launch a frontal attack on the social and constitutional order. The employers attempted a rollback across the whole spectrum of social policy, hence a revision of the Weimar compromise also affecting politics. The measures taken included mass lockouts, in violation of state arbitration practices, during the "Ruhr iron dispute" of November–December 1928, the worst labor conflict that Weimar would have to endure.[16] And all this occurred before the Great Depression struck the following year.[17]

From the very onset, the social-political conflicts in Weimar Germany were marked by the old regime's desire to strike a debilitating blow at the republican and parliamentary order. These conflicts threatened to destabilize the country's institutions. The encroachment of economic and social policy on the constitution and form of government was largely due to the state having assumed increasing responsibility for regulating the labor market.[18] In England and France, events took a different turn; their political systems revealed themselves as less imperiled during the international economic crisis. In Germany, the situation had worsened since 1928; it threatened to spin out of control with the onset of the Great Depression in 1929, which left millions unemployed. The worldwide disruptions compounded long-smoldering difficulties, and crisis followed crisis.[19]

Even England, whose time-tested parliamentary democracy made it the most stable country in Europe, was faced with a severe domestic crisis in 1931. Like Hermann Müller in 1930, Ramsay MacDonald and his Labor-led government were forced to adopt drastic social measures to deal with the state's deepening financial difficulties. In accordance with a "sound money" policy, painful cuts in unemployment insurance were necessary. And as in Germany, the Labor MPs, closely bound to organized labor, withdrew their support for the prime minister in August.[20] Instead of resigning, however, MacDonald turned against his party and assembled a government with the Conservative opposition and the remaining Liberals. The fact that he and his entourage were now excluded from their party did not intimidate the Labor leader. To the contrary, he announced new elections, which he and his National Government won by a large margin in October. For its part, the Labor Party was decimated, the only reelected Socialist MPs being those who had proclaimed their allegiance to the prime minister. Given his new majority, MacDonald passed a program of cuts in social spending and guided England through the crisis.[21]

Much has been written about the difference between British and Continental polities. The central question is what were the traditions and institutions saving England's society and political institutions, despite some severe buffeting, from the convulsions besetting other states in the 1930s, casting some into the abyss? (A similar question can be posed regarding France's Third Republic.) Ancient traditions and divergent social-political constellations here clearly played a role. In Germany, the Depression hurled the Weimar government's decade-old parliamentary institutions into catastrophe. But not much analysis is needed to recognize that British history is guided by long-term continuities while Germany's historical hallmark is recurrent rupture.[22]

In 1931, the collapse of the world economy had actually plunged England into an unprecedented political crisis. In May 1926, it had already experienced a labor struggle—the miners' general strike—that, as it were, immunized the polity against what was to come. The strike was called to protest draconian wage cuts instituted by the mine owners with the approval of the Baldwin government. The TUC (the British association of individual trade unions) then rallied to the strikers' support, resulting in a work stoppage by virtually the entire unionized workforce, with England's key industries being hardest hit.[23] The strike was discontinued after ten days, having revealed two things: first, a remarkable physical self-control on the part of both the workers and the Conservative government's officials, in the context of a highly politicized labor struggle; and second, the drastic nature of the decision that had brought about the strike.[24] More generally, the upheaval of 1926 revealed a profound structural crisis in the British economy—one that was homemade and that went far beyond economic fluctuations and employment cycles. It differed from dislocations affecting other economies in that it was an expression of the "English disease"—the late result of an industrial prominence that the world's first industrial power had gained in the nineteenth century—a prominence that eventually proved detrimental to continued modernization, leading to stagnation.[25] The branches of British industry that were traditionally strongest had already lost their dynamism by the turn of the century. Strong impulses for growth were no longer driving industries such as coal, iron, steel, shipbuilding, and textiles. Expansion lay elsewhere, in the chemical, electrical, and automotive industries, but here Germany and the United States had already taken the lead, their relatively late industrialization offering a distinct advantage. Also, Britain had introduced few production innovations. Its shipbuilding, for example, was slow to adopt electric welding. Likewise, goods were overpriced, partly owing to the trade unions and their organizational structure. The diverse processes involved in manufacturing a single product were handled in different plants by different union groupings, which frustrated initiatives for modernization. Such deficiencies weighed heavily on the British economy and contributed to mounting mass unemployment in the 1920s.[26]

Against the backdrop of such troubles, the general strike of May 1926 exemplifies England's political culture of moderation and restraint. While bloodshed accompanied similar confrontations on the Continent—in France and Germany—nobody was killed or injured in England, on either side of the struggle. The union leaders represented in Parliament insisted on abiding by both the constitution and the government's duty to punish any breach of public order. While the TUC urged its members not to resort to violence against strikebreakers, the government, though prepared for confrontation and a possible state of emergency, tried to preserve calm and reason and even endeavored to maintain a semblance of neutrality. Stanley Baldwin, who shortly before, in Parliament, had accused the unions of trying to provoke civil war, now publicly expressed regret at the government's uncompromising approach. In trying to convince the public that the Conservatives did not represent the class interests of one side or the other—that, to the contrary, their chief concern was the common good[27]—he was following a Tory tradition established by Benjamin Disraeli: not to appear as the party of the rich but rather to speak in the name of all.[28] After the war, a new social policy had been introduced by the Liberal-Conservative coalition under David Lloyd George, involving measures such as the Housing and Town Planning Act of 1919, which affirmed the right to public housing, and the socially more significant Unemployment Insurance Act of 1920.[29] To be sure, in contrast to the moderate unions, the Conservative government under Baldwin had done little to avert the May 1926 strike. A year earlier, however, it had sought to alleviate the misery of the needy by passing the Pension Act. This measure guaranteed state benefits to the poorest of the poor—widows, orphans, and the elderly—and was supported by the minister of health at the time, Neville Chamberlain. Though pioneered by the Conservatives, it is regarded as one of the cornerstones of the comprehensive welfare-state system established by the Labor Party after World War II.[30]

The traditional moderation of the political actors in Great Britain reflected the country's proverbial contractualism, a form of exchange between workers and employers prevalent since the end of the eighteenth century. In Germany, it was customary for the worker to sell his labor, with the employer covering his living expenses in return; in England, the fiction was maintained of an exchange of goods in which the worker sold the product he made.[31] Hence although the employer provided the worker with the equipment needed to produce the product, the worker formally controlled his own labor power. To that extent, he was a free man who could contract with another free man in an act of exchange. Correspondingly, his freedom as owner of his own labor power was transferred to the representatives of the workers' collective interests, the trade unions.[32] This idea of equal exchange was reflected in early British recognition of the unions, which were legalized in 1824, their legally protected scope for action then steadily expanding. This process included the 1875 law protecting workers from being prosecuted for taking part in labor disputes and the 1906 regulation shielding trade unions from damage claims resulting from strike action. During the late nineteenth-century depression, employers did not exploit the moment to suppress the unions but rather tried to reach an arrangement with them.[33] Hence even in the grip of a crisis, they maintained a bargaining ethic. Having thus been socially integrated at a relatively early date, the labor movement would then be politically integrated with the rise of the Labor Party, which first came to power briefly under Ramsay MacDonald in 1924—a development that did not take place in France until the emergence of the Popular Front in 1936, when the French workers' movement finally reconciled itself with the state.

The British labor movement's moderation yielded results. The living standard of wage earners, especially unionized workers, rose steadily. This in turn encouraged the unions to choose leaders who knew how to preserve and increase the successes won through restraint and perseverance. Radical demands aimed at overcoming and revolutionizing the existing order, the state and its system of government, had no chance. The tradition of moderation also placed a check on Communist temptations in the

interwar period. Both as a party and in the trade union movement, the British Communists were in a hopeless position[34]—
despite its combativeness, the British working class was basically
immune to calls to action based on ideological creed. Lenin was
badly mistaken in 1920 in supposing that the action committees
formed during the Polish-Soviet War and the refusal by the British
dockers' union to load weapons and munitions on ships bound for
the Polish forces reflected a revolutionary stance.[35] The dockers'
union was led by Ernest Bevin, later a great socially oriented politician and, as foreign minister beginning in 1945, architect of Western militancy in the early stages of the Cold War. Even the threat
of a general strike by the TUC, when, in light of General Tukhachevsky's advance on Warsaw, England had begun preparing for
intervention against the Soviets, was less an expression of solidarity with the Bolsheviks than a protest against British meddling in
the affairs of others (i.e., other states).[36]

The social legislation introduced in Britain in the 1920s was based
on an assumption that the conditions stamping the Victorian and
Edwardian eras would continue unchecked. Britain had emerged
from the Great War without any major social or political upheavals. There had not even been a change of government after
the armistice and peace negotiations, merely a reshuffle of Lloyd
George's Liberal-Conservative coalition following the "khaki election" of December 1918, which gave the Conservatives an overwhelming victory. This was the first election in which all men over
twenty years of age and all women over thirty had the right to
vote. Lloyd George, armed with a range of emergency powers,
had guided Britain through the troubles of the Great War since
1916; he remained prime minister after England's victory. Everything seemed to be following the norms of British tradition.[37]

But the impression of continuity was deceptive. The "English
sickness" was actually manifest everywhere. Although British political institutions were shielded from shocks grounded in social

misery, there was serious potential for conflict in the economic sphere. The problem of mass unemployment seemed insoluble. After the collapse of the postwar boom in the winter of 1920–21, the number of jobless individuals doubled within a few months; in March 1921 it reached 16 percent of the workforce. But despite the high unemployment level and the strikes that accompanied it, the government's authority remained unchallenged. Lloyd George now tried to ease the social and economic crisis through foreign policy initiatives;[38] most importantly, he widened exports to stimulate production and reduce unemployment. In the same manner, the Conservative government's reintroduction of the gold standard in 1925, with gold being sold at prewar parity, was aimed at guaranteeing currency convertibility and thus stabilizing world trade.[39] No matter that such a policy overvalued the pound and led to increases in export prices, and consequently to a further rise in unemployment; to expand international trade, traditional relations with former trading partners—Germany, the Continental industrial locomotive, and newly Bolshevik Russia—had to be restored. London thus now tried to reach an agreement with the two ostracized powers within Europe's new security order. Both Britain's compliant policy toward Berlin and its attempt to restrain France on the question of reparations can be explained against this background.[40] Britain expressed regret over the occupation of the Ruhr by Belgian and French troops in January 1923, calling it a blow to world economic recovery.

By 1925, British industrial output barely exceeded that of 1913, and exports continued to plummet—a situation exacerbated by the deflationary effect of the gold standard. Furthermore, to increase trust in the City of London by the international financial community, the government had begun pursuing a policy of high interest rates.[41] These measures were detrimental to exports. The government mistakenly believed it could adequately address unemployment through an adroit deflationary move. But the pound's high value deterred British industry from introducing new manufacturing methods and products, which further aggravated joblessness. During the worldwide boom of 1925 to 1929, when worldwide production rose around 25 percent on average, British production maintained levels slightly below those of 1913.[42] Nevertheless, the political impact of unemployment in Britain remained limited, especially since it was largely confined to certain sectors of the economy. British manufacturers sought to offset the higher prices of their products in the world market with a policy of wage cuts at home.[43]

From today's perspective, it seems odd that in this period the British did not attach much importance to the unemployment problem. Employment policy was secondary to classic factors such as free trade and import tariffs, as well as maintenance of a solid currency, a balanced budget, and industrial efficiency. Even the trade unions regarded unemployment as less important than wage policy and the struggle to maintain unemployment benefits.[44] In fact, this view was widespread on the Continent as well, with adherents on both the left and the right. French prime minister Raymond Poincaré, returned to office in 1926, was a firm believer in orthodox economic theories calling for rigorous austerity and stabilization measures to counter the monetary and budgetary crisis. So was Chancellor Heinrich Brüning, whose strict deflationary policy led to disastrous unemployment, a contributing factor in the demise of the Weimar Republic.[45] Rudolf Hilferding, the Marxist financial doyen of German Social Democracy, believed that the effects of a policy of tight money at high interest rates amounted to a necessary consequence of a crisis of readjustment—the deus ex machina of the utilization of capital.[46] John Maynard Keynes' *General Theory of Employment, Interest, and Money* (1936), which was a reaction to the mass unemployment of the 1920s and 1930s, would of course eventually provoke a rethinking of such economic theory. But by that time it was too late.[47] The disaster had taken its course, even though trade-union circles had long been discussing ideas about adapting an actively anticyclical economic policy that would stimulate job creation. Notably, in Germany the Social Democrats opposed such notions. Like the British Conservatives, they believed that measures designed to stimulate employment would fuel inflation.[48]

As indicated, the British government had tried to revive lagging exports by promoting a drastic cut in wages; the general strike of 1926—the fiercest social conflict in modern British history—resulted from the knife being applied to the coal-mining industry. Announcing their intention of abrogating the 1924 national wage agreement, the mine owners referred to fantastical wage cuts of between 13 and 48 percent—not in order to reap splendid profits but to offset ruinous losses.[49] No mediation could prevent a confrontation. In May 1926, it culminated in a test of strength in which the workers were forced to concede defeat.[50]

While the general strike was still basically a labor conflict, the Great Depression threatened the fabric of the British system of government. Hoping to protect the parliamentary-democratic order by moderating the nation's social antagonisms, Ramsay MacDonald formed a national government,[51] a solution that in effect meant the British people accepting an authoritarian regime. On the one hand, the model of a government without opposition contradicted the traditional values and practices of British parliamentary culture. On the other hand, this exceptional solution, supported by an overwhelming majority of the electorate, gave expression to another powerful tradition in British society: solidarity in hard times. MacDonald, who "betrayed" his Labor Party by joining with the Conservatives in a policy of social dismantling, believed he was acting to preserve the workers' interests. In the summer and fall of 1931, he feared possible financial collapse, with consequences for the working class going far beyond the necessary cuts in social expenditures and wages. Also, in that critical August he was convinced of one thing in particular: that after struggling for years to gain power, through its intransigent stance his party was now forfeiting its fitness to govern. It would thus be irresponsible to act solely with union interests in mind, a sectarianism other Labor leaders had already confronted. But MacDonald's ideas of socialism were oriented more to community than class; his agenda stressed service to the community, mutual dependence, integration, prudent action, security for the poor and underprivileged. He wanted a just distribution of the social burden and participation by everyone in the political community's institutions.[52] The precondition for such goals was naturally a stable government, which was his overriding aim—if need be, even at his own party's expense.

In this way the British answer to the Great Depression was stability and integration.[53] The class struggle was neutralized by its representatives being voted out of Commons, MacDonald's coalition gaining 554 seats, the overwhelming majority Conservative, and the actual Labor Party reduced to a mere 53. The Liberals and others managed to win only 9 seats. In a situation of crisis, many traditional Labor Party voters had thus chosen a policy of national unity and social cutbacks over their own particularistic interests. With a resounding mandate, the National Government instituted the cuts it thought necessary, especially in social services. It was unable to achieve another of its objectives, preserving the pound's value, and the gold standard was once again abandoned. At the same time, a century-old tradition of free trade was abandoned with the introduction of protective tariffs.[54] The result was a more-rapid recovery than that of other countries. Consequently, in 1934 it was already possible to reverse the earlier cuts in unemployment benefits. Nobody tried to maintain the social sector's economizing measures simply because they had been passed into law a few years earlier. With government support, more than a million poor individuals were now furnished with housing. Before coming apart during the transition to a war economy, the National Government thus succeeded in politically neutralizing mass unemployment.[55]

This experiment in solving economic crisis through "soft" methods had highly unusual consequences. The Tories became

increasingly convinced of the advantages of state intervention
and the need to curb unbridled capitalism through governmental regulation. The Conservative Stanley Baldwin, a minister in
MacDonald's cabinet, even affirmed that laissez-faire, like the former slave trade, was now passé.[56] Also, he voiced his respect for
the Labor opposition, acknowledging a common objective: preserving British tradition on the basis of the (uncodified) constitution and parliament. Such crisis management through social consensus was virtually inconceivable on the Continent. Continental
political culture lacked the tradition of moderation that was a
British hallmark; it lacked parliaments committed to reaching
consensus—even one marked by self-imposed authoritarianism.
Britain was a democracy in which an optimum of stability was
assured—a stability expedited by a somewhat less than fully democratic electoral system.[57]

In the early 1930s, Britain's moderate, consensus-based political culture together with a relatively aristocratic plurality-based
voting system preserved a nation shaken by a twofold crisis from
even graver troubles. The consensual politics and voting system
were closely, even systemically, linked. In contrast to proportional
representation, the system of majority vote does not offer much
electoral equality: marginal parties and particularistic interests
are clearly at a disadvantage. All votes beyond the majority ob-
tained by the successful candidate, no matter how many, are only
of statistical interest. Given the likelihood of casting a "wasted"
ballot, voters avoid parties that have little chance of winning a
mandate. Reflecting these structural constraints, the electoral will
thus gravitates toward a two-party system. Since success can only
be gained by attracting the floating vote, and thus by espousing a
more centrist position, the majority system effectively cancels out
the diversity of political views and particularistic interests that
are, inversely, promoted by the system of proportional representation. England's political forms and symbols of legitimacy have
likewise been oriented in this centrist, consensual direction, with

differences of opinion tending to be limited to strictly public issues. Questions of worldview and ideology couched in a discourse of sectarian ardor, and truths promulgated in a similar manner, are considered suspect and illegitimate. Extremist parties thus have little chance of winning a seat in parliament, but rather are consigned to irrelevance. Even at the height of the ideological decade, this proved a formidable barrier to Britain's Communists and Fascists.[58]

The situation was entirely different on the Continent, where ideology and worldview exerted a lasting impact on political institutions. Undecided voters, playing a crucial role in the British electoral system, were far less important here. Instead, solid bloc formations reflected prevailing political realities. In some places, the parties gained the contours of religious orders. They were similar to ideological armed camps and tended to affirm the validity of traditional affiliations and milieus rather than offer pragmatic, flexible, and changing perspectives. If voters switched parties, this was due less to the success or failure of the government in power than to a change in their underlying political disposition. And while the "landslide" was integral to the plurality system, radical shifts in the system of proportional representation augured revolution.[59] This was evident in Germany during the period of the presidential cabinets, when governments ruled by emergency decrees and arbitrary decisions. Brüning's deflationary policies, introduced almost without Reichstag participation, produced hordes of unemployed workers and unsettled broad segments of the population.[60] Given these deteriorating conditions, every election was bound to have disastrous results. There was consequently nothing surprising about the Nazis being able to increase their Reichstag representation from 12 to 107 delegates in the elections of September 1930; in the elections of July 1932, they succeeded in more than doubling this figure to a dizzying 230.

The system of proportional representation cannot be blamed for all the era's afflictions. Nor can one specific electoral system be imposed on states with very different political traditions. As the history of the Kaiserreich strongly suggests, even with a plurality system, the territorial, religious, and ideological divisions in Germany would have produced more than two parties in the Reichstag vying for the voters' preference.[61] Nevertheless, such a system in Weimar would not only have encouraged the electorate to behave in a different way; at the same time, it would have resulted in a Reichstag whose overall composition strongly favored the parties of the Weimar coalition.[62]

The effects of the Great Depression were different in France than in Germany or England. France being a state in the Continental tradition, politics tended toward polarization, and party disputes were ideologically motivated. In times of crisis, the French had a certain predilection for street violence. The variety of parties represented in the Chamber of Deputies was testimony to the benefits of democracy but also to the various disadvantages of the system of proportional representation introduced in 1927.

France's postwar economy was stable and prosperous. It offered a diametrical contrast to the British economy, since its dynamism was fueled by the fall of the franc, which stabilized at a very low level.[63] Both workers and employers benefited from this situation, while the main losers were pensioners and others on a fixed income. The undervalued franc spurred exports and guaranteed full employment. On the eve of the Great Depression, production had risen by some 50 percent over the levels of 1913, while incomes were higher by a third.[64]

France was indeed affected by the global economic crisis, but this happened relatively late and by degrees, leading to stagnation instead of shock.[65] That may have been due to the fact that France's foreign debt was relatively limited. Also, its economy was still mainly agrarian and thus far less export-oriented than Germany's or England's. While joblessness in Germany and England reached epidemic proportions, it remained relatively low in

France. The structure of France's labor market may also have been a factor at work here: in the crisis, large numbers of foreign laborers who had arrived after the war from Southern Europe and East Central Europe were dismissed and presumably sent home; in any case, they did not appear in the unemployment statistics.[66]

Before the Great Depression, France had enjoyed not only favorable economic conditions but also a reasonably stable political structure. The frequent changes in governments and cabinets in these years are deceptive, since they took place without a need for requiring new elections—although they point to a certain unrest in the French system, it had a solid enough foundation. Despite the Third Republic and its constitution having arisen, like Weimar's, from military defeat and severe territorial loss—that of the 1870–71 Franco-Prussian war[67]—the social-political situation stabilized relatively quickly afterward. Under these circumstances, the republic was already able to prevail against its opponents at an early point,[68] and a tradition thus coalesced within the structure of its political system.[69] This system held its ground for three generations, until finally succumbing to the *étrange défaite* of 1940. During its long existence, patterns of political behavior had evolved that contributed to a significant degree of harmony between France's historical parties, the parties of the notables.

The stability of the Third Republic during the great crisis is in fact far more noteworthy than its often accentuated opposite. The republic stood firm despite all the threats and shocks besetting its political system, street battles, strikes, and authoritarian decrees, which could have resulted in a transformation of its parliamentary democracy. There were certainly plenty of temptations. Prime Minister André Tardieu, who had entered from the left and shifted to the right, envisioned a Bonapartist regime appealing directly to the masses, thus reducing both the importance of the party machines and the influence of the notables, an enduring hallmark of French political life. His downfall in 1932 marked a reversal for authoritarian ambitions, but it also marked the onset of a chronic crisis in the French executive.[70] Such authoritarian tendencies were also evident toward the end of the 1930s, when it became customary to govern by means of so-called *pleins pouvoirs*. It is difficult to say what would have happened in the end if the war had not intervened.[71]

Consensus was also evident in the unusually strong integrative influence of the parliamentary committees, whose deliberations were closed to public scrutiny.[72] In these deliberations, the traditional bonds of the "political class" were highly effective, with both compromises and less laudable arrangements being crafted across party lines. Such camaraderie outside parliament's public arena proved advantageous, old ties now serving as bulwarks against the tide of political passion in the crisis years of the 1930s. Although the committees were derided in the street by antiparliamentarian groups on the far right, this vociferous scorn could not undermine France's admittedly precarious political stability.[73] The public was all the more generously served with heated debate in the plenum. Here ideological confrontation seethed, with politicians addressing the people from the podium while actual decisions were being made in the private committees. This role playing between the National Assembly plenum and the closed-door committees encouraged the emergence of supportive decision-making authorities mediating between the government and the opposition,[74] a generations-old tradition that made it possible to keep sharp political and ideological differences in check in the years of crisis. If that crisis threatened to carry open conflict from the street into the parliament, the chamber protected itself by issuing *décrets-lois*, emergency decrees circumventing the ideologically influenced decisions of the plenum and thus the public forum. A surface layer of parliamentary tradition that had evolved over decades disposed the legislature to grant *pleins pouvoirs* to the executive during an emergency, thus freeing it from the need to seek approval for every new measure. This approach, while unsavory from an institutional perspective, nevertheless benefited French democracy in stormy times. It protected the Third Republic from more far-reaching perils.

Operating in a gray zone of parliamentary legitimacy, the committees were one pillar of French democracy. The other pillar was the Radical Party in its balancing role. On the one hand, the party, whose name was misleading since it was neither radical nor left wing in a traditional way, served a conservative function in its capacity to enter into coalitions with either the left or the right. On the other hand, it was a bastion of French republicanism, thus standing in the grand tradition of the revolution, defending its achievements as a status quo emerging from the time-honored past.[75] This was the source of the party's singular duality. As champions of France's republican ideals, the Radicals were progressive when it came to political issues: those concerning state and government reform, freedom and equality, the separation of church and state, the preservation of democracy and parliamentarianism. But they were conservative, even reactionary, when it came to social and economic issues, particularly issues tied to the stability of the franc. In this respect, they represented the small independent landowners whose ancestors had profited from revolutionary secularization: the independent farmers, tradesmen, small shop owners, public officials, and self-employed professionals, the journalists and artists. Their traditional adversaries were the representatives of Catholicism and high finance and the great landowners.[76] The Radicals in fact represented the very milieu that in Germany lent massive support to the Nazis, the basic, defining difference being that the Radical Party opted in France's crisis for political freedom rather than its opposite.[77] This underscores the long-term impact of differing traditions of political culture.

In this way, through their amalgam of social conservatism and political progressivism the Radicals provided a guarantee against civil war.[78] In 1936, when it was imperative to protect the Republic from the far-right Fascist leagues, they joined the left-wing forces, including the Communists, in the Popular Front without suffering any loss of face.[79] Their leader, Daladier, even resorted to Marxist rhetoric in publicly affirming that as a representative of the lower middle class, his aim was a natural alliance with the proletariat.[80] But when the left began extravagantly assailing traditional property owners with social legislation and lavish wage hikes, the Radicals shifted back to the right, putting an end to such projects. In 1926, 1934, and 1938, this left-right oscillation led to different majorities emerging in the Chamber of Deputies. It was especially during the crisis period and its aftermath that the Radical Party's policies had a decisive impact on French politics. The chamber elected in 1936 not only produced different governments through party realignment but also diametrically opposed economic policies: a policy of social progress that was introduced by the Popular Front in 1936, and a policy of social conservatism and monetary orthodoxy in 1938. The Radicals belonged to both majorities.[81] Pursuing their partisan interests, they helped assure the system's stability.

In Germany there was no radical-republican, socially conservative party. The task of defending the Weimar Republic's democratic and parliamentary institutions basically fell to the Social Democrats. Yet the SPD remained a party of social reform that made use of radical socialist rhetoric.[82] Although practically the guardian of the Republic, it was just as much a party of partisan ideology and interests as most of the other parties. It, too, had a constituency to serve. While the Radicals occupied the middle ground in the French Third Republic's play of forces, the republican-minded SPD leaned left of a political center defending parliamentarianism, hence Weimar's status quo. The party saw itself as protector of the November 1918 revolution's sociopolitical achievements, as codified in the Stinnes-Legien Agreement between employers and trade unions. It felt itself obliged to fulfill this "social-conservative" task.[83]

It would be unfair to reproach the SPD for its policy of protecting vested interests: it was an "old" party that had emerged from the conditions of Imperial Germany, and in the "Second German Empire" the government was accountable to the kaiser, not the Reichstag. In that period, the Reichstag thus focused on promoting particularistic interests, not on maintaining a system in which its participation was restricted. In common with the other "old" parties, the SPD brought this way of proceeding to the Weimar Republic: its conduct was defensive and passive, as if it could unite within itself the dual role of being both a government and an opposition party.[84]

Parties that have evolved by representing specific social interests have difficulty in acknowledging their responsibility to the system as a whole. This is already clear in the case of Great Britain. Even under the far more favorable conditions of its electoral and party system, realizing this "national" responsibility still required Ramsay MacDonald's unconventional move away from the special interests to which the parties were committed. In Germany after the disaster of the September 1930 elections, the SPD thought it necessary to support Brüning's orthodox economic policies, even if only indirectly, by siding with the government in the no-confidence motions brought against it in the Reichstag. But it was acting under the pressure of circumstances, in the certainty that a new vote, loudly demanded at every opportunity by the Nazis, would only worsen the situation. Moreover, the SPD was obliged to support the coalition with the Center Party. Had Brüning (a member of the Center Party) been toppled by SPD misconduct in the Reichstag, this would have entailed extremely unpleasant consequences for the Prussian government, composed of the Social Democrats in coalition with the Center Party.[85]

As is well known, in March 1930, the Weimar Republic's last parliamentary cabinet, the Great Coalition under SPD chancellor Müller, had fallen over the issue of unemployment insurance.

This involved an abdication of the party's republican mission due to the special trade-union interests dominant in its parliamentary faction. The perception that what was here at stake was a choice between mere partisanship and the good of all, in other words the fate of the republic, is not a historiographical reconstruction. Rather, it corresponds very closely to the perception of the time. The expert in labor law Hugo Sinzheimer thus praised the parliamentary faction's decision to reject Brüning's proposed compromise on the issue by arguing that defense of the republic was "secondary" to defense of social rights and socialism. Rudolf Hilferding, by contrast, mindful of Reich President Hindenburg's executive powers and seeing what was coming, denounced the decision as an evasion of republican responsibility.[86]

With historical perspective, set against both the stance Ramsay McDonald embraced against his own party, facilitated of course by Britain's electoral and party system, and the downright "natural" barrier raised by the French Radicals against the right-wing challenge, it is clear that Germany lacked a credible force at the center truly committed to defending the republic and parliamentary democracy. Certain personalities marked an exception: Otto Braun the long-time Social Democratic Prussian prime minister, thus urged his party to fill the political vacuum.[87] But the SPD, the most republican party in Weimar, found itself overtaxed by the demands of such a mediatory role—that of defending both the republic and the social gains it had achieved. It was not up to coping with such a strain.

It is striking that the only European polities to emerge from the convulsions of the international economic crisis as functioning democracies were those that had been democracies before World War I: France and Britain. All the other polities turned authoritarian, dictatorial, or Fascist in the interwar period.[88] Most of the democratic parliamentary regimes in Europe had no need of the crisis of the 1930s to shed the governmental forms they had been induced to adopt by the Allies at Paris in 1919. Especially in East Central Europe, the Balkans, and Southeastern Europe, states had already cast off the blessings of democracy and parliamentarianism by the 1920s. While the reasons for this differed, the overall picture suggests that these states, newly created or expanded after World War I, turned to authoritarian solutions to cope with shrinking external markets, chronic agrarian troubles, smoldering social conflicts, and problems of nationality.[89] These polities—for instance, Poland under Piłsudski and Yugoslavia under the royal despotism of King Alexander—were "functional dictatorships," mainly concerned with preserving the state.[90] Aside from Czechoslovakia, which notably maintained its democratic parliamentary system, all the new or expanded states in Central, East Central, and Southern Europe became authoritarian or Fascist. But strikingly, among the modern, industrialized states, only Germany veered from democracy to dictatorship. This deserves an explanation.

Germany's transformation into a very special type of dictatorship cannot be explained by pointing to other countries, such as Lithuania, Poland, or Hungary, that established authoritarian regimes in the interwar period. Evocations of a deep-rooted "special path" should also be viewed with skepticism. In political history, such long-term strands are not much use in interpreting short-term sequences of cataclysmic events. In the face of these events, a group of facts clearly remains crucial: In 1918–19 Germany underwent a change in both its political system and its form of state;[91] at the same time, Europe's constitutional monarchies, including Belgium, the Netherlands, and the Scandinavian countries, survived the international economic crisis while preserving their political systems. Moreover, except for Britain and Belgium, none of these states was involved in the Great War; and both Britain and Belgium counted among the victors. France, Switzerland, and Finland had both a republican form of state and a parliamentary system of government, but otherwise differed substantially from

Germany: France was another victor, Switzerland remained outside the war, and in our context Finland's case has no importance.

Germany's situation was different from that of the other nations. The Reich had accepted defeat reluctantly. Until the very end, the German army's supreme command encouraged public belief in an imminent victory by the Central Powers.[92] With defeat, the monarchic form of state was not so much consciously and willingly renounced as simply lost; not even the Social Democrats really envisaged the Reich's transformation into a republic, even though that had been one of their official aims. Ultimately, they were "monarchists of reason."[93] Philipp Scheidemann's cry of "long live the German republic" to the crowd amassed in front of the Reichstag was in fact an "accidental" proclamation, primarily meant to forestall a radicalization of the situation in the streets, where the Spartacist Karl Liebknecht, it was believed, was about to pronounce a Socialist German republic. The widespread longing for a monarch remained; the misgivings of the constitution's liberal fathers, "republicans of reason," regarding the internal stability of a parliamentary republic were addressed by creating the office of a Reich president with expanded powers. Finally, the forces of the old regime managed to tie the system's transformation through the "October reforms" to military defeat: the formation of a parliamentary government in Germany had been an Allied, in other words Wilsonian, precondition for the armistice; and indeed, the Allied intention had been to raze the last autocratic bastion in Germany, rendering the government accountable to the people.

Nevertheless, a parliamentary government did not emerge in Germany solely as a response to external pressure. The parties in the Reichstag's "interfactional committee" had already demanded it in September 1918, which thoroughly reflected the will of the parliamentary majority.[94] Even in a monarchic framework, steps toward democratic parliamentarianism would have had a powerful political impact. But both the crown and the army were dead set against any further constitutional limitations on their power, and Wilhelm II was not prepared to abdicate in favor of a Hohenzollern prince not heir to the throne.[95] With the proclamation of the republic on 9 November 1918, the monarchy's abolition meant the loss of a basic element of national tradition. And the inability of the new republic to gain the kind of peace expected of it in Paris discredited it in the eyes of a great many Germans.[96]

For those raised in the Wilhelminian tradition, Germany now seemed a different country, the Reich staggering from one crisis to another, robbed of its once-enshrined ties. But making a historical necessity out of the path from such an inauspicious starting point to Hitler's seizure of power is not very illuminating. We should here keep in mind that the latter event took place nearly fifteen years after the Great War, following a phase of recovery and stabilization. This forms a contrast with Mussolini's march on Rome, which took place in 1922, with *la vittoria mutilata* at one's back and the revolutionary unrest sparked by the war before one's eyes. Classical Fascism's historical matrix is located in this immediate postwar phase. The events of January 1933 in Germany do not, in fact, appear to have mainly constituted a reaction to the Great War, defeat, and the Versailles Treaty. While the treaty was indeed broadly perceived as a national humiliation, its stringent conditions regarding reparations and rearmament had already been eased during the period of the presidential cabinets—that is, before Hitler's accession—and were in the final stage of further revision. In the final analysis, despite all that came before, it was the Great Depression that hurled Germany into the abyss.[97] The aftermath of Black Friday simply swept away the institutions of a republic that had been unable to adequately consolidate themselves, to develop a political tradition, or to gain widespread popular acceptance in the short period between World War I and the global economic crisis.

The successive presidential cabinets represented an attempt, long prepared behind the scene by the forces of the old regime, to transform parliamentary democracy along authoritarian lines. But only the Great Depression supplied the social and economic conditions allowing such a political intent to become reality. With the parliamentary stalemate having led to a successive transfer of power, in accordance with Article 48 of the Weimar Constitution, from the republican institutions—and especially from the legislature—into the hands of the Reich's president and hence to the executive, a new institutional reality had emerged in Weimar. Although a government relying on presidential authority might conceivably have been brought down by a parliamentary majority, in those days of deepening crisis such a constellation became continually less feasible. Apparently, the state's power had slipped into the blurred corridors of the old régime's ruling elites.[98]

The direction taken by the presidential cabinets tended to enhance the autonomy of the government, increasingly detached from the parties and parliament. The ground for this disentanglement had been laid by a basic dichotomy at work in the Weimar constitution between the sovereignty of parliament, whose possible "absolutism" was feared by the constitution's authors, and the sovereignty of the president's office, especially as manifest in his emergency powers.[99] Both forms of sovereignty were legitimized by general elections, and in normal situations there would have been no reason for parliament and president to thwart each other. Their evolving confrontation was chiefly a result of that increasingly evident parliamentary stalemate, which is to say of the parties' structural inability to set aside their special interests and form a stable government. In general, the less the parties agreed among themselves, the weaker the government and the greater the powers wielded by the president. The intensifying crisis burdened the party system with mounting radicalization; the crisis favored extremist parties and those opposed to the "system" while paralyzing the Reichstag.

The collapse of the system was ushered in by presidential cabinet measures that took the form of emergency decrees—measures thus no longer really sanctioned by a sovereign parliament.[100] Deflationary policies and an accompanying surge in unemployment further aggravated the situation. In this manner, during the crisis years of Weimar's presidential cabinets antidemocratic defiance grew precisely in that ostensible stronghold of democracy: the parliament. The September 1930 and July 1932 elections, held during ominous economic crises, led to a huge increase in the number of Nazi deputies. The Reichstag had now become a convocation of the existing order's sworn enemies: together the Nazis and the German Communist Party controlled a negative majority.[101]

The Weimar Republic had maneuvered itself into an impasse. From the republican perspective, the parliament was overflowing with parties hostile to the system, while forces ill-disposed to democracy surrounded the Reich president. Further events unfolded between the fearsome representatives of these two authorities. On the eve of Hitler's accession to power, there were two possible alternatives: the establishment of an authoritarian presidential regime, which risked violating the constitution and thus provoking civil war; or a return to parliamentary sovereignty and the formation of a Reichstag-backed government—a possibility that made the Nazis, now the strongest faction in parliament, a much-courted partner. As a result of secret right-wing machinations and intrigues, the two alternatives were combined. Hindenburg appointed Hitler chancellor in the expectation that he could muster a parliamentary majority; doing so would have freed the president from a burden of daily political accountability resulting from the cabinets being only responsible to him—a responsibility in accordance with the notorious "dictatorial" Article 48 of the Weimar Constitution.[102] For his part, Hitler insisted on being appointed chancellor in a presidential cabinet since he did not want to depend on coalition partners in a parliamentary cabinet that could topple him at any moment. It was left to the previous chancellor Franz von Papen to obscure the difference between the alternatives, deceive Hindenburg, and launch Hitler's cabinet. This was a result a more aware Hindenburg probably would not have accepted.[103]

That cabal and deception, idiosyncrasies and resentment could have such a decisive impact on Germany's fate and the world's has its source in the circumstances surrounding the Weimar Republic's downfall. With the collapse of democratic-parliamentary institutions and the location of power in a place where it was at the mercy of the moods, preferences, and machinations of a small coterie surrounding the president, the political vying for power took on atavistic and courtly forms. Consequently, the republic's most dramatic moments, in all their world-historical significance, resembled a burlesque. That such a shameful charade was possible cannot be explained by simply pointing to one or another characters; it had to have deeper roots. But acknowledging this does not mean we can avoid considering what actually transpired during those fateful days—or asking if what finally came to pass was not to be avoided. At the same time, scrutinizing Weimar's last phase offers more than insight into the stumbling and excesses of mediocre personalities. Rather, we confront fundamental questions involving the relationship between historical tradition and the circumstances of political action, between possibility and reality, contingency and necessity, personal character and structure. The short stretch from Weimar's agony to Hitler's assumption of power is a morality play in two senses: it offers lessons about both the realization of the worst of all possibilities and the meaning of history itself.

To again take up our narrative: by refusing to accept the "Brüning compromise" regarding unemployment insurance, the Social Democratic faction in the Reichstag brought about the collapse of the Müller government, Weimar's last parliamentary cabinet. But the Social Democrats were not solely responsible for that collapse. Although a majority of the DVP faction had endorsed the compromise at the last moment, this was essentially a tactical move: the SPD was meant to shoulder the blame for breaching the coalition. Word had got out that Hindenburg was not prepared to either grant Müller plenary powers—based on Article 48 of the Weimar Constitution—or accede to parliament's dissolution. The cabinet, it was reported, would thus have no choice but to resign. In its place, the ideas of the enterprising Kurt von Schleicher, head of the Wehrmacht Office in the Reich Ministry of Defense, were being adopted. Schleicher had been trying to usher in a change of regime for some time,[104] his aim being a cabinet based on the bourgeois parties with the "backing" of the Reich president. "Backing" was here a euphemism for separating the government from the parliament, in other words, restructuring the constitution and the state along authoritarian lines. State secretary Meißner intimated as much when he casually informed Center Party minister Josef Wirth that President Hindenburg would refuse to sanction *this* government, again based on Article 48.[105]

The DVP was thus aware of the growing prospect of a "Hindenburg cabinet" detached from parliament. Under such circumstances, it was not particularly disposed to reach an understanding with the SPD. At the same time, Heinrich Brüning and the Center Party, which had given parliamentary democracy a last chance with the Great Coalition, were also familiar with the basic plan. Confidants of the president had already initiated contacts with Brüning in the spring of 1929. It is thus not surprising that the Center Party politician and his parliamentary faction believed that if this last effort at a compromise failed, the fate of the cabinet and indeed of this form of government would be sealed.[106]

With Müller's resignation, the SPD made it easier for its political and social opponents to embark on a presidential path whose course had already been set. This path led to major changes in monetary, economic, and social policy; it led to an authoritarian regime whose open aim was to drive the SPD from the corridors of power. Yet Brüning, having assumed administrative control directly after Müller's fall and soon installed as presidentially appointed chancellor, only realized this aim in a limited fashion once the Social Democrats decided to tolerate his government in response to the catastrophic September 1930 elections. The SPD ensured his parliamentary position by thwarting attempts to topple the cabinet with a vote of no confidence. By opting for this strategy, designed to prevent new elections and even worse, the SPD was stigmatized for associating with a "hunger chancellor" whose deflationary policies sought to free Germany from the burden of reparations at the cost of a growing horde of jobless workers.[107] Brüning in turn forfeited Hindenburg's confidence, failing, in the president's view, in his task of ridding himself of the SPD and securing a "national" majority; he fell, as he himself put it, "a hundred meters short of the goal."

It would be up to Brüning's successor, Franz von Papen, to bring the Nazis, whom Hindenburg considered plebeian but still part of the national camp, into "participation in the state."[108] The Brüning cabinet had received parliamentary support through the SPD's policy of toleration. But the Papen "cabinet of barons" aroused intense mistrust in the Reichstag when it reconvened in September 1932, following a disastrous set of elections in July in which the Nazis more than doubled their mandates, making them the strongest faction in the Reichstag. With an order from Hindenburg for the dissolution of parliament in his pocket, Papen hoped to buy more time for his government. Lacking a majority, he was in a legally precarious position, mainly because his advocate Kurt von Schleicher had failed in behind-the-scenes negotiations to convince Hitler to back Papen's cabinet. After his overwhelming victory at the polls, Hitler insisted on being named chancellor. His demand was rejected by Hindenburg in a brusque and humiliating fashion after a short meeting between the two in August. Hindenburg had nothing but contempt for Hitler; moreover, he considered the reckless demagogue a political danger and feared he would establish a party dictatorship. Appointing him chancellor was completely out of the question. And while

Schleicher was trying to bring the Nazis into the government and thus tame them, Hitler was adamant, obsessively bent on a strategy of "all or nothing."[109]

This strategy proved detrimental to his party. There was widespread discontent when the Nazis were not granted a role in the government after the July elections. And when new elections were held in November, a clear shift became evident: the wave of popularity for the Nazi Party had begun to ebb. Though it remained the strongest single party in the Reichstag, its electoral losses had been substantial—some two million votes. Also, the party's coffers were rapidly becoming depleted; further elections would bring financial ruin. Finally, the signs that emerged in autumn that the economy was recovering—even if this still was having no perceptible impact on the labor market—boded ill for the Nazis. Sooner or later a weakened party would back the government, without Hitler having been awarded the prize he so ardently desired— thus Schleicher's calculation.

Kurt von Schleicher has often been described as a modern reactionary. In contrast to the conservatives, he did not wish to resuscitate the Wilhelminian era. He also did not consider "sitting on bayonets," in other words open military dictatorship, to be any kind of alternative. He was well aware of the drastic changes that came with modern mass society.[110] In his thinking, a temporary breach of the Weimar Constitution, namely, setting a date for Reichstag elections going beyond the limit prescribed by Article 25 of sixty days following parliament's dissolution, could be realized through a consensus of various social groups, especially the trade unions. In this, his ideas differed considerably from those at work in Papen's "emergency" project. Papen not only cultivated wild plans for an authoritarian "new state" but also intended to install a regular "battle cabinet" in opposition to the Reichstag.[111]

Schleicher tried to stabilize the situation by increasing public backing for his emergency plans, proposing a "trade-union axis." He approached Hitler's deputy, Gregor Strasser, whom he introduced to Hindenburg as a possible vice chancellor, while concurrently conducting talks with the leadership of the League of German Unions (the ADGB); his aim was to remind the unions of their "national duty," a process resembling the crisis management that had taken place during World War I. The SPD leadership rejected this initiative.[112] Tensions had surfaced everywhere between the Social Democratic Party and the free trade unions. These tensions were only partly due to the party's reduced influence resulting from its exclusion from the Reichstag; more importantly, there had been a realignment of interests. The ADGB was operating across the lines of the hostile camps and—in a direct reversal of the situation in March 1930, when it allowed Hermann Müller to fall—was now cooperating with those it had traditionally disdained. The common concern was implementing an unconventional policy to reduce unemployment; for its part, while biding its time the SPD continued to espouse positions that were ideological and legalistic. Already in October 1932, Theodor Leipart of the ADGB had publicly affirmed the free unions' willingness to cooperate with a presidential regime.[113] Schleicher had gained their support by agreeing to revoke Papen's September decrees, which gave employers the option of paying less than the agreed-on wage levels. Long-term measures to generate jobs were planned to alleviate the crisis—a project under discussion in the ADGB but stubbornly opposed by the SPD, which believed it would only fuel inflation. But such fears would prove unfounded.

A *Reichskommissar* had meanwhile been instructed to agree with the Reichsbank on far-reaching plans for a crash program to create employment.[114] This program, however, failed to fulfill the expectations aroused by Schleicher. The economic upturn finally perceptible in the spring of 1933, from which Hitler would profit, was due to more than job creation schemes, although these did send out positive psychological signals to the population. The plan, attributed to Schleicher, of a corporatist "cross-front" in which the employer organizations of the otherwise politically hostile parties, the party militias, and the entrepreneurs would operate in tandem, was still undeveloped, though Schleicher enjoyed being dubbed the "social general."[115] The East Elbian Junkers suspected him of trying to institute a kind of "countryside Bolshevism" when he proposed that heavily indebted estates be requisitioned for settlement purposes—the same "eastern relief project" that had earlier been Brüning's undoing.[116] On the other hand, Schleicher had little to fear from heavy industry, whose leaders were receptive to his stabilization policies; later, they would regret his fall.[117]

As a man of the Reichswehr, Schleicher was revisionist in his views on foreign policy and the eastern frontier; he envisaged a possible war with Poland. In view of approaching German parity in rearmament policy, he saw the storm-troop battalions and the Stahlhelm as grateful partners in his scheme to "transform" the Reichswehr, enlarged by militia units—a step leading to general conscription.[118] The Reichswehr's rearmament was always Schleicher's main priority. He had engineered the system of presidential cabinets in order to neutralize the SPD, which was opposed to defense, and to promote the army's interests in the disarmament negotiations.[119] At the same time, he devised some unconventional solutions to the political crisis. That none of these was realized and instead Hitler was appointed chancellor by the Reich president is the great enigma of German history.[120]

The man who finally opened the gates to Hitler's chancellorship was Franz von Papen, whose government succumbed to a no-confidence vote in September 1932 under dishonorable circumstances. Papen had succeeded Brüning in June. Considered an extreme reactionary, he had managed to incur the wrath of most of the country's interest groups. He had resigned from the Center Party to preempt his expulsion from it. He had estranged the workers and their movement by arbitrarily cutting unemployment benefits and forcing applicants to submit to a rigid and demeaning review. By contrast, he had appeased the employers with a series of tax relief measures and the above-mentioned possibility of setting new workers' wages below the agreed-on levels. Also, he had made himself unpopular through various plans to change the constitution. In the eyes of the republican parties, he was the chancellor of a looming civil war.[121] Derided as a "gentleman rider," he seemed ready to risk a general strike and further escalation when, faced with another hostile parliament as a result of the November elections, he tried to persuade Hindenburg to dissolve the Reichstag once again in order to circumvent the sixty-day constitutional limit for calling new elections. But Schleicher and the other cabinet ministers were not ready to risk an open battle in the streets. It was imperative, they believed, to preserve both state and Reichswehr from civil war, hence from Papen's planned declaration of a national emergency.[122] Schleicher's "Ott Scenario," a simulation played out for the German high command, was meant to show that Papen's adventurism would end in horror. Along with civil war, this scenario included a Polish invasion of the Reich. Incapable of coping with its internal and external enemies, the army would be destroyed. A shaken president now decided he was too old to assume responsibility for a civil war, thus foiling Papen's scheme to breach the constitution; Papen was obliged to resign. Hindenburg accepted the decision, but reluctantly, since a relationship of deep mutual trust had evolved between the two men.

When Hindenburg appointed Schleicher chancellor in December 1932, he asked Papen to continue offering him advice. Also, at the president's request Papen was allowed to retain his official residence in the chancellery. He thus remained in Hindenburg's immediate proximity, since the latter had temporarily relocated to the chancellery while the presidential palace was being renovated. Through this direct access, Papen assured himself a substantial measure of courtly power, now a determining factor in the arena of national politics.[123] Papen knew how to take full advantage of his political capital. In order to destroy Schleicher, a former mentor and sponsor who had engineered his downfall, he was prepared to press for Hitler's appointment by Hindenburg as chancellor.

By early January 1933, it was clear that Schleicher's support was crumbling. In this atmosphere, Hindenburg let himself be persuaded by his political camarilla, especially by his confidant Papen, to withdraw his trust from Schleicher and name Hitler chancellor.[124] That the president, the only remaining authority between Hitler and the chancellorship, finally abandoned his resolve to deny state power to the "Bohemian corporal" was partly due to Papen having deceived him regarding the makeup of Hitler's cabinet. Hindenburg had been unwilling to grant the leader of the largest faction in the Reichstag a presidential government for which he would have had to assume responsibility. He was thus willing to suppress his misgivings about a Hitler chancellorship only in the case of a government appointed by the Reichstag. A majority consisting of Nazis, German Nationals, the Center Party, and the Bavarian People's Party was statistically conceivable.[125] But Hitler had no intention of relying on the moods of a Reichstag majority, which could withdraw its parliamentary support at will. He wanted to head a presidential cabinet and, armed with a presidential decree, to dissolve the Reichstag, declare new elections, and gain a comfortable parliamentary majority as the legitimate state power. The Reichstag would then pass an enabling act granting him a free hand and disencumbering him from the objections of both president and parliament. The path to dictatorship would lie open—and this in a legal constitutional manner.[126]

To reconcile Hindenburg's wishes with Hitler's nonnegotiable demand for a presidential government, Papen resorted to duping the elderly president. In league with Hitler, he presented Hindenburg with a list of names for a cabinet in which the post of minister of justice was still vacant. This gave Hindenburg the impression it would be filled after negotiations with the Center Party, which was slated to join the coalition.[127] To underscore his point, Papen observed that even in the case of Müller's Great Coalition, the Center Party had only joined later. At this time, Hitler knew that the head of the German National People's Party (DNVP), Alfred Hugenberg, himself known for his antiparliamentary views and opposed to the Center's social demands, would not insist on its inclusion in the coalition. And Papen correctly assumed that Hindenburg would not rescind his decision once the cabinet had been sworn in and was functioning de facto on presidential authority. It seemed necessary to act without delay: rumors were rife that Schleicher and Hammerstein (commander of the Potsdam garrison) were scheming to have the Potsdam garrison arrest the president and his family, a military putsch to be forestalled by prompt inauguration of the new government and, above all, of its minister of defense. Such false reports played their role in the investiture of Hitler's cabinet. The following day, 31 January 1933, Hitler, newly appointed as German chancellor, raised untenable demands leading to the breakdown of negotiations with the Center Party—negotiations that in any event had only begun for purposes of show.[128] Armed with a presidential decree, Hitler dissolved the Reichstag on 1 February and set new elections for 5 March. The fate of the Weimar Republic was sealed.

Hitler had thus succeeded in breaching the dike around the president, in penetrating his carefully guarded inner sanctum of power. This access to the august potentate proved decisive for Germany's fortunes. Like a dwarf from the netherworld, the mediocre figure of Franz von Papen had wielded the key to Hindenburg, which he decided to pass on to Hitler so that the latter could gratify his greed for power. Hitler, in turn, had installed himself in Papen's inner chamber in order to win Hindenburg's trust. The dice were thus tossed within a narrow circle of individuals— Papen, Hindenburg, Meißner, and Hugenberg—whose decisions were determined by personal feelings,[129] namely, feelings of vengeance, hatred, ambition, and opportunism. Although the transfer of state power to Hitler thus occurred in circumstances evoking bygone eras of court intrigue, the historical consequences were monstrous. This conclusion might be unsatisfying to an observer whose perspective has been sharpened by the structures of modern mass societies. But in fact, such a regression could occur only against the backdrop of a mass society whose institutions lay dying. In such a situation, with society's representatives no longer able to fulfill their tasks, it became possible to do away with the president's powers.[130]

Hitler's play for power was veiled; few perceived what was taking place. Even some of those hastily summoned to the chancellery to be sworn in as ministers were unsure until the last moment whether Papen or Hitler would head the cabinet. Neither the public nor the parties expected a transfer of power to Hitler. The danger that many dreaded was a second Papen cabinet. Papen was thought capable of the worst, which at the time meant suspending the constitution, precipitating a civil war, and establishing a dictatorship. The representatives of the Weimar Republic's two remaining founding parties—the SPD and the Center—watched the unfolding legal procedures virtually paralyzed. Would it come to a breach of the constitution in the form of a proclamation of national emergency? It was well known that Schleicher was contemplating such a move. But for various reasons, Hindenburg could not be persuaded to dissolve the Reichstag without first setting a legal date for a new poll. Schleicher's plans would involve a flagrant breach of the constitution, based on the hope that a parliament with a functioning majority could emerge from a later election (perhaps in autumn), in the midst of an improved economy. The Reich president was probably still under the sway of the persuasive Ott Scenario, with its bloody vision of civil war.

Schleicher had also been quietly informed of another, "soft" approach to breaching the constitution. This was a notion first submitted in 1928 by the legal theorist—and eventual "crown jurist of the Third Reich"—Carl Schmitt. He suggested a constitutional interpretation in which a negative majority that might bring down a government would be obstructed if it was not in a position to establish a government by itself. Such a desired "constructive vote of nonconfidence," not envisioned by the Weimar Constitution, would defy any further "act of obstruction," paralyzing the parliamentary system.[131] Schmitt's point was that the political parties should be deprived of the possibility to vote down a government by this means. Such a negative majority, he argued, was meant to be ignored; despite the loss of its parliamentary margin, the government could continue to rule until a new cabinet had been installed.

Schleicher did not make use of this proposed constitutional interpretation when he asked the president on 28 January for a decree dissolving the Reichstag—without, however, requesting a delay in new elections. He no longer dared to press Hindenburg that far. When the latter refused to issue the decree, and Schleicher realized he was facing dismissal, the only option he could imagine was that Papen would be called on to succeed him, a danger he and the Reichswehr were determined to forestall at any cost. "Chancellor Hitler" seemed preferable to the prospect of another Papen government.[132]

The SPD and the Center Party were also inclined to this view. In November 1932, the Center deputy Joseph Wirth, who had exclaimed following Rathenau's murder that "this enemy is on the right!" informed SPD faction leader Rudolf Breitscheid that the Center was contemplating a coalition with the Nazis to prevent the dismissal of the Reichstag and the destruction of democracy and basic civil rights.[133] Some voices in the Center's sister party, the Bavarian People's Party, were even prepared to consider Hitler as chancellor.[134] In the face of the state's dire crisis, the arguments advanced by the Social Democrats were no less legalistic and inadequate. In contrast to the Center, the SPD categorically ruled out any coalition with the Nazis. But the party considered a parliamentary government under Hitler an acceptable alternative to Schleicher's unconstitutional proposal and certainly preferable to Papen's dangerous experiments with the constitution, which risked civil war. Already in conversations at the end of November, Breitscheid had informed Schleicher that the SPD would fight with all necessary means against a breach of the constitution.[135]

In January 1933, that fateful month of German history, everyone's priority appeared to be the defense of legality. The SPD executive announced that the proclamation of a "so-called national emergency" by the Schleicher government would create an unlawful situation and should be opposed by all means.[136] The Center's press justified the party's legalistic preference of a parliamentary government under Hitler to a state of emergency established by Schleicher by arguing that an "emergency dictatorship" would be based on a narrow political stratum, that of the Stahlhelm and the German Nationals,[137] which could only lead to unrest and bloodshed. On 28 January 1933, the Social Democratic paper *Vorwärts* aired the view that although Schleicher's imminent downfall would not mark an end to the reactionary course of events, it would at least spell an end to the "maniacal phase of reaction." In the Reichstag, the paper indicated, the SPD would resolutely oppose the anticipated constitutional government of Hitler, Hugenberg, and the Center.[138]

At the end of 1932, the SPD clearly believed that Schleicher posed a far greater threat to the state than Hitler. This is not at all surprising. In November it seemed that Hitler was defeated; the SPD executive issued an "all clear."[139] The Social Democrats had the impression that their consistent opposition to Hitler and his cohorts over the years had finally proven successful. Their toleration of Brüning had also derived from this basic policy, although it had cost them dearly.[140] The increase in votes for the Communists at the expense of the SPD was due at least in part to that party's strategy of backing the "hunger chancellor" Brüning against the Nazis. Still, the SPD had waged five electoral campaigns under the banner "Beat Hitler!" and it viewed the results of the November 1932 poll as a significant achievement. Nobody could now seriously imagine a Hitler dictatorship.[141] That was not just the attitude of the Social Democrats; it was the general consensus.

The Nazis also believed that their chances of seizing power were vanishing. On 15 January, they had managed to achieve a small victory in local elections in the small state of Lippe-Detmold; they had mobilized the entire party leadership, complete with a military parade by the SA. Although they tried to see this as a source of courage and confidence, for experienced observers the results were not very convincing. The NSDAP had not rebounded from its November setback. Even among party activists, the impression was growing that it would be best to avoid further elections in the Reich.[142] It is thus not very surprising that in expectation of Schleicher's fall, *Vorwärts* commented in late January that Germany was faced with one alterative: either "Carnival Chancellor Hitler" or the return of "Papen the Gentleman Rider."[143]

The view that a parliamentary cabinet under Hitler was a lesser evil than a declaration of national emergency by Schleicher or even Papen was the result not so much of political blindness as of moods and perceptions that at the time were thought realistic. Why not give preference to a parliamentary solution, even if it was called "Hitler"? The restoration of parliamentary government meant the return of the parties, which, excluded from responsibility in a regime of presidential cabinets, had been languishing for nearly three years. Moreover, the Nazis had been weakened. That was at least the prevailing view. It was also likely that the economy would soon begin to recover,[144] which would sound the death knell of the NSDAP, as a party of the desperate; it would contract to its former dimensions. In any case, there would be no real prospect of a presidential cabinet under Hitler; Hindenburg's profound aversion to the Nazi leader was well known. On the other hand, the threat of a renewed presidential cabinet under Papen seemed very real indeed. And while Papen could only be disposed of by physical force, even perhaps through a civil war, Hitler could be toppled by a vote of the Reichstag; his party only controlled a third of the deputies. And what despite all differences seemed right to both Weimar Republic parties, the SPD and the Center, was also fine with Schleicher and the leadership of the Reichswehr. On the day he resigned, Schleicher tried to persuade Hindenburg to appoint Hitler instead of Papen, who in his view was the greater threat to the state.

From a historical perspective, this view of things seems hopelessly out of focus. Hindsight makes the events that followed—the catastrophe that the Third Reich and Hitler's policies brought upon the world—into a basis for judgment. Already soon after Hitler's accession, it became clear that a change of the highest order had taken place and that earlier views had been deeply mistaken. Since then, the disaster resulting from Hitler's takeover has reconfigured its prehistory and functions as a mnemonic vortex from which neither historiography nor the consciousness of posterity can escape. In history, contingencies are continuously swept up in a torrent of seemingly inexorable necessities, a process also shaping the narrative describing Hitler's path to power. Given the events that transpired, this has probably been inevitable, even if such a perspective runs counter to the situation of those who had to decide how to proceed. In its basic approach, the questions it poses, and the methods it employs, the historiography of Weimar tries to somehow shield these people from the approaching catastrophe—to counsel them on the proper course of action. The belated perspective at work here can only be alarmist and teleological; against such a backdrop, historians tend to seek out traces that might have given the events a different turn, yielded a different outcome. In this manner, the historical consciousness seems constrained to both grant necessity to what happened and repel that necessity. In its own volte-face, it thus resists the vortex of the apparently unavoidable by stressing the element of chance attending the events.

The account of what happened is then narrated as a concatenation of such "chance" turns. And there are plenty of contingencies in the events leading up to 30 January 1933.[145]

The historical cornerstones of the transition from Weimar to Hitler are thus composed of accidents. As such, they become the emblems of a historical paradox. Historiography makes use of these emblems without openly admitting it: an ironic stylistic means to satisfy the desire for what did not occur. The events of the last three months before the transfer of power to Hitler, in particular the final days of Weimar, resemble a panopticon of the grotesque: the above-cited characterization of Hitler, at the end of January 1933, as "carnival chancellor" in the SPD journal *Vorwärts;* or Papen's effusive chatter to the effect that Hitler had been "hired" and would in a few months be pressed into a corner until—understood, like a rat in a trap—he squeaked. Or the choreography of the morning of 30 January, when the illustrious band comprising Hitler's future cabinet was guided by Papen, who was familiar with the grounds, through the Reich chancellery gardens to the building's rear entrance to elude the rumored imminent attack by the Reichswehr. Or the dispute between Hitler and Hugenberg over a further Reichstag election, which could only result in further losses for the already decimated German National People's Party and on account of which Hugenberg, the stubborn party chairman, threatened to torpedo the entire business of working with Hitler. The swearing-in ceremony was scheduled for 11:00 a.m. The hour had already come and gone in bickering, interrupted by state secretary Otto Meißner, who warned Hitler and Hugenberg that Herr Reichspräsident could no longer be kept waiting. The gentlemen then followed him into Hindenburg's office. The president administered the oath. This scene reflects like none other the emblematics of contingency at the Weimar Republic's end.

Fate is the metaphysical equivalent of chance. Against a backdrop of inevitability, the observer is struck by events imbued

with a sense of contingency. This accrual of moments of random-
ness and contingency corresponds to the political conditions in
Weimar's final phase. Rule by a small group of individuals bound
only to the letter of the constitution, not to its spirit, took the form
of a court intrigue that was neither regulated nor publicly transparent, and that was certainly beyond control. Once the institutions had become unanchored, anything was possible. In such circumstances, an arbitrariness prevails that, in a setting stamped by
the habitual procedures, forms of social communication, and cal-
culability of modern industrial mass society, takes on the character
of blind chance. To both contemporaries and posterity, an appointment of Hitler as chancellor following the July elections, in
August or September 1932, could only seem the logical outcome of
an unavoidable process that had begun in 1930, if not earlier. Few
signs of accident could be found here. While the catastrophe's impact would here endure undiminished, one might at least seek con-
solation in reflections on historical inevitability. In January 1933,
however, Hitler's appointment as chancellor took on the character
of something contingent, since it ran counter to general expectations and the general thrust of developments. After his cabinet was
sworn in, Göring hurried breathless out of the chancellery and reported to those waiting outside that a miracle had occurred. Many
leading Nazis viewed Hitler's ascension to power as so unexpected
and uncanny that Hindenburg, precisely because he had always
resisted Hitler, was now seen as an "instrument of God."[146] What
appears to posterity as chance was for the Nazis a stroke of fate.

Focusing on the role of key actors in the events of January
1933 also encourages a sense of historical contingency. But with
methodologically imposed distance, the importance of individuals
fades. It simply seems unreasonable to attribute the destruction of
the Weimar Republic in the phase of the presidential cabinets to
the actions or failures of specific persons.[147] Structures, traditions,
and mentalities thus come into the picture; the discourse concerning Germany's special historical past thus continues to unfold. For

clearly, that history's duration cannot be measured against the short-term rhythm of unfolding events—in weeks, days, and hours. But again, it remains difficult to imagine the consequences of the long historical movements that led to this catastrophe without considering Hitler's person. Indisputably, Hitler managed to become chancellor through a personal strategy of "all or nothing," in defiance of a demoralization besetting his party after the November losses. Paradoxically, then, it was precisely Hitler's maneuvers against the political current that brought him to power. Unquestionably, it was ultimately factors of historical of *longue durée* that made him and his success possible. But without his person, the factors would not have produced the results they in fact produced. Historical possibility and concrete reality are two different matters.

The final weeks, days, and hours of Weimar, as well as their historical treatment, are fitting material for a didactic play on the writing of history—its procedures, modes of representation, and choice of perspective. But the possible approaches are by no means arbitrary. The topic itself prescribes limits to the range of interpretations. Due to the swift pace of events, Weimar's final phase can hardly be described in terms other than those of political history. Such a description examines the conduct of the actors in view of conceivable alternatives, thus addressing issues of guilt and responsibility. In this respect, an approach focused on structural history can have only limited usefulness, since it is not very well suited for probing human inadequacies, idiosyncrasies, and other unpredictable characteristics. Such an approach might indeed offer an adequate account of why the Weimar Republic, with its specific prehistory, was doomed from the start. But it cannot shed light on the difference between the dictatorships that were possible at this historical moment, although it is precisely here—in the difference between dictatorship and dictatorship—that we can locate the key epistemic question regarding the end of Weimar. The enigma of German history is not that Weimar was buried but rather *the identity* of those who dug the grave.

4

Cataclysms

Genocide and Memory

Eastern Questions / Ethnic Cleansing / Greeks and Turks /
Armenian Catastrophes / Poland's Demography / Germany's
Ideology / Eastern Expansion and Holocaust / Opposing
Perspectives / Memory and Narrative / Hierarchy of
Remembrance / Nazism and Stalinism / Labor and Death /
Genocide and Class Extinction / Comparison and Perception

❖

In the less-than-happy chronicle of Turkish-Greek relations, 15 May 1919 is an especially grim day. On this day, Greek troops landed in Smyrna, on the western coast of Asia Minor. Furnished with a mandate from the Supreme Council of the Allied and Associated Powers in Paris and accompanied by an Allied naval squadron, these troops had until recently served under French command in the anti-Bolshevik interventionist forces in southern Russia. Now they were being steered toward a more patriotic task. Under the pretext of preempting an Italian scramble for Western

Anatolia, they attempted to incorporate this territory, filled with ancient Hellenic landscapes but now inhabited by Orthodox Greeks and Muslim Turks, into the expanding Greek nation-state.[1]

These expectations would be disappointed. The Greek attack on the Smyrna region and its thrust into the interior ended in bitter defeat at the hands of the Turks under Kemal Pasha. What followed was the flight and expulsion of well over a million ethnic Greeks from the Turkish nation-state taking shape in Anatolia.[2] The enterprise of national aggrandizement, driven by visions of a Greater Greece, had resulted in catastrophe.

What ended so dreadfully in 1922 with the flight and expulsion of Greeks from Asia Minor, Thrace, and the Hellespont had already begun on an ominous note. The entire operation amounted to a massacre perpetrated by the Greek expeditionary forces on the Turkish population of Smyrna. The catalyst had been a single shot fired from the top of a derelict Ottoman administrative building as two columns of Hellenic soldiers were advancing from the harbor toward the city. The soldiers responded immediately, firing indiscriminately into a fez-wearing crowd standing by.

With scant knowledge of local customs, the Greeks considered the fez, the standard local male headdress, to be exclusively Muslim, which is to say Turkish. During the Balkan wars, especially during the Greek conquest of Macedonian Salonika in November 1912, Muslim fez-wearing males had been singled out and expelled to the East.[3] In Smyrna, after two days of bloodshed in which local Greeks plundered and set fire to the houses and property of their Muslim neighbors, the fez had disappeared from the heads of Muslims, Greek-Orthodox Christians, Armenians, and Jews.[4] The interethnic violence in Smyrna spilled over into the countryside. Incited by reports of atrocities by Greeks against Muslims, Turks took gruesome revenge on their Greek neighbors in Aydin and the surrounding villages. Intense violence now engulfed the Orthodox populace; men, women, and children were slain indiscriminately. As the struggle between Greeks and Turks penetrated deeper into the interior, the atrocities became more organized, especially where enemy military offensives were anticipated or one's own forces had suffered a reversal.[5] The spreading violence took the form of demographic warfare along constantly shifting fronts or else of a blind will toward vengeance after defeat.

The conduct of an ethnic war, with its atrocities and expulsions, evoked the violence in the Balkan wars of 1912–13 in various ways.[6] While in Anatolia between 1919 and 1922 the lines of conflict were clearly drawn between Orthodox Christians (Greeks) and Muslims (Turks), the situation in ethnically mixed Macedonia had been more complex. During the Second Balkan War of 1913, in which Turkey participated in the anti-Bulgarian alliance, largely Orthodox polities fought over the territorial spoils they had previously wrested from the Ottoman Empire. The conflict was ethnic in that for the sake of their various territorial claims the belligerents announced themselves as national saviors, bringing deliverance to their imagined brethren among the diverse populations of Macedonia, brethren to whom they were bound by ties of language, religion, or some fictive notion of origin.[7] In this way, the Slavic-speaking Muslims of western Thrace, the so-called Pomaks, were declared lost Christian sons of Bulgaria who had been forcibly Islamicized centuries before. Brutality served to remind the Pomaks of their putative origins. Their return to Bulgarian Orthodoxy was quite harsh indeed: under a hail of blows from canes and cudgels, they were forced to confirm their conversion by publicly eating pork.[8]

Macedonia had been a bone of contention between Serbia and Montenegro but especially between Greece, Bulgaria, and the Ottoman Empire. The type of violence unleashed by the Macedonian question and in the associated Balkan wars would later become common currency as "ethnic cleansing." This violence would not be confined to the Balkans, but rather would spread from the Ottoman Europe to Anatolia, emerging there as a struggle between Greeks and Turks of Asia Minor. In turn, that struggle would culminate in 1922 in the flight and expulsion of the Anatolian Greeks from the land they had inhabited for millennia.[9]

The beginnings of this tragedy are normally traced to events of 1908, a paradoxical date, standing for the revolution of the Young Turks, initially welcomed enthusiastically by Muslims, Orthodox Christians, Armenians, and other subjects of the sultan.[10] All Ottomans, regardless of ethnic or religious affiliation, were finally free from the despotic yoke of Sultan Abdülhamid II and could unite in equality and fraternity. But these expectations were to prove illusory, for the Young Turks in the Committee for Unity and Progress soon displayed Turkish chauvinism, a metamorphosis less surprising than normally supposed.[11] Despite proclamations by the revolutionaries to the contrary, such intolerance had actually been basic to the revolution from the start; it had been unleashed not simply to restore the liberal constitution of 1876 but above all to preserve the Ottoman Empire. By introducing reform, the Young Turks hoped to forestall the loss of the three remaining Rumelian districts, Kosovo, Monastir, and Salonika.[12] The extent to which their revolution was driven by dislocations tied to the Macedonian question is reflected in the fact that the events were initiated in the Macedonian garrisons of the Ottoman army as a military enterprise, and this without any coordination with the Salonika-based Committee for Unity and Progress.[13] In many respects, then, Macedonia had become an Ottoman region of profound importance for maintaining the further territorial integrity of the empire. The fact that the founder of modern Turkey, Kemal Atatürk, originated from Salonika is more than incidental to his biography.

The 1912–13 Balkan wars were Macedonian wars. In the First Balkan War, the Ottoman Empire, weakened by the Tripolitan War against Italy in 1911, was attacked by the four members of the Balkan League: Serbia, Montenegro, Bulgaria, and Greece. Their aim was to wrest the remaining Rumelian territories, primarily

Macedonia, from the empire. The First Balkan War resulted in the brutal expulsion of the Muslim inhabitants of these territories. Hundreds of thousands of Turkish refugees fled eastward toward Istanbul, where government offices established for that purpose directed them to Anatolia. There they were resettled in the countryside, mainly in the Aydin region.[14]

But the absorption and relocation of these Rumelian refugees did not bring the chain of brutal events to an end. Rather, the atrocities suffered by the Macedonian and Thracian Muslims now befell the Anatolian Greeks in turn. Incoming Muslims, assisted by indigenous Turks and the local police, set about terrorizing the Greek Orthodox population of Western Anatolia, a process peaking in the spring of 1914, when entire Greek communities were robbed of their possessions and driven from their homes and land in reprisal for the outrages committed against the Macedonian Muslims. The Turkish action was not totally unplanned. Its systematic character was especially apparent along Asia Minor's shore, where the Aegean islands, under Greek sovereignty since the Balkan wars, were adjacent to costal regions inhabited by Anatolian Greeks. Within a few months, more than 150,000 Greeks were forced to emigrate to the Greek nation-state, and another 50,000 were displaced to the Anatolian interior.[15]

Before the expulsions and deportations were halted, the intent had been to extend them to the major Greek centers of Anatolia such as Smyrna and its surroundings. This was because talks had begun between the Greek and Turkish authorities concerning a possible "transfer," in other words a regulated population exchange, similar to what had been arranged between Bulgaria and Turkey in 1913, even if that precedent had only confirmed already-realized expulsions.[16] A transfer between Greece and the Ottoman Empire would, to be sure, have to be far more ambitious, involving an exchange of the Orthodox Greeks in Thrace and Western Anatolia for the Muslims in Macedonia and Epirus. In the summer of 1914, both states announced their readiness for the transfer. But they could not agree on a suitable procedure, and so the accord was not ratified.[17] Furthermore, the Great War—the "European War," as it was called in the Orient and the Levant—had begun.

When Greece entered the Great War on the side of the Entente in 1917, the Ottoman authorities resumed deportations of Orthodox populations into the interior, prompted by a desire to secure the empire's coastline. Greeks living along the Aegean and the Sea of Marmara, areas susceptible to possible Allied amphibious assaults, were relocated deep in the hinterland. The Ottomans were not alone in choosing to depopulate a region considered militarily sensitive. In czarist Russia, it was common practice during World War I to remove populations considered unreliable from sectors adjoining the front. Thus the Galician Jews, believed to harbor sympathies for the Central Powers, were deported to the East. Ethnic Germans received similar treatment. In the Baltic, hundreds of thousands of Jews were likewise relocated.[18] In Rumania, the Jewish populace, allegedly sympathetic to Austria-Hungary, was subjected to similar oppressive measures.[19] The fate of some half-million Turkic-speaking Central Asian nomads, the Kazakhs of the Kirghiz-Kazakh Federation, was particularly horrible. Stripped of their herds and possessions, they were driven by the Russians into the desert and mountains in the dead of winter, where they perished miserably. A plea on their behalf by Duma deputy Alexander Kerensky went unheeded.[20]

The genocide of the Armenians in 1915 took place at the juncture between two displacements: the gradual formation of the Turkish nation-state from the decaying Ottoman Empire and the upheaval accompanying the war on the Caucasus front.[21] The government-inspired deportations and massacres were occasioned by earlier Armenian uprisings and ethnic clashes in mixed areas of settlement as well as by Armenian sympathies for Russia, the archenemy of the Ottoman Empire. This mix of old and new conflicts ended in the annihilation of well over a million Armenians.

The persecution of the Armenians began in the wake of the crippling defeat of the Third Ottoman Army near Sarikamis in January 1915. War minister Enver Pasha had deployed this ill-prepared army on the Armenian high plateau during an exceptionally harsh winter, the aim being to confront far better equipped Russian forces under excellent command, in order to then advance into the oil-rich region of Baku. With four legions of foreign Armenians in the Russian army having fought with distinction against the Ottomans, the Armenians were held responsible for the defeat of the Ottoman troops. In this context, the radical, highly nationalistic, and pan-Turkish faction within the Committee for Unity and Progress seized upon the Armenian military role as a pretext to launch deportations of the Anatolian Armenians that resulted in genocide.[22]

As a first step, the generally loyal Armenian soldiers serving in the Ottoman army were disarmed, demobilized, and reassembled in labor battalions. Then all Armenians living in Eastern Anatolia were ordered to surrender whatever weapons they had. When the deportations from Zaitun began in April 1915, members of these labor battalions were herded together and killed.[23] On instructions from interior minister Talat Pasha, thousands of Armenian community leaders were arrested on 24 April, and many were executed. Armenian notables in Istanbul and Smyrna, in the westernmost reaches of the empire, far from the Russian front in the Caucasus, suffered the same fate. From May to June 1915, Armenians living in the eastern provinces were "resettled," that is, the men were largely murdered on the spot, while the elderly, the women, and the children were forced to leave on foot or shipped off in trains as far as the rail network allowed. Along the way, they often fall prey to marauding Kurdish bands. Most died of exhaustion, hunger, or thirst. The destination of these deportations was the Aleppo region; from there the trek continued on to Deir ez Zor. Those who had managed to survive this ordeal were driven into the Syrian Desert abutting the Euphrates area. From here there was no escape.

The Great War and the dubious accusations leveled by pan-Turkish members of the Committee for Unity and Progress furnished the genocide's immediate pretext. But the real sources of this horrifying event lie deeper, are bound up with the slow dismemberment of the Ottoman Empire over the course of the nineteenth century. At work here was a highly complex process of religious ethnification: the transformation of the empire's religious communities, the so-called *millets,* into nations.[24] Within the empire, the traditional principle of personality was steadily supplanted by territorial notions of order. With the introduction of even limited local representation, the various regions gradually assumed a "national" tint. Relations between "majority" and "minority," previously having little relevance within the state's imperial structure, gradually gained prominence.[25] By the end of the nineteenth century, the nationalization of groups whose identity had hitherto been religious had raised the issue of the empire's "national" character. The Turkicizing Muslims were increasingly becoming the group whose ethnic attributes stamped the physiognomy of the state. In contrast, the Orthodox Christians of various denominations and the Armenians were being increasingly viewed as outsiders. This generations-long process, in which Ottoman subjects of the sultan with differing religious affiliations were transformed into members of diverse nationalities, soon developed a murderous political dynamic. Around the turn of the century, it led to hopeless conflicts between Orthodox Christians and Muslims, as well as among Orthodox communities with different languages and rites.[26] It produced seemingly interminable conflicts between Turks and Armenians and between Turks and Greeks, with all the accompanying distress. To the Armenians, it brought genocide.

In this manner, what came to a climax during the Great War was the outcome of a more long-term development. It is here important to note that, toward the end of the nineteenth century, what passed as the civilized world had already learned of massacres of Armenians in the Ottoman Empire. Between 1894 and 1896, they had been murdered by the thousands, the atrocities beginning in Sassoun, in the *vilayet* of Bitlis, than spreading to several other provinces. In total, there were between 90,000 and 250,000 victims. Missionaries and consuls apprised Europe of the events, with questions soon raised about the causes and those responsible. Pastor Johannes Lepsius, who was instrumental in gathering evidence of these early massacres as well as of the later genocide, suspected that a central administrative hand was behind the bloodbath.[27] Other authors have attributed it to spontaneous reactions by resettled Muslims who following the Russo-Turkish War of 1876–77 had gradually reached Anatolia, where they encountered Christian Armenians purportedly sympathetic to Russia.[28] The Armenian and other minority questions were discussed at the Berlin Congress of 1878, reforms now being demanded of the Sublime Porte. The Armenian problem had become an international problem requiring repeated action by the leading powers. In turn, Muslims in the Ottoman Empire began to identify the Armenians and their demands with foreign interests. In the aftermath of the Young Turk Revolution and especially after the 1909 counterrevolution, twenty-thousand Armenians in Cilicia were murdered by gangs. In 1912 Russia raised the Armenian question anew; in February 1914 it reached an accord with the Ottomans for institutional reform in the region, to be implemented under the supervision of two European inspectors—a form of intervention reminding the Ottomans of their earlier, unfavorable agreement on the Macedonian question.[29] This generated fear among the Muslims that resettlement and expulsion might become their fate in the eastern provinces as it had been in Rumelia.[30]

At the outbreak of the Great War, the Ottoman Empire's Armenians found themselves in an extremely precarious situation. A chain of events leading toward the genocide began to unfold. The events involved Ottoman territorial losses occurring, paradoxically, after the Young Turk's revolution.[31] First, there was the final declaration of Bulgarian independence from Ottoman rule in September 1908, followed by the Austro-Hungarian annexation of Bosnia-Herzegovina, the Tripolitan War of 1911 against Italy, and the Balkan wars of 1912–1913, resulting in the loss of the empire's last European territory, together with the expulsion of Muslims from Macedonia and Thrace and a constant influx of Muslim refugees from the Caucasus, who could only be resettled in Anatolia with great difficulty. These developments accelerated the transformation of the Ottoman Empire into an increasingly homogeneous Turkish nation-state. The territorial losses radicalized the Young Turks, while the steady decline in numbers of the empire's other Christian subjects through further territorial losses deprived the Armenians of the traditional protection offered in the empire by multiethnic and multireligious diversity. On the eve of the "European War," the Armenians, once known as the most loyal of the Sultan's *millets*, stood nearly alone in facing the increasingly Turkicized Muslims in Anatolia.[32] Only the Greeks in Asia Minor and the Hellespont still continued to inhabit their ancient homeland,—at least until their final expulsion in 1922. But there was a basic difference between their situation and that of the Armenians: namely, the existence of a Greek nation-state in near proximity, capable, if necessary, of absorbing desperate, threatened Orthodox Greeks. This was something the Turkish nationalist and pan-Turkish extremist factions in the Committee for Unity and Progress could rely on, hence the agreement to this effect under discussion in the summer of 1914. The Armenians, to the contrary, had no place of their own to flee to.

The Armenians of Anatolia were consequently doomed. One-third of the Ottoman Armenian population survived—some six hundred thousand persons, including the Armenians in Lebanon and Palestine (both still part of the empire). Many had fled from Anatolia to Russian territory before the deportations began; others, the legendary defenders of Musa Dagh, were evacuated by Allied ships; still others managed to survive the camps in the Syrian Desert. The Armenian inhabitants of Constantinople and Smyrna also survived the ferocious persecution, something clearly due to the presence of many European legations in both localities—not least the German military mission headed by Liman von Sanders. Generally, however, the Ottomans' German and Austrian allies kept a low profile. After the crimes became known, the Entente threatened to punish those responsible. As much as possible, the Young Turk government tried to conceal the true scale of the events; but leading personalities such as defense minister Enver Pasha acknowledged the crime in private conversations, for example, with American ambassador Henry Morgenthau.[33]

The territorial secession of the Rumelian Christians from the Ottoman Empire, the expansion of the Greek state in the aftermath of the Balkan wars, the reciprocal expulsions of Muslims and Orthodox Christians in the course of the Greek-Turkish confrontations between 1919 and 1922, and the Armenian genocide were manifestations of a single process: the formation of ethnically homogeneous nation-states from the disintegrating body of a multireligious, multinational empire. This phenomenon was not limited to the territories of the Ottoman Empire and the Eastern Question. With the Great War's end and the Paris Peace Conference of 1919–20, national and ethnic questions emerged with similar sharpness in the heart of the Continent, in Central and East Central Europe.[34]

In East Central and Eastern Europe, issues of church affiliation, so crucial in the Balkans and the Levant, were secondary to those of ethnic affiliation. This was very much the case with the new or expanded states that had emerged from the dynastically legitimized multiethnic and multinational empires. Although hardly less diverse than the empires they had successfully disrupted, they strove for the political ideal of national homogeneity.[35] The situation with the Russian Empire was strikingly different: even after the political upheaval of 1919, multinationality was able to subsist there in the framework of Bolshevik internationalism; albeit in Communist guise, Soviet Russia and the later Soviet Union remained committed to the empire's universal character.

Each of the new states in Central and East Central Europe was plagued by constant tensions between the titular nation and its minorities. The great powers in Paris tried to regulate interethnic and border conflicts by demanding that these newly expanded states sign formal accords protecting minority rights. But over the long term, these accords were unable to shield the minorities from persecution by the ruling nation.[36] Increasingly, the minorities fell victim to social, political, and institutional discrimination. Already in the 1920s, a chronic agrarian crisis had produced authoritarian and dictatorial regimes in East Central and Southern Europe; this, in turn, exacerbated the condition of the minorities.[37] In particular, Jews in East Central Europe faced a seemingly hopeless situation.[38] In Poland, 35 percent of the total population consisted of non-ethnic Poles; Jews comprised over 10 percent of the population. In that context, the intensifying social antagonism between city and countryside had damaging consequences for Poland's Jewry. For example, when applying for work in government-held monopolies and other state enterprises and agencies, ethnic (Catholic) Poles who had migrated to urban areas were given preference over urban Jews.[39] At the same time, the United States, which at the turn of the century had left its gates open for an unlimited immigration from Southern and Eastern Europe, now introduced drastic restrictions. In the 1930s, such restrictions, shared with other potential lands of asylum, would prove fatal for the Jewish populace of Poland.[40]

In the 1930s, the dangers facing the Jews of Germany were of a different character than those menacing their coreligionists in Poland.[41] Polish Jews were a numerically significant segment of Polish society. They had encountered both their own government's discriminatory policies and popular, everyday anti-Semitism. They could relate their misery largely to structural problems, especially poverty, inherent in the social reality of the new Polish polity. In contrast, the Jews of Germany, comprising less than 1 percent of the total population, seemed neither to present a social problem nor to challenge Germany's territorial or ethnic integrity. In interwar Poland, Polish integrists considered all the ethnic minorities to pose a permanent danger to the very existence of an independent Poland. In certain Polish nationalist circles, the Jews were reviled as a "fourth partitioning power." And they were repeatedly accused of conspiring with other ethnic minorities, including the Ukrainians, the White Russians, the Lithuanians, and the Germans, to undermine the country's sovereignty through appeals to the clauses in the Polish constitution, approved by the League of Nations, that guaranteed minority protection.[42]

The East Central European nationalities question, mass poverty, and popular anti-Semitism thus formed the context for the Polish government's effort to rid itself of what it considered a "surplus" of Jews by encouraging migration to, for instance, Madagascar or Palestine. In contrast, the Nazis' own, far more radical anti-Jewish measures, an apparent attempt to force all Jews out of Germany,[43] were ideologically grounded in a rigid racist weltanschauung, hence located beyond considerations of utility and—what will become clear later—even their own self-preservation: a reality eventually leading to the destruction of European Jewry. In the end, it would not even be enough to expel the Jews from the territories under German control. The Nazis thus not only surpassed previous excesses of ethnic cleansing but transformed, in the course of territorial expansion, the very logic of expulsion into its opposite. The Nazi aim, it turned out, was to locate all the Jews living in Europe and assemble them logistically for "eastern settlement"; eventually, this became a concentration for the sake of annihilation. Particularly in that last stage, the process involved something categorically different than trying to achieve ethnic homogeneity by transporting populations beyond one's own national borders. The deportation of fewer than eight hundred Norwegian Jews to Auschwitz is a phenomenon beyond the "ethnic cleansing" that had already taken place in Europe.[44] That in July 1944 the Germans shipped the Jews of Rhodes to their annihilation even as they were abandoning their heavy military equipment testifies to an assault on their own most basic interest, on a human instinct for self-preservation widely considered an anthropological commonplace.[45]

While the thrust of National Socialism's ideologically driven Jewish policy was toward annihilation, this does not mean it was programmatically steered from the start. But ideological willingness in that regard had settled into everything that appeared to be tied to contingency, coincidence, or circumstance. It impregnated a mode of action ostensibly under the sway of practical constraints, thus generating collective will. It consisted of both active, ideologically driven factors and passive elements following the situation's dictates in opportunistic fashion. This form of willingness headed toward annihilation *as if* programmatically steered there from the start.

Along with an ideological propensity, the destruction of European Jewry required an advent of unpredictable circumstances in increasingly extreme situations. These circumstances themselves stemmed from both the special character of the Nazi regime and the rapidly unfolding phases of its expansion. Historians have defined the regime's special character as that of a "polycracy" producing "institutional chaos" and leading in turn to a spiral of self-created radicalization;[46] the consequences of such radicalization in any case do not have an intentional appearance. This was the case as well, it is argued, for the mass annihilation, carried out less for reasons of ideology than because of specific circumstances. To be sure, the Nazis ignored neither racial origin nor other stigmatizing factors in selecting their victims, but such factors were secondary to the circumstances, which produced the actual choice of the groups to be sacrificed. This choice was consequently not the principle consideration in carrying out the Holocaust.[47]

In many respects, this sort of historical argument is plausible. It certainly generates insight into the structures and processes of the Nazi power apparatus. Nevertheless, its ultimate explanatory value is dubious, especially in light of the fact that the very selection of the groups to be victimized reveals an ideological disposition to deal with them as they were finally dealt with.[48] For the victims were, emphatically, not individuals chosen at random, thus mistakenly consigned to the death mills of a totalitarian regime. Rather, they belonged to certain groups whose stigmatization derived from supposedly immutable genealogical features. It was precisely because of that shared genealogy that they were consigned to a common fate. Again, the victims were not chosen haphazardly, irrespective of collective affiliation, for utilitarian or other practical reasons. Specific persons and groups—Jews, Gypsies, and others—were exterminated for reasons of ideology or from pseudoscientific motives.[49] In contrast to what the circumstantial or structuralist-functionalist approaches imply, the choice of groups doomed to death can indeed disclose the causes of their destruction. But at the same time, it is crucial to acknowledge both background motives and external circumstances that allowed the monstrous deed to be carried out, for this juncture between motive and circumstance points the way to the Holocaust. The juncture was itself reflected in the direction of Nazi expansion: while it proceeded from west to east, the extermination began on the easternmost edge of the expansion, moving from there in the opposite direction, east to west. The extermination began with conventional mass killings reminiscent of massacres and culminated, pressing westward, in the total genocide of European Jewry.

The topography of annihilation can be delineated as follows: Until November 1938, the Jews of Germany were subjected to harsh discriminatory measures whose purpose was to ensure social isolation and thus induce emigration. The "annexation" of Austria, the first step in Nazi Germany's expansion, led to genuine expulsions soon extended into Germany proper—into the *Altreich*. The outbreak of war and the conquest of Poland in 1939 led to the ghettoization of the Jews in the annexed and occupied territories. The actual extermination began in 1941 in tandem with the specifically anti-Bolshevik mode of warfare characterizing Operation Barbarossa. In the areas of the Soviet Union falling under German control, the killing passed through several stages of intensification, culminating in large-scale genocidal massacres. By the end of 1941 or the beginning of 1942, after the rather illusory notion of transferring the Jews to the East had been abandoned due to the inauspicious progress of the Russian campaign, the bureaucratically organized and industrially implemented process of annihilation got under way. It began with the Polish Jews and gradually encompassed all of European Jewry.

Hence until the Kristallnacht in November 1938, the German authorities sought to rid their nation of Jews, whose presence they considered intolerable, by means of forced emigration. This policy was carried out by conservative officials in the relevant ministries in coordination with the remaining Jewish institutions and organizations.[50] Of course, emigration could only be successfully achieved if immigration into another country was assured. But in the stressful process of searching for acceptance by another country, potential Jewish émigrés had to meet certain conditions, for instance, learning a new useful trade. Leaving Germany was thus an extremely laborious procedure requiring adequate time and planning. Both the Jews and the responsible officials in the Ministry of

Economy and Finance believed that under the existing conditions of international peace and relative stability, the procedure would require more than twenty years.[51]

But the conditions favoring such a long-term project soon vanished. The expulsions following the Austrian *Anschluß* in March 1938 undermined the basis for orderly emigration. Faced with a flood of refugees lacking valid papers or possessions or a suitable vocation, the countries of immigration became increasingly reluctant to receive them. They feared, justifiably, that pressure on Jews to leave Germany and Austria would soon mount.[52] The conference initiated by Franklin D. Roosevelt in Evian in the summer of 1938 was meant to encourage such countries, especially those in the Western Hemisphere, to grant entry to the Jewish refugees. But the conference's American organizers were also aware of one possible result of any general declaration of readiness to accept new Jewish immigrants: increased pressure by the governments of Poland, Rumania, and Hungary on their Jewish citizens to leave. These East Central European governments had markedly little sympathy for the Jews; and indeed, the planned American conference had encouraged government circles in Warsaw to press ahead with their own long-standing plans to get rid of "surplus" Jews by means of emigration.[53] For this reason, the organizers decided to term the Evian conference the Conference on Political Refugees from Germany and Austria. The title was to contain no specific reference to Jews, although they were its main concern.

After war broke out in September 1939, orderly emigration became unthinkable—all the more so with the considerable expansion of the number of Jews under German rule that accompanied the conquest of Polish territory. Even if there was still no clear intention to liquidate all the Jews, the conditions that the Nazis created already pointed in this direction. The prewar process of forced emigration and expulsion was now supplanted by internal deportation to the east and a local concentration of the Jewish populace. Between December 1939 and April 1940, Jews from the

Reich, the Protectorate of Bohemia, and the annexed Polish territories were deported to the newly created "Generalgouvernement" of Poland, which was declared a "collateral territory" *(Nebenland)* of the German Reich in June 1940. In comparison with the previous forced emigration, these deportations were a qualitative leap in the direction of annihilation. While emigration, even when less than voluntary, generally involves a prospect of maintaining or even improving one's social status and living conditions, deportation is a forced change of living place involving loss of civil rights and restrictions on mobility to the point of total subjugation. Deportees are deprived of control not only over their own decisions but even over their own bodies. Consequently, the Jewish emigration westward and following deportations eastward were antithetical in terms of both status and fate.[54]

At the same time that barriers were being raised against emigration, the expulsions and deportations were intensifying in the annexed territories. This was especially the case in the Polish region the Nazis now called the "Wartheland," under its enterprising *Gauleiter,* Arthur Greiser, who was particularly eager to Germanize his satrapy. Poles, Jews, and Gypsies were summarily expelled, while ethnic Germans from the Baltic were brought "home into the Reich" and resettled there.[55] As part of an enterprise of national-racial homogenization, these events evoke earlier ethnic cleansings and population transfers. Initially, both Poles and Jews were ousted from the annexed territories, but that practice was soon discontinued.[56] To the east, in the nonannexed but German-occupied Generalgouvernement, a distinction was drawn between Poles with "Aryan" papers and Jews. This would later mark the line between life and death. Beginning in 1940, Jews were concentrated in special residential "ghettos," preferably near railway junctions or in localities affording access to a rail network, since they were not meant to remain in the Generalgouvernement permanently. The Nazis wanted to devise a "territorial solution" to the "Jewish Question." In October 1939, there had been provisional talk about creating a "Jewish reservation" in eastern occupied Poland, around the Lublin district and Nisko on the San. According to Reinhard Heydrich's casual formulation, a "Reich ghetto" was to be established.[57] But this casual form of speech harbored increasing radicalization.

The radicalizing process is manifest in the history of the first ghetto—the Łódź ghetto in the "Warthegau," created because deportations to the Generalgouvernement had been temporarily halted. Hans Frank had successfully protested against any further importation of Jews, so those arriving from the west were concentrated instead in Łódź. Somewhat later, ghettoization began in the Generalgouvernement. The Warsaw ghetto was set up in October 1940, followed by other, larger ghettos the following spring. The Jews in the ghettos were meant to be kept ready for further transport to the "east."[58]

Ghettoization was introduced as a temporary measure; the ghetto was meant to be a place of transit. But to where? And how long, and under what conditions, would this situation continue? These remained open questions. This extended provisionality soon shifted onto another level of radicalization. On 16 July 1941, hence even before the offensive in the Soviet Union had stalled, Gauleiter Greiser's office broached the idea of a "humane" solution for the "non-able-bodied" Jews packed into the Łódź ghetto. Mounting problems with food supply and the threat of epidemics made it urgent to dispose of these Jews by some "expeditious means."[59]

Before such measures were applied and the Jews were gassed en masse as part of "Operation Reinhard," a "territorial solution" was considered once again, In June 1940, just after the fall of France, officials in the Reich Central Security Office became enthused over another reservation scheme, this time in Madagascar. The island, part of the French colonial empire, would absorb the Jews of Europe who had come under German jurisdiction.[60] From the outset, however, the project was wholly unrealistic.

Transporting millions of persons, already confined to ghettos and deprived of all means of livelihood, across the ocean, then resettling them on an inhospitable island lacking adequate infrastructure and other essentials was logistically unfeasible. When it became clear that the war with England would yield neither a quick victory nor an accord, the "Madagascar Plan" was shelved.[61] The Jews would thus continue to be kept ready in the ghettos of occupied Poland for deportation to the "East" once the "Russian campaign" began. Meanwhile, the provisional situation was steadily corroding the living circumstances of the penned-up Jews. The misery of these individuals, torn from their social milieu and thrown into confinement, further deepened after rations were reduced and disease began to spread. Gradually the state of affairs came into being that Greiser's staff had foreseen in the summer of 1941 and that had led to proposals to liquidate the Jews for reasons of "humanity." That was, in the end, "more pleasant than letting them starve to death."[62]

The "humane" solution of killing had been introduced some time before by the highest echelons as "secret state policy." Hitler's chancellery was directing the "euthanasia" program inaugurated in the fall of 1939: the elimination of "life-unworthy life"— *lebensunwertes Leben*—in other words, a covert and systematic execution of physically and mentally disabled Germans.[63] The eugenic practices preceding euthanasia had little in common with the parallel anti-Jewish measures instituted in the 1930s. On the one hand, aside from the forcibly sterilized Rhineland Germans of partly black descent,[64] the victims of euthanasia were by and large "Aryans," to be eliminated according to the demands of "racial hygiene." On the other hand, although the Jews were ostensibly murdered for being "non-Aryan," indeed subhuman, in actuality, for all the Nazi's racial ideals and anthropological-physiognomical theory, the Third Reich's legal definition of who was a Jew was necessarily based less on racial criteria than on religious affiliation.[65]

Consequently, the real linkage between euthanasia and the murder of the Jews involved not a unified racial-hygienic argument but relatively secondary factors.[66] While the machinery devoted to killing "life-unworthy life" was justified by medical-biological principles, there was no direct linkage between eugenic theory and the onset of mass murder of Jews in the East. To be sure, their extermination would be carried out using the *technical* means developed for the euthanasia program—"Action T-4." After the latter was halted in August 1941 in the wake of popular protests, its personnel was transferred to the East on account of its "expertise," in order to process the Jews "deported" from the ghettos in Poland to death mills as part of Operation Reinhard. Hence the industrialized murder began with the arrival of the "Action T-4" cadre; with the construction of the death camps, regular slaughterhouses for human beings were up and running.[67] But they did not *initiate* the extermination, which can be traced back to the summer of 1941 and large-scale conventional massacres of Jews during Operation Barbarossa—hence in the framework of the ideological war against Bolshevism.[68]

There is an evident causal nexus between Nazi anti-Bolshevism and the murder of the Jews in the East. The difference between Nazi anti-Bolshevism and its Western, liberal-democratic counterpart already emerged during Germany's revolutionary insurgencies of 1918–19 and their counterrevolutionary suppression; it was especially manifest in the ideological synthesis of class and race stamping the National Socialist movement. Within the Nazi weltanschauung, the racial dimension of anti-Bolshevism predominated over its political dimension. In Nazi eyes, Bolshevism was not the rule of a certain class or a form of dictatorship by a self-declared proletariat avant-garde, but was rather a racial-ideological composite of "Jewish intelligentsia" and "Slavic subhumans."[69] As a result, the Nazis perceived the Soviet Union's Bolshevik regime as a variant of Jewish world domination. That perception is one reason the Soviet Union's military staying power and its capacity to resist the German war machine could be so badly underestimated. The attack on the Soviet Union was launched in the firm conviction that the Red Empire would soon collapse.[70]

Anti-Bolshevism as a racist worldview determined the war's conduct. This can be seen in the increasingly broadened orders given the Wehrmacht, particularly Hitler's so-called Commissar Decree of March 1941.[71] Political commissars in the Red Army, officials of the Comintern and the Communist Party, as well as other agents of Soviet power were to be summarily executed—in extraordinarily intense acts of enmity commonly associated with civil war. And yet Nazi policy did not halt at this ostensibly political selection of victims. The shooting of Jewish males was soon extended to the annihilation of all Jews;[72] the putative class war became a war of race. In keeping with its racist-ideological character, the commander of the German Sixth Army, Walter von Reichenau, issued orders in October 1941 making the true nature of the "war in the East" unmistakably clear to German soldiers. The campaign would be guided not by earlier rules of war but by an "inexorable *völkish* idea" that would be imposed on the "subhuman Jews."[73] As "Slavic subhumans," millions of Soviet prisoners-of-war were exposed to starvation and subfreezing temperature and thus themselves abandoned to a grim mass death.[74]

Despite its connection with the euthanasia program, the onset of the extermination of European Jewry was closely bound up with the "eastern campaign" and its anti-Bolshevik, race-ideological orientation.[75] In many respects, Nazi anti-Bolshevism presented itself as a variant of anti-Semitism. Albeit possibly unconvincing to some, the repeated assertion of a dire threat stemming from a "Jewish intelligentsia" working together with "subhuman Slavs" provided the SS's *Einsatz* units, the police reserve battalions, and units of the Wehrmacht with a useful rationale for their murderous activities.[76] The ideological blight had especially murderous consequences when orders were ambiguous. In August and September 1941, the threshold between an anti-Bolshevik ideological war and genocide of the Jews was crossed imperceptibly; this was followed by growing pressure to totalize the process. Germany's entire administrative apparatus was now steadily drawn, as if by an invisible hand, into a vortex of visionary planning.[77] Soon the "total solution of the Jewish Question" had become an exclusively technical question, the main concern being to make it easier for the murderers by creating bureaucratic and spatial distance between them and their victims, while at the same time industrially accelerating the process. This was the context in which the euthanasia experts were to play their parts.[78] The Jews in the Polish ghettos were now caught up in the factory-like killing machinery; death camps in the close vicinity—Belzec, Sobibor, and Treblinka—were the destination of the "deportations." These "human slaughterhouses"[79] were in constant operation from the spring of 1942 to October 1943. By the time the large industrial complex at Auschwitz had reached its maximal killing capacity, Polish Jewry had thus already been largely eradicated. Deportees to Auschwitz were now transported from the remaining reaches— western, central, southern—of German-occupied Europe.[80]

On 29 November 1941, Reinhard Heydrich invited middle-level personnel in the state and Nazi-party bureaucracy to attend a meeting on the "Jewish Question" that later became known as the Wannsee Conference, a reference to its venue in the lakeside villa of an affluent Berlin suburb. The meeting, which took place on 20 January 1942, was not aimed at passing a formal resolution[81]— none was needed, since the annihilation of the Jews was already well under way. Typical of the "Final Solution" in its entirety, the mass murder had itself proceeded by degrees.[82]

What was the actual purpose of this ominous meeting, held not during normal business hours in the Reich Security Main Office, but rather at noon in a secluded villa? There is circumstantial evidence supporting the idea that Heydrich wished to receive some special authority on the "Jewish Question" from his colleagues in other agencies. But this explanation is inadequate, for the Wannsee Conference seems to have been much more significant than that.[83] First, the intention to simulate a bureaucratic procedure to secure administrative legitimation for a mass-murder process that was long under way is evident. Furthermore, by bringing in representatives from a variety of responsible offices in the state and party apparatus, the simulated procedure could contribute to the bureaucratic rationalization and thus acceleration of the genocidal enterprise. Through the conference, Heydrich was able to enlist the governmental and party bureaucracy for a task until then solely within the competence of the Reich Security Main Office, the SS, and the Wehrmacht, but without surrendering overall control. He thus succeeded in "nailing down" the involvement of the state secretaries and office heads who were present, as Eichmann put it during his interrogation in Jerusalem.[84]

The timing of the Wannsee Conference is significant. The rapid succession of events between August and December 1941 point to various processes and individual decisions at work in the "Jewish Question" that fed into the Final Solution. Among these were the expansion of killing actions by the *Einsatz* squads into genocidal murder of all Jews they could get their hands on, the decision to include German Jews in the deportations, the construction of the Belzec extermination camp, the declaration of war against the United States in December 1941, the first systematic killings in Chelmno in the Wartheland, and so forth. These decisions and processes suggest a "caesura"[85] in the entire complex of unfolding events; from that point onward, the entirety of European Jewry was to be exterminated. It remains doubtful whether a clear, administratively effective decision, traceable to specific officials, rests behind the killing process's sequential intensification. This is the case despite the fact that on 12 December 1941, one day after declaring war on the United States, Hitler informed the *Reichsleiter* and *Gauleiter* elite assembled in the chancellery's private quarters that his "prophecy" would now be fulfilled: the Jews, who bore ultimate blame for the war, would be "destroyed."[86]

The declaration of war against the United States and the expansion of the conflict into a world war probably further radicalized the approach to the "Jewish Question."[87] In Hitler's fantasy, the Jews were, after all, an international power that exploited both Bolshevism and Western plutocracy to enhance their domination.[88] This ideological projection had now become ubiquitous: in the media, in propaganda, in public declarations, and in the Führer's unrelenting anti-Jewish rhetoric. Within his closest circle, there was certainly no doubt about his intentions. He repeatedly tied the ever-widening war to the Jews; this in turn generated an array of increasingly severe measures against them. The intensification of activities in the chancellery in this period is striking. In particular, Himmler's calendar entry for 18 December 1941— "Jewish Question / to be eradicated as partisans"—appears to strongly suggest that such a decision was reached in consultation with Hitler.[89]

Nevertheless, as indicated, doubts persist regarding the existence of a decision or order clearly demarcating the threshold where the Holocaust began. The total annihilation of the Jews by *Einsatz* squads and similar formations had already begun in formerly Soviet territory long before America's entry into the war and the accompanying posturing and rhetorical hyperbole.[90] To· stress again: what appears to have unfolded was a kind of gliding escalation, the limitless extension of a practice of extermination already established in principle. When, following mass executions in an area stretching from the Baltic to the Black Sea, the deportations were extended to the German Jews in the fall of 1941, the fate of Polish Jewry had long been sealed, their liquidation only a technical question, initially addressed in November with the construction of the Belzec death camp.[91]

The Wannsee Conference thus represented an institutional legitimation of ongoing mass murder. Heydrich was probing to see if the bureaucracy would offer some resistance to his "solution of the Jewish Question." In this regard, the conference was a complete success. None of the bureau chiefs expressed any reservations regarding his competency. Nor had he been obliged to coordinate with other offices in matters regarding the Final Solution. As things turned out, including the bureaucracy in the process ensured its further radicalization.

At first glance, then, the Wannsee Conference's choreography appears to have been designed to confirm Heydrich's competence—a competence otherwise infringing on the prerogatives of almost every agency. But that was not all there was to it, for the conference was held in the context of those liminal events, in the autumn and winter of 1941, heralding the transition from annihilation of the "Bolshevik" Jews in the East to the Final Solution. The conference, then, marks the "caesura" during which the complete destruction of European Jewry was set in motion. On the administrative level, there was a need for a symbolic act; the transition to the Holocaust was to have its bureaucratic signet. But there was no official resolution sanctioning action, and it is not surprising that the state secretaries and bureau chiefs participating in the meeting were later at a loss to say just what had come out of it or why it had been held in the first place. Heydrich, on the other hand, was in a much better position to gauge its success. Relieved, the plenipotentiary for the "total solution of the Jewish Question," a man who normally eschewed alcohol, enjoyed a glass of cognac with his paladin Adolf Eichmann.[92]

It would be mistaken to conclude that the decisions leading to the Final Solution amounted to a deplorable but still in the end basically negligent procedure. Even when what is at stake is a series of distinct but interrelated deeds rather than an elaborate plan driven by a declared will to act, intense deliberation and ideological motivation can be manifestly present. This disarticulation of intention contributed significantly to the Holocaust's relatively smooth implementation. Also, the fraying of accountability served to foil later attempts to prosecute the crimes before a court of law.[93] And yet no matter how detached and disconnected the execution of the Final Solution may have seemed to its principle agents, the fact that it constituted a gross violation of all ethical norms must have been obvious to all of them. On the threshold of horrendous crime, these agents found it necessary to seek reasons to justify their actions. Here absolving themselves by transferring responsibility to superiors or supralegal authorities—appealing, for example, to the "will of the Führer"—may have been convenient.[94] We would be seriously underestimating the role of justification as a basis for action if we considered a particular weltanschauung important only when it follows a comprehensive program or a political itinerary pursued down to the smallest detail. This is not how ideology operates. Rather, it works through osmosis. It spreads a thin veneer of justification over events and can perform a useful service in allaying doubts or overcoming moral inhibitions when under social pressure. To this end, neither ideological conviction in the sense of an overall worldview nor a pervasive anti-Semitic animus is necessary, contrary to what some wish to argue.[95] Instead, it suffices simply to appeal to the ideology in moments of doubt or inner conflict. Of course, any such justification of nakedly criminal acts comes up against limits when the victims are persons with whom one feels a bond of kinship or ethnicity, as revealed in the popular protest against euthanasia or the case of the "factory Jews" in Berlin successfully shielded by their "Aryan" wives.[96] Killing is easier if perpetrated against groups of outsiders, especially if they are transformed into a pliable mass and, if possible, proscribed as an "eternal enemy."[97]

When one tries to understand the events leading to the Nazi extermination of European Jewry, two apparently separate factors are of special importance: first, a characteristic institutional process of Nazi agencies, an effort unfolding in extreme situations to solve problems of their own making, tending to generate intensification and radicalization; second, the precise groups against whom the increasingly radical measures were to be directed.

Despite the Nazi regime's institutional chaos, there was in fact little doubt about who was to be persecuted and finally subjected to "special treatment." Initially the victims—Jews, Gypsies, the disabled, and others—were stigmatized; only later were they subjected to the corresponding treatment. There was no threat from the regime toward Germans who belonged to the "national community" (the *Volksgemeinschaft*). The only doubt was whether a specific individual should be assigned to a stigmatized group.[98]

The identity of the victims is important for identifying a broader intentionality—that not only of the crime's initiators but also of perpetrators on the middle and lower levels—driving the annihilation. In contrast to the criminalizing of individuals, collective stigmatizing reveals, by its very nature, the underlying motive for an act of persecution. And the presence of a motive itself attests to a widely denied intentional action. Many have tried to escape accountability by claiming not to have known *what* was happening to the Jews. But it is difficult to maintain convincingly that they did not know that *something* was happening to the Jews. In these deplorable proceedings, a motive emerges that must have been present latently and independent of the regime's official proclamations, again without necessarily being articulated openly and with ideological fervor. It was enough to signal passive readiness through indifference. For the deed's realization, it was immaterial whether either initiators or perpetrators were motivated by a strong sense of inward conviction. What mattered far more was that they acted *as if* they were so motivated. Consequently, the anti-Jewish measures did not require an anti-Semitism of firm conviction. The murder of the Jews was an anti-Semitic act in that it needed no other motive than the fact that Jews were involved.

Looking backward, we can divide perception and interpretation of the Holocaust into two contradictory perspectives, attached to two different realms of experience and memory. These realms lead, in turn, to antithetical questions about the past. The question about the circumstances culminating in the Holocaust, the question of *how* it could happen, is asked above all by those who have adopted the perpetrators' viewpoint, whether out of emotional shock, intellectual curiosity, or a sense of collective belonging. These individuals tend to universalize their question, citing similar events in the hope of understanding what happened, and exploring—as it were, anthropologically—various factors that might allow similar events to recur. The contrasting perspective tends to adopt the viewpoint of the victims. The fact that the horrifying crimes of the Holocaust were emphatically not inflicted on persons irrespective of origin, but rather on a specific group of people stigmatized on grounds of ethnicity, encourages a focus on the motives of the perpetrators. The question then asked about the Holocaust as a historical event is *why* it happened. Or more particularistically: *"Why us?"*[99]

These central, epistemologically contrary historical questions asked about the Holocaust—on the one hand, the question of its circumstances, its *how;* on the other hand, the question of its causes, its *why*—can be classified according to origin, antithetically generated historical images, and associated narratives; by definition, they profoundly influence the event's historical reconstruction. In the ultimative terms of their couching, the very nature of the mass annihilation seems to be confirmed.[100] Strikingly, this unfolding antithetical historical discourse appears to follow the pattern of statement and counterstatement between plaintiff and accused characterizing a court of law.[101] Although thoroughly confirming the basic facts of the case, the accused will still be tempted to offer cogent reasons for not being guilty. In view of the complex events that led to the mass murder, the accused may sometimes succeed in such an endeavor, especially in regard to the decision-making processes, but also to the obscurity resulting from the genocide's division of labor. Above all, the accused will here be tempted to minimize anything suggesting intent or subjective readiness—the centrality, for instance, of virulent anti-Semitism in the infliction of pain on stigmatized human beings. In general, they will downplay the importance of ideology. Attached to the collective memory defining their ethnic affiliation, they will maintain that the horrific events resulted from negligence rather than guilt.[102]

It is different for those belonging to the collective of victims. For them, the perpetrators' guilt is proven beyond a reasonable doubt. Intent is undeniable. After all, the victims were singled out for annihilation solely on the basis of their origin. There were no other reasons, since the victims were totally blameless. And this sole reason, origin, evokes the question of *why*, a *why* pointing to remote pasts. This is the locus where the question's answer appears to lie hidden—within a pre-past, reaching back into religious myth.[103]

Such reasoning is by no means misguided. In justifying their actions, the perpetrators themselves repeatedly referred to religious and secular preconditions.[104] With the Holocaust thus supercharged with polarized prehistories stored in cultural memory, citing trivial circumstances as its underlying cause seems tantamount to a cheap apologia.

To have murdered the Jews out of anti-Semitism seems to be far more dramatic, while impregnated with a higher meaning than doing so out of caprice or sheer negligence. For undeniably, throughout Western memory the Jews have stood for more than themselves. In the self-identity of Christendom, they have long occupied an exceptional position—immemorially, quite independent of the Holocaust. For Christianity, they are the Other par excellence; this Other is constitutive of the Christian religion.[105] In Christian memory, there is thus an inevitable linkage between the physical destruction of the Jews and their metaphysical importance. Consequently, the Holocaust becomes more than one genocide among others—all the more so after Christian memory has shed its sacred vesture and assumed a secular, universal form.

Likewise, within that memory, the Jews clearly differ in their significance from *other* victims of the Nazi mass murder, a hierarchy of
victimization thus crystallizing in posterity's consciousness. This
hierarchy certainly reflects not the real relative worth of those
killed but only their relative vividness—hence the Jewish genocide's dramatic resonance—in the self-awareness of the West.

In his interrogation in Nuremberg, which led to his conviction
and sentencing to death by hanging, Viktor Brack, one of the
guiding figures of the euthanasia program, accepted full responsibility for the killing of the physically and mentally disabled but
denied any role in the murder of European Jewry.[106] After the
American examiner confronted him with a letter he had signed
and sent to Himmler in June 1942 proving beyond doubt that he
had proposed selecting two to three million of the approximately
ten million Jews slated for extermination, consigning them to
forced labor, and thereby rendering them "incapable of reproduc-
ing," Brack burst into tears. Was this because he viewed the murder of the disabled differently? Or was it because he believed that
behind the victors stood the Manichean power of World Jewry?
Or was it rather that the Jews a priori had some exceptional status
owing to their position in Christian myth? Whatever the reason,
the proof of his participation in their annihilation seemed to stir
special feelings in him.[107]

Cultural memory assigns different values to different groups
of victims. The greater the significance of a group for one's own
identity, the more space it seems to occupy in memory. Because
the Jews and their associated myths are constitutive of Christian
memory, it seems that their extermination involved more than
the death of the Jews themselves. Also, the Christian or Christian-
hued sense of self is implicated. Thus the special commemorative
rituals for the Jewish victims of the Holocaust may also have
another function: to re-appropriate lost elements of Christian tradition. Hence although the murder of the Gypsies is also tied in
memory to ancient realms of European culture, it seems to burden

the conscience less than does that of the Jews; despite centuries of vilification and mistreatment, the Gypsies comprise an ethnic group belonging to the Christian religion, and thus stand on this side of the line separating Christians from Jews.[108]

In view of the enormity of the Nazi mass murder, it seems paradoxical that historically transmitted, whenever possible religious mnemonic patterns play a greater role in constructing the Holocaust's memory than do the actual events. These patterns have furnished an imagistic arsenal centered on a phenomenon that, owing to its horror, its abstractness, its relatively brief duration, but, above all, its literal defiance of reason, eludes proper description. This is all the more the case in that through their act the Nazis succeeded in confirming, as it were in negative distortion, just those cultural spheres of recollection with their mythical and historical patterns—for example, the notion of Jewish election. Consciousness cannot escape an evocation of such patterns.

Memory of the past is bound up with the operation of collective memory. In looking back at real or fantasized events, a group of individuals accumulates a mnemonic canon; others in turn identify with it and pass it on.[109] Duration is fundamental to the weight and impact of this sort of memory: it needs several generations to crystallize into a "community of solidarity." Over time, the canon condenses, rationalizing itself as a history of descent— as an ethnos. An enduring memory, rationalized in terms of origin, differs in a basic way from the sort of memory producing ad hoc cohesion. The latter mainly characterizes social or political groupings, as well as institutional entities, which are unable to preserve memory over the long term. It fades especially quickly when the circumstances that brought the individuals together do not lend themselves to being continued. This is evidently the case with forced collectives, those whose cohesion is imposed from without. The victims of euthanasia and their relations cannot form a sense of collective memory for the simple reason that the stigmatized attributes of their affiliation are not transmitted further.[110] No feelings of continued belonging can develop; no genealogy of re-membrance can coalesce. The recollection is in any case preserved passively, etched in the memories of those guilty of the crime. Passing on such recollections as history requires professional insti-tutions devoted to preserving and expanding knowledge, not to maintaining the canon of memory constituting an ethnos.[111]

In this manner, the memory of "sociocide," class murder, is archived, not transmitted from one generation to another as is the case with genocide. The mnemonic rituals practiced in Germany to commemorate the Nazi crimes thus markedly differ from the passive memorializing of the victims of Stalinism in the former Soviet Union. The reasons for this discrepancy are obvious. On the one hand, Hitler's crimes are perceived as atrocities commit-ted by Germany *against others*. They have entered the collective memory of the Germans and been preserved in the memory of others as German crimes. The Nazi period is considered an inte-gral element of German history; as such, it is indelibly engraved in collective memory. On the other hand, the crimes of Stalin and the Soviet Union's Communist regime can hardly be construed as *Russian* crimes. Furthermore, a distinctively Soviet memory is hardly sustainable, especially since the peoples of the former Soviet Union have distanced themselves from a defunct confed-eration that, in any event, was merely an administrative frame-work.[112] While in Germany Nazism succeeded in fusing nation and regime, seeking its victims mainly *outside* the *Volksgemeinschaft*, the Soviet populace was the main victim of its own regime. And while Hitler waged his war as a German war against adversaries mainly beyond Germany's borders, Stalin's war was internal—a catastrophe ostensibly launched as a social upheaval, appropriat-ing the idiom of class struggle and civil war. Hitler's racial mania drew on the narrative and terminology of integral nationalism. As a consequence, Nazism, dressed in distinctively German col-ors, was able to contaminate German memory with the crimes of the Nazi regime. They are preserved in the canon of memory of Germans and others as *German* crimes.

The formation of a post-Soviet memory in which the crimes of Stalin and the Communist regime are preserved in their full enormity is intrinsically problematic. How can crimes eluding ethnic and hence long-term memory be kept collectively alive? Can actions perpetrated not in the name of a collective, such as the nation, but in the name of a social construct, such as class, be commemorated in a suitable form? What earlier narratives must be evoked in order to admit these crimes into memory?

To the extent that they have not been incorporated into individual long-term memories, the crimes of Soviet Communism threaten to fall into oblivion, at least outside the realm of academic history.[113] On the other hand, it is clear that those nations whose memories retain traces of their fierce struggle against old imperial Russia have tended to be more successful in recollecting the Stalinist past. These are peoples whose histories of suffering under Soviet domination can be tied to the various narratives of their earlier resistance to the czarist empire. Above all the Poles come to mind here, together with the Hungarians and even to a certain degree the Germans, in whose eastern provinces postwar Soviet rule established itself as distinctively "Russian," thus burdening itself with memories of both world wars.

The Polish example clearly illustrates a fusion of the present with narratives drawn from the past. More than any other nationality, the Poles have been able to incorporate Soviet oppression into a long concatenation of historical events. Their amassed arsenal of memory reaches back to the uprisings of the nineteenth century, the partitions of the late eighteenth century, and further back to the seventeenth century's Polish-Muscovite antagonism, manifest in its extreme religious form in a confrontation between Orthodoxy and Roman Catholicism.[114] This entire prehistory has converged into the image of the slaughter of fifteen thousand Polish officers by the Soviet NKVD in 1940 in the Katyn Forest near Smolensk. In this manner, crimes by Poland's Communist regime have been converted in collective memory to crimes committed by Russia against Poland.

In Hungary, a historical soundboard has been provided by the 1848–49 revolution and its suppression by Russian troops.[115] This emblematic experience became somehow amplified by the 1956 events in Budapest. Likewise, Finland's special position in the Cold War cannot be genuinely understood without the prehistory of the Finno-Russian War of 1939–40. And the former Baltic Soviet republics themselves possess enough historical material to identify czarist Russia in Soviet domination. In various ways, the situation is quite similar to that of other peoples of the former Soviet Union, for the Soviet regime's "social" crimes, perpetrated in the language of class, have been assimilated to ethnically constituted memories and narratives: those of imperial Russian crimes of expansion, colonialization, and forced Russification. This process is especially marked in the case of the "persecuted peoples" such as the Tartars, the Kalmucks, and the Volga Germans, who were subjected to a Stalinist policy of mass deportation and resettlement.[116] With the exception of the approach taken to the highly urbanized Jewish population, whose intelligentsia was accused of "cosmopolitanism" and thus of high treason in the late Stalinist period and then subjected to anti-Semitic persecution and murder, Stalin's regime presented itself to those it ruled in its pure form: as a despotism relying on mere arbitrariness and devoted to an ambitious social experiment whose results were catastrophic. But in an ironic reversal, in post-Soviet Russia—and not just on the extreme fringes of the political spectrum—Soviet Communist rule has often been given an ethnic cast and depicted in terms of rule by non-Russian nationalities: by Jewish, Caucasian, Baltic, and other ethnic minorities.

A conversion of episodes from Soviet Communism's social experiment into a form of national narrative is especially pronounced in the Ukraine. The consequences of the forced collectivization between 1929 and 1933, and particularly the terrible famine of 1932, are preserved in national memory as an act of intentional genocide.[117] Throughout the "black earth" region and other agricultural areas of the Soviet Union such as Kazakhstan, the events of the period of forced collectivization and "de-Kulakization" have been transposed to earlier narrative and interpretive structures, thus integrated into historical memory. The narrative of the Russian Civil War here plays a strong role. For the Ukraine, southern Russia, and the northern Caucasus were not only harmed by forced collectivization and the subsequent famine but had already been ravaged by the civil war and foreign intervention.[118] For their part, the Soviet authorities, including party representatives and the People's Commissariat for Internal Affairs, had repeatedly imagined in the early 1930s that they were being threatened with acts of sabotage by members of the White Guard, veterans of the White Armies, landowners, New Economic Policy profiteers, clerics, and other counterrevolutionaries, thus defining the horrors of forced collectivization they themselves were perpetrating as an extension of the civil war. The agricultural areas of southern Russia and the Ukraine were thus transformed into a battle zone of internecine conflict, a zone in which, with the characteristic despotism of the Soviet regime, anyone could be depicted as a saboteur and class enemy. In the search for scapegoats to explain the results of economic mismanagement, inefficiency, and theft in the coercively established collective farms, suspicions and accusations spread like an epidemic; the mood resembled that surrounding the witch hunts of an earlier era. National and local conflicts fed into this general mélange of distrust.[119]

Styled into "class struggle," the persecutions, arrests, executions, and deportations took the form of "social purging" in former areas of the civil war. Paradoxically, the process followed a principle of lineage, not in the ethnic sense, but in respect to the status and position of a person's ancestors—a kind of social genealogy, offering ideological justification for the abuse and punishment of purported delinquents.[120] Such "biologized" class origin was enough to be accused of counterrevolutionary acts, or at least to be suspected of subversive intent. Supposedly reactionary fathers and grandfathers had their "sins" visited upon their sons and daughters and grandchildren. As "objective" class enemies, they were consigned to the mills of social purging.[121] Anyone branded a class enemy was subject to the caprice of the authorities and the machinations of his fellow citizens. In this atmosphere of rank suspicion, every conceivable local conflict—from personal enmity to rivalries based on social envy—was rationalized and legitimized by means of the terminology and ideology of class struggle. At times, such conflicts reached back into the prerevolutionary period; they were resuscitated during the civil war and continued into the era of the New Economic Policy. There was, in fact, plenty of tinder for conflict, and it was easy to exploit the dominant legitimizing code to harm others. The terror kindled from above was further fanned from below. Hence in a climate of fear and mutual distrust, the arbitrary power epitomizing the Stalinist system destroyed the last remnants of social solidarity, producing a total atomization of society.

Their self-perceptions notwithstanding, Communism and Nazism are linked by striking similarities. Seen from the vantage of liberal democracy, with its institutional safeguards for civil rights, its separation of powers, legal security, and, above all, division between public and private spheres, both regimes exemplify a totalitarianism intensified by ties to a charismatic leader. Both were driven by worldviews grounded in the philosophy of history— tribunes of legitimization for political action highly suspect to Western polities. In accordance with Communist belief, Stalin's regime sought to accelerate historical time; it was ready to sacrifice the past and the present to a supposedly better future. Nazism intended to halt time's current through a biologistic social fiction, in other words: race. In the historical-philosophical project of either accelerating or stemming time's flow, the individual is superseded, simply grist in a mill. The project is of a utopian nature, whether projected in the name of universal humankind or of a race to be bred, and requires the exercise of tremendous institutional force for its realization. Hence owing to their horrific crimes, both the Nazi and the Stalinist regime are engraved in our memory of the twentieth century as twins of terror.

Still, if we leave the obvious parallels behind and examine the question more closely, a more complex picture emerges. A comparative counting of victims is complicated by the fact that the Nazi regime lasted twelve years and was destroyed from without, while the Soviet regime lasted more than two generations, until it collapsed from within. Also, the crimes of the Nazis were largely committed during the war and were directed against those defined as *Fremdvölkische,* "alien peoples"; the crimes of Stalinism were committed in peacetime, with a terrible climax in forced collectivization and mass starvation, exacting a toll of countless millions of lives.[122] This social war was waged almost entirely against the agrarian classes, whereas the purges in the Communist Party, the military command, and the technocratic class between 1936 and 1939 mainly affected members of the elite—a kind of prophylactic civil war.[123] An internal relaxation only set in during World War II; in the "Great War for the Fatherland," the regime appealed to the patriotic sentiments of the populace. Repression was substantially reduced, though not rescinded. After the war, the number of Gulag inmates burgeoned, only declining in the "thaw" after Stalin's death.[124]

The important temporal and numerical differences do not make quantitative comparison easy. There are also difficulties in qualifying the victims, a problematic procedure in the best of cases. But one thing is clear: compared to the Nazi regime, the Stalinist system was notable for its extreme despotic caprice. Not even its highest echelons were exempt from periodic and systematic persecution. Participation in power and rule involved exposure and jeopardy; it certainly offered no security.[125] The political elites, held accountable for constant failings and aberrations, were executed as scapegoats. The recurrent comparison between the Kirov affair and the Röhm putsch is misguided, if only because the "night of the long knives" was exceptional in the relatively brief annals of the Nazi regime, while similar episodes were chronic in Stalin's Soviet Union.[126] In the heyday of Stalinism, despotism and fear were the elixir of rule. Anyone could fall victim: the regime's opponents, its supporters, Stalin's henchmen, sycophants and lackeys, the members of special units involved in mass executions, together with respectable citizens and comrades with no inkling why they had been drawn into the mills of the "Red Inquisition."[127]

Compared with this arbitrariness, Hitler's rule gives the impression of order, even of legal security. After all, the criteria for persecution were "objective."[128] Everyone could be certain of his fate, one way or the other. In any event, the *Volksgenossen*—"national comrades"—who did not actively oppose the regime were allowed to go about their lives unmolested. Hence for members of the *Volksgemeinschaft*, the regime was far less totalitarian than Stalin's Soviet Union was for its own population. At the same time, thanks to its initial successes, the Nazi regime enjoyed relatively broad support during the war. To a significant degree, it was a system of rule *with* the people rather than against them. As for those excluded from the *Volksgemeinschaft*, it was made clear to them that they were unwanted. Generally, those affected were apprised in advance of the tightening noose of restrictions and other oppressive measures.[129] There was nothing capricious here, although they were indeed kept in the dark concerning their final fate.

Probably the most clear-cut difference between the Stalinist and the Nazi regime was the nature of the deaths of their victims. At the heart of this difference was the use made of labor. Apart from those who died of starvation, millions were subjected by Soviet Communism to forced labor. This type of exploitation developed from the system of forced military labor introduced by

Trotsky; it soon supplied an array of sectors and enterprises with cheap labor.[130] The responsible office, subordinate to the Commissariat for Internal Affairs, had access to a virtually limitless pool of workers, replenished by a constant influx of new "delinquents." In this way, political and legal despotism went hand in hand with the system of compulsory labor in Stalin's Soviet Union—a reality with horrific consequences. Due to the unlimited and regularly restocked fund of slave labor, there was a tendency to disregard the minimum of nutrition and rest necessary for the workers' physical survival.[131] Worn to the bone, they were forced to meet performance quotas exceeding their physical limits.

The Nazi regime was also familiar with slave labor. It was performed, however, by *others*, not by ethnic Germans, for Nazism's exploitation of slaves was closely bound up with its campaigns of expansion and conquest.[132] In conjunction with the Nazi utopia, Nazi enslavement offers an idea implemented in the course of its campaign, in conjunction with the Nazi utopia, of what would have happened if Germany had emerged victorious from the Second World War: a hierarchy of races and labor. In Eastern Europe, entire peoples would have been reduced to helotry.[133] For the time being, the regime was focusing on the war economy in its slave-labor policies. Some of the slaves were literally worked to death, but they were doomed in any event. In the Stalinist forced-labor system, the death of the slaves was likewise considered part of the bargain, but it was not a specific and central aim.[134]

In any event, the fundamental difference between regimes becomes particularly clear in that locus where individuals were annihilated beyond all exigencies of labor. The Nazis, as suggested, killed for the sake of killing. In the extreme case of their genocide of the Jews, they made use of labor merely to create an impression of utility. For this reason, Stalin's Gulag cannot be compared coherently with full coherence to Hitler's death factories—his plants for the production of corpses, beyond any rationale of exploitation and economic benefit. The Final Solution was a project annulling even what are broadly considered universally valid standards of self-preservation. Stalinism had nothing comparable to offer.[135]

Stalinism and Nazism were basically distinct systems emerging from different cultures under dissimilar conditions. That they were locked in a global struggle—real, partial, or only ostensible—has always posed challenging questions. And yet inquiring into underlying motives is far more to the point than any juxtaposition of the systems. A need for comparison is by no means self-evident; rather, it seems to derive from specific, culturally determined memories that feel compelled to counterpose atrocities. To that extent, the modes of comparison are not universally valid. Instead, they stem from particularistically grounded collective memories, converting events such as state-perpetrated crimes into the canon and narrative of the ethnos.

As indicated, the process of converting crimes *by* a regime into crimes *against* an ethnic collective becomes strikingly clear in the case of Poland. On the basis of a geopolitical location between Germany and Russia and an associated—tragic—history, two types of suffering have fused in Polish memory: a suffering caused by regimes perceived as totalitarian; and a suffering that stems from the oppression of the Poles as a nation.[136] Consequently, with national interpretation of the Katyn massacre drowning out its significance as a state crime committed by Stalin, its recollection has remained vivid to the present day, keeping Poland ever vigilant toward Russia. That vigilance does not arise from fears regarding a possible resurgence of Communism in Moscow, but rather from the long memory of Poland's tragic history with the Russian Empire.

Why there has been a tendency in Germany to systematically compare these two totalitarian systems is a particularly complex question. The main reason would appear to be that in its actions beyond its borders, Nazism has served for the Germans as an example of exaggerated nationalism rather than of a regime comparable in its despotism to Stalin's.[137] The attack on the Soviet Union begun in 1941 entered collective memory as the "Russian campaign": at the time of its launching, enmity toward the Soviet Union as a regime was of less consequence than an acutely racist nationalism; its professed anti-Bolshevism appeared in a national rather than a universal-political guise.[138] In Soviet wartime memory also elements linked to the regime's Communist self-identity were downplayed; instead, there was intense emphasis on the patriotic—Russian—character of the war against the German invaders, combined with a Russification of Soviet memory. Concepts such as "Hitlerism" and "anti-Fascism" remained in currency, but they steadily lost their political meaning. And the closer the Red Army came to German territory in its westward thrust during the war's final phase, as atavistic horrors perpetrated by "the Russians" spread fear and anxiety among the Germans, ideological motives further yielded on both sides to national and ethnic ascriptions.[139]

The postwar flight and expulsion of the German populace from areas now incorporated into Poland in the east, as well as from the Sudetenland, which reverted to Czechoslovakia, were prompted by ethnic and not social motives. This process cannot be compared to crimes of the Communist regime such as the "social purges" carried out during the forced collectivizations of the 1930s. Rather, although a reaction to Nazi oppression, resettlement, and genocide, the process had much in common with "ethnic cleansing," with the tradition of the nationality conflicts that took place between the Great War and World War II. And this is actually the way the expulsions have been engraved in Germany's collective memory. They cannot, in any event, be at all construed as resulting from a struggle between regimes, in the sense of the epochal confrontation between Bolshevism and anti-Bolshevism. Against the background of the experiences of the interwar period and the war instigated by Hitler, the Western allies sanctioned these population shifts as a solution to festering problems of nationalities and minorities.[140]

In postwar Germany, the sufferings of the Germans were not publicly remembered. There was virtually no mention of the victims of postwar deportations or the destruction inflicted by strategic Allied bombing. Those who fell in action went officially unmourned. There were probably a number of reasons for this, one being of crucial importance: a shared intuition that the crimes committed by the Germans in the name of Germany were of such magnitude they commanded a collective silence — an expression of justice weighed and removed from any claim to balance.

The collective memory of the Germans searched for ways to overcome this paralysis.[141] Accusations against the West were taboo in the early postwar decades. Because of the German question — closely bound up with the deepening Cold War — the memory of the Anglo-American bombing was sealed, although it would be revived by a later generation as new and allegedly similar events unfolded elsewhere in the world.[142] The Soviet Union offered a more valid mnemonic terrain for comparison. As has often been suggested, this may well have been due to the Cold War's political-ideological constellations. Especially in a divided Germany, with the East German state viewing its legitimation solely in terms of class and withdrawing as an anti-Fascist polity from any collective German memory, a comparison between the systems was made on the basis of confronting values and worldviews. The political enmity between East Germany and West Germany resuscitated images and concepts developed in the clashes of the Weimar Republic, the Communists in the East — in keeping with their unshakable philosophy of history — equating their adversaries in the West with the ogre of "Fascism."[143] Amid the ideological rhetoric, traces of collective memory still managed to surface, for example, when representatives of the East German regime were branded traitors and henchmen of the "Russians" or when West German politicians were denounced as lackeys of the "Anglo-Americans," who were ultimately blamed for the destruction of the German cities.[144]

In Germany's collective memory, the comparison between systems in the East and the West has itself been projected backward onto the screen of the "Russian campaign"—an intense and brutal ideological war that in the period of its launching had, for its part, been mnemonically rendered into an exclusively anti-Bolshevik crusade. For after all, other European nations had themselves participated earlier in militarily defending the Occident against the Soviets. Inscribed in this constellation, the "Russian campaign" could be registered as the decisive front in a universal civil war, the crimes committed during Operation Barbarossa thus being balanced against the crimes of the Soviet regime, the emblematics of Stalingrad's horror against those of Stalinism's terror. Two factors appear to have been at work in the backward projection of the postwar period: on the one hand, the Cold War emerging after 1945 seemed to support such an interpretation; on the other hand, there was the fact that the crimes of Nazi Germany had been, finally, directed against *others*, those of the Soviet regime against its own population.

The German wish to convert the crimes committed by Nazi Germany into crimes of a regime runs against the collective memory of those who lived in the Soviet Union and their descendants. In the first half of the twentieth century, the Soviet populace was victimized by both of the century's most oppressive regimes: the regime grounded in the violence of Communist utopian ideals and their experiment with humanity; and the regime grounded in the violent ideal of racial purity and in racial warfare with an anti-Bolshevik rationale. In keeping with the collective memory's tenets, both regimes are widely perceived as having been directed against the Russian people, though in different ways: on the one hand, through crimes based on class; on the other hand, through crimes based on race. To an extent, this distinction corresponds to the modes of memory manifest in the former East German state, in that a link has been forged there between the effects of Nazi rule and those of the Communist regime that followed. While ethnic Germans may perceive the two regimes as totalitarian variants, for those who had been excluded from the German *Volksgemeinschaft* on grounds of race and then managed to survive the extermination project, the Communist regime, despite its despicable totalitarian features, can hardly be compared with it.

On the Continent in the interwar period, Fascism and Communism, the twentieth century's dominant ideologies supplying meaning and orientation, were arrayed against each other in civil-war formation.[145] Especially in the realm of ideas, it was hard to avoid the confrontation, even if the century's conflicts were driven by other impulses as well. Today the contours of the debates unfolding then have lost their interpretive power. Nevertheless, they continue to exert an influence on efforts to grasp the past, in particular the enormous crimes against humanity committed by both Nazism and Stalinism. Understanding these crimes seems akin to reaching a judgment concerning the century itself. Otherwise, it would be hard to explain the passion accompanying debates on this issue; their discursive mode of *ultima ratio* suggests deep-seated motives emerging from the memory space of religion.[146] As soon as the debate turns to the status and significance of the crimes, the religious contours of the discourse become unmistakable. This is particularly true in relation to the Holocaust, for the question of its possible singularity seems to recapitulate earlier disputes about the idea of Jewish election. While the need to compare and the resulting anthropologizing of the crime seem to reflect Christian modes of narrative discourse, the insistence on singularity would appear to reflect their Jewish counterpart.[147] In this way, the features of religious narrative have strongly stamped an unfolding, ostensibly secular historical discussion. We may thus suspect that any effort at doing historical justice to the reality of what happened will have trouble escaping a vortex of prelayered narratives that move in the direction of final causes.

5

Dualisms

Decolonization and the Cold War

Translatio Imperii / *Britain and America* / *Geography and Ideology* / *Greek Questions — Far Eastern Answers* / *Asian Crisis and Western Freedoms* / *Worlds Divided — Worlds Apart* / *Mao Zedong and Chiang Kai-shek* / *Dulles and Mendès-France* / *Dien Bien Phu and European Integration* / *History Neutralized — History Revived*

꘏

On 21 February 1947 — a late Friday afternoon, just before closing-time — Loy Henderson, head of the newly established Office for Near Eastern and African Affairs in the U.S. State Department, received an urgent telephone call from the British Embassy informing him of the first secretary's imminent arrival. About an hour later, Herbert M. Sichel appeared and delivered two extremely important documents: the British government's formal announcement of its intention to end its engagement in the Balkans and the Levant as of 31 March; and an accompanying diplomatic note stating that England no longer saw itself in a position to continue providing support for Greece and Turkey.[1]

In historical perspective, this routine diplomatic event represents the end of one epoch and the beginning of another: a *translatio imperii* of our time.[2] This was meant to be more than a mere relaying of the imperial baton from one naval power, Great Britain, to another, the United States. Rather, beyond that transaction, it marked a shift from the traditional ciphers at play in world events, based on a philosophy of balance of power, to an order relying on ideological values.[3] From that point onward, the Soviet Union and the United States would find themselves at loggerheads in a traditional area of the game of nations— confronting each other in the perpetually critical region of the Straits and the adjacent area of Greece and Turkey—a confrontation duly replacing the historical antagonism between Russia and England. This conflict over values, the opposition between East and West, thus emerged in the zone of traditional European and imperial antagonism, extending then from the Balkans to Central Asia. From there it would turn global.[4]

With its cradle lying in the Straits, the Cold War's birth certificate was issued by Harry Truman on 12 March 1947 in a dramatic speech to a joint session of Congress. On this occasion, Truman solicited support for Greece and Turkey while announcing American readiness to defend principles of freedom wherever they were menaced by totalitarianism. Without specifically naming the adversary, he spoke of a conflict between two ways of life, one based on self-chosen institutions, the other on the exercise of power by a minority. At the present moment in history, he stated, every nation had to choose between these alternatives.[5] And he pledged American support to all who resisted totalitarian assault. Greece and Turkey, in especially precarious situations, were to be given generous aid.

The Truman Doctrine and the announcement the following June of the Marshall Plan for Europe's economic recovery soon encountered resistance from the emerging Eastern bloc. In September 1947, representatives of the European Communist parties agreed to establish the Cominform.[6] Out of consideration for his Western allies, Stalin had dissolved the Comintern in 1943. The institution of a new Communist information bureau itself signaled the reactivation of an ideological conflict that had been held in abeyance. Andrey Zhdanov, in charge of ideology and propaganda, saw two worlds pitted against each other: the "imperialist and antidemocratic camp" and the "anti-imperialist and democratic camp."[7] In this way, the Communist side reacted to the challenge of the Truman Doctrine with its own, quasi-theological, "two worlds theory." A power-political opposition thus now assumed an ideological cast.[8]

The Truman Doctrine signaled the end of America's intentions to demobilize its forces and leave the Continent.[9] The ensuing Cold War would be based on a nuclear bipolarity between East and West persisting over four decades and marked by a fusion of two dimensions of conflict revealing different degrees of intensity: the traditional great-power struggle and the new ideological antagonism over values and worldviews.[10] The antagonism had no fixed boundaries; it would influence both domestic and foreign affairs. Still, it is striking that it crystallized precisely at those points where the continental power of Russia and the maritime power of Britain had collided for generations.[11]

That the imperial insignia would be transferred from Great Britain to America was not self-evident. As the United States saw its own historical role, it was not at all clear it was meant to succeed Britain, especially in the eastern Mediterranean, where England has been defending the lifelines of its empire, above all its ties with the Indian crown colony. Such concerns were alien to America: an inveterate opponent of colonialism and a sponsor of free trade—of most-favored-nation status, the "open door," and an "undivided world market," in contrast to the policies of restricted markets and protectionism pursued by the colonial empires. In

America's view, it was not proper to maintain these empires; they were ballast best jettisoned.[12]

During World War II, and in light of events in the Far East and Southeast Asia, the United States became convinced that the dissolution of the colonial empires was a matter of urgency. In their advance southward, especially when they encountered Europe's colonial possessions, the Japanese had made use of a transparent but effective anticolonial rhetoric.[13] The speed with which the Japanese overran French, Dutch, and British colonies was not lost on Franklin D. Roosevelt. The indigenous peoples had seen no reason to fight for the interests of their European masters. The situation grew critical when the British bastion of Singapore fell in February 1942 and an Indian uprising erupted the following summer—the greatest threat to British rule since the Indian Mutiny of 1857–58.[14]

Mindful of the danger of a Japanese attack on India, Washington tried to persuade London to accommodate the demands of India's national movement. Roosevelt referred to America's own struggle for independence and its anticolonial tradition. Indeed, according to Article 3 of the Atlantic Charter, the right of self-determination was to be extended to peoples under colonial rule.[15] But in a decisive speech to parliament in November 1942, Winston Churchill rejected such a notion, remarking famously that he had not become His Majesty's prime minister in order to preside over the liquidation of the British Empire.[16] England spared no efforts in its bid to win American support for its view. Thus, for example, Lord Halifax, appointed British ambassador to Washington in 1941, had served (as Lord Irwin) as viceroy of India between 1926 and 1931. He seemed especially well suited to explain the British view of the Indian situation to the Americans.[17] Still, it was virtually impossible to postpone the unraveling of Britain's rule over India. The process would not be initiated by Churchill, voted out of office in 1945, but by the Labor cabinet of Clement Attlee, who was weary of empire and concerned with building a welfare state at home.[18] On 20 February 1947, Attlee publicly announced Britain's imminent withdrawal from India; he also let it be known that his country was renouncing its control over Burma and Palestine. The next day witnessed the delivery in Washington of the documents speaking of Britain's inability to hold the historical line on the "northern tier" in Greece and Turkey.[19]

The English decision to dissolve the empire had been preceded in 1946–47 by one of the harshest winters of the century.[20] Heavy snowstorms had buffeted the British Isles, and record low temperatures had caused critical energy shortages. Production had stagnated dramatically. In view of January's catastrophic impact, chancellor of the exchequer Dalton warned that the country was facing financial collapse and that cuts in spending were urgently needed. The cabinet thus decided to halt aid payments to Greece. Nevertheless, such turmoil caused by nature was not really the source of the power transfer from England to America. The process had already begun in the wake of the Great War and had been visible to all sides during the interwar period.[21]

Nevertheless, in the face of British urging and predictions of the loss of Greece and Turkey to real or imagined Soviet machinations, America hesitated to take up the burden. To many in Washington, the British appeal was far less ingenuous than it seemed on the surface. Some accused Britain of trying to manipulate America,[22] suspecting a ploy by "perfidious Albion" to buttress its tottering empire with the help of American troops and dollars. While exaggerated, such suspicions were not entirely baseless. With the proclamation of the Truman Doctrine, Washington had committed itself to confronting Communism everywhere, and this could entangle it in conflicts contrary to its own interests and anticolonial ethos. In particular, alliance obligations could draw the United States into the colonial affairs of its European partners.[23] Such apprehensions would later prove well founded, especially in what became known as the Third World, where anticolonial nationalist movements would be led by Communist parties.

Conflicts of ideological origin thus threatened to fuse with the desire for national liberation.[24] Such entanglements could become ubiquitous, especially where the United States was saddled with allies like France, which would spare no efforts in trying to offset the disgrace of capitulation to Germany in 1940 through an aggressive colonial policy in Indochina and Africa.[25] The British, of course, had much less to compensate for, and the decolonization of their possessions could be facilitated by the tradition of indirect rule.[26] Paradoxically, precisely because of its universalist and assimilationist traditions, French colonialism would become entangled in exceptionally violent conflicts, with the indigenous populations pressing for complete independence from the Union Française. France's *mission civilisatrice* would drown in torrents of blood—in Madagascar, Indochina, and Algeria.[27]

In an era of renewed universal civil war between freedom and equality, the confluence of an anticolonial struggle unfolding under the aegis of national liberation with social-revolutionary aspirations would work to the benefit of the Eastern bloc. The United States tended to read this struggle in terms of the civil war, thus becoming involved in disputes for which it had a traditional distaste. In this way the anticolonial impetus within the national liberation movement would shift to the side of the Soviet Union and the emerging socialist camp.[28] The People's Republic of China would lay claim to the most direct link between Communism and national liberation; for some time the incipient conflict between North and South in the camp of international Communism would remain hidden from view.

Especially in Vietnam, Communism and national liberation underwent a complex fusion. Here American involvement diverged from its anticolonial tradition, but the involvement was hardly a historical accident. The United States had already been engaged in conflicts in East Asia and along its Pacific rim during

World War II.[29] It had played a decidedly active part in the arc of crisis stretching from China and Korea to Indochina that began to emerge at the end of the 1940s. The manifold conflicts in that region soon fell into patterns corresponding to the ideological opposition between Communism and anti-Communism. In that context, during hot phases of the Cold War the region could serve as a real battlefield for an ideological struggle whose epicenter remained in Europe. The significance of far-removed, secondary theaters in the universal civil war of ideologies and values would only increase during the most anxious phase of nuclear deterrence. In the 1960s and 1970s, the main arenas would shift from Asia to Africa, where it would overlap with zones in which late colonial conflicts were still raging, as in the Portuguese domain. As the confrontation extended across the globe, the superpowers avoided the main front running through Central Europe. In the eye of the hurricane, military calm prevailed.

The confrontation had emerged from a traditional zone of political crisis in Europe: the zone of the Eastern Question and the nineteenth-century Great Game. In Asia Britain had enclosed its Indian and neighboring possessions with a security cordon, the "northern tier" as it came to be known. Russia was determined to protect its southern flank, open to the Black Sea, from possible attack by the naval powers.[30] Such fears were by no means baseless. Each side could cite a series of events confirming its sense of peril. Thus in the Crimean War of 1853–56—the nineteenth century's world war, or, as Disraeli called it, the "Indian War"—the naval powers of Britain and France, bolstered by a Piedmontese detachment, had penetrated into the Black Sea to repel Russia's attack on the Ottoman Empire and a possible breakthrough into the Mediterranean.[31] Under Palmerston, the English hoped to eliminate their Russian rival once and for all as a prospective sea power, driving it back to its historical boundaries as a land-locked continental power.[32]

These ambitious British plans would not be realized. The Crimean War ended more or less in a military stalemate, even if the subsequent peace accord rendered Russia defenseless on its Black Sea coast.[33] But already in October 1870, following the Battle of Sedan in the Franco-Prussian War, Russia abrogated the humiliating "Pontus provisos" and began once again, as a redoubtable land power, to interfere in the affairs of Europe and Asia. The Crimean War experience had left it with an awareness of the vulnerability of its southern flank in the face of the great naval powers.[34] This lesson would be reconfirmed during the Russian Civil War of 1918–20, when Britain and France again penetrated into the Black Sea region, advancing into southern Russia in support of the White civil war armies. And the plans of Britain and France in 1940, when World War II was still confined to Europe, to open a further front against Germany and Russia in the Black Sea area served to reinforce this sense of vulnerability. The Soviets justified their repeated demands for border revisions and changes in the status of the Straits by referring to the trauma of the Crimean War and the West's intervention in the civil war. In their political memory, these past events had taken on the iconic significance of an attack by naval powers on a vulnerable land power.[35]

The main actors in the early phase of the Cold War, Churchill and Stalin, paid special attention to this region, if only on account of their own political pasts. Both men had been closely connected personally with the fate of southern Russia, the Black Sea, the Caucasus, and naturally the Hellespont.[36] During the civil war, Stalin, the Georgian, had been entrusted with political supervision of the struggle against Wrangel in the south. As head of the Soviet negotiation team, he had concluded the border treaties of 1921 with Turkey and Persia, which allowed him to demonstrate his intimate knowledge of the region.[37] Stalin was exceedingly distrustful of Turkey under Kemal Atatürk, and unlike Lenin, he had supported the establishment of the short-lived Azerbaijani Soviet Republic of Gilan on Persian soil. For his part, as First

Lord of the Admiralty (1911–15) Churchill had promoted the installation of oil-fired engines for the British fleet and had played a decisive role in 1914 in acquiring the majority of shares in the Anglo-Persian Oil Company for the British navy. During World War I, he had organized a joint land and sea operation in a bid to break through the Dardanelles and restore physical contact with the Russian allies. This led in 1915 to the legendary Gallipoli campaign.[38] The expedition encountered heavy German-Ottoman resistance and ended in disaster; it was an Allied defeat in which Mustafa Kemal Pasha played a decisive role as commanding officer.[39] During the Russian Revolution and subsequent civil war, Churchill became a spokesman for the interventionists; as colonial minister after the war he had to grapple with questions concerning the eastern Mediterranean, Persia, and the Near East—the very region in which Britain and Russia had traditionally come into conflict. It was thus obvious that the 1941 alliance between London and Moscow had been concluded on a basis not of concord but of geopolitical necessity. This relation between the two powers on the flanks of Europe was strategically dictated; they had set aside their ideological differences for the sake of joint defense against a hegemonial threat from the Continent's center, from Germany. In a union that bore all the hallmarks of being forced, genuine agreement could not be expected.

Against this backdrop, the alliance that emerged in the 1941–45 period can be understood as reflecting a provisional truce in the universal civil war of values. Indeed, just before Germany's attack on the Soviet Union, the alignment had been completely different. In line with Russian-British antagonism in the Straits and elsewhere, the Soviets had drawn closer to the Anti-Comintern Pact, an alliance increasingly directed against Britain, while insisting to Nazi Germany on their historical interests in the Straits and the Balkans, especially Bulgaria. Stalin was acting according to the same, traditional Russian aspirations, already explained to Hitler by Molotov in Berlin in November 1940, when he approached the Western allies with similar demands just after Stalingrad.[40] Indeed, the decisive Soviet victory at Stalingrad would be followed by increasing signs of a return to the traditional antagonism between Britain and Russia in the Straits, the Transcaucasus, and Iran, where the two countries had long confronted each other as power-political rivals. In particular, the pressure that Moscow was beginning to exert on Turkey evoked political contours that were familiar from the past.[41]

Immediately after the revolution, the Bolsheviks had loudly distanced themselves from the traditional imperialist aims of the czarist empire. But in August 1939, the Soviets again pressed for a role in supervising the Straits, an intention running contrary to the accord reached at Montreux in 1936. Turkey categorically rejected the Soviet request, instead signing a treaty of mutual assistance with France and Britain in October.[42] The treaty's motivation was by no means ideological; along with its anti-Soviet component, it was also directed against Italy. Moscow now denounced Ankara and the Western powers as warmongers. It even kept up the pressure after the Nazi German attack in 1941,[43] insisting that Turkey declare war on the German Reich—a notion that the far weaker Turkey rejected, with British agreement. Moscow then accused the Turkish government of colluding with the Axis powers.[44] The Turks repeatedly tried to elude Soviet insistence upon an alliance—an understandable effort, since the Soviets had linked their declaration of war on Germany with a demand to station Soviet troops on Turkish soil. The Turks suspected, not without reason, that such troops would not be withdrawn once the war was over.[45] But Moscow was also well advised to maintain a degree of mistrust toward its southern neighbor. Apparently wishing to exploit an opportune moment, Turkey concentrated troops on its Russian frontier just when the Soviet Union had its back to the wall at Stalingrad.[46]

From a wider historical perspective, Turkey's situation bore a striking resemblance to Poland's. For geopolitical and historical reasons, Turkey feared it would suffer a similar fate, succumbing to a Russian attack. In his meetings with Allied representatives after 1939, the Turkish foreign minister repeatedly cited the Polish precedent. For the Turks, the breaking of relations between Stalin and the Polish government-in-exile after the exhumation of mass graves at Katyn in 1943 and the problem of Poland's eastern border made the Polish question a touchstone for their own security.[47] They believed they could see the contours of Turkey's future in Poland's present reality. This perspective was bolstered by historical recollections reaching back to the eighteenth century. Since the unfavorable Peace of Kuchuk Kainarji (1774), which followed the sultan's crushing defeat by the Russians, a dismemberment of the Ottoman Empire along the lines of the first Polish partition (1772) had been easily imaginable. The fact that it had not occurred in the nearly 150 years preceding World War I was due to the European balance. Not least of all, the intensifying antagonism between England and Russia since the 1830s had guaranteed the Ottoman Empire's continued survival.[48]

But the Eastern Question concerned more than the fate of the Ottoman Empire. Poland, which at the height of its power had stretched from the Baltic to the Black Sea, itself comprised an Eastern question.[49] But while Poland had ceased to exist as a state in the aftermath of successive partitions, the Ottoman Empire had remained largely unscathed. In any event, the last Muslim universal empire could preserve itself intact as long as it remained a cornerstone of a peaceful European order and the sea power Britain and the land power Russia held each other in check.[50] With Turkey's entry into the war on the side of the Central Powers in 1914, this historical constellation came to an end, and Turkey suffered the same fate that had befallen Poland at the end of the eighteenth century: partition. Poland's lot, like Turkey's, was thus closely bound up with Russia's power, which was expanding toward the south and the west. After a temporary weakening of the Russian Empire by world war, revolution, and civil

war, a development favorable for both the restitution and eastward expansion of Poland and the reconstitution of the Turkish
state, Russia in the garb of the Soviet Union reassumed its historical role in the course of World War II—and now with an enormous increase in power. Neither Turkey nor Poland could remain
indifferent to this turn of events. Being so well aware of the historical parallel between their fate and the Poles', the Turks looked
Argus-eyed to the north, seeking to draw some conclusions regarding their own future based on the West's stance toward Russia.[51]
To this extent, Poland was indeed a touchstone for Turkey.

After the turning point at Stalingrad, the antagonism between
the partners in the anti-Hitler coalition, which has been set aside
in 1941, became conspicuous again. And with the war's conclusion, it erupted in full. Nevertheless, something fundamental had
indeed changed, for the Soviet Union had emerged from the conflict with far more power. This was in striking contrast to Britain,
whose power had obviously ebbed. Furthermore, with Germany's
absolute defeat (as well as Japan's in the Far East) and the drastic
demotion of France, Russia had become Europe's sole remaining
continental power. Also, it had gained enormously in prestige as a
result of its victory over Nazi Germany, since it had paid a higher
price in suffering, misery, and sheer effort than any other country.
Hence after 1945 the Soviet Union benefited from a mutually rein-
forcing increase in both power and moral standing. Both in Eastern Europe and in the area of the "northern tier," Stalin seemed
eager to exploit this combination, whether for reasons of expansionism or an inflated need for security. On the Soviet Union's
western flank, in much of Eastern Europe but especially in Poland,
the Western allies believed that Stalin had confronted them with
a fait accompli. They sought to offset the Soviets' one-sided advance in a terrain far more suitable to the maritime Anglo-
Americans: in the Levant, where Russia faced a substantially
weakened but still intact Britain hoping to maintain its imperial

hold in the eastern Mediterranean and coastal region, especially in Greece and Turkey. When Western discontent grew in the aftermath of the Potsdam Conference and Truman declared in 1946 that he was tired of pampering the Soviets, the confrontation that would hold the world in suspense for more than four decades was under way. That the zone in which it crystallized was the Straits, the Transcaucasus, and Iran suggests a kind of historical recidivism: immediately after World War II, the great powers had reassumed the positions that they had inherited from the previous century.

Three areas of conflict here emerged as prominent: the confrontation between the Anglo-Americans and the Soviets in Iran; the tensions between the former allies due to Soviet pressure on Turkey; and the frictions arising from the Greek Civil War, including territorial demands by Greece on its northern neighbors Yugoslavia and Bulgaria (and vice versa). Here, too, the mold was familiar: the Balkan hostilities followed the contours of the historical Macedonian question. In the area of the "northern tier," it seemed that nineteenth-century conflicts persisted and only the political semantics had changed. The diction of geopolitical antagonisms, of a challenged balance of power, and of ethnic conflicts had been converted into the diction of universal ideological struggle. The Eastern Question had thus returned as the Cold War's midwife.

1945 was marked by the advance of the Soviet Army. In Eastern and Central Europe, Russia now established itself as a hegemonial power. The first region to come under its sway was the Baltic, where the situation existing in 1940 was restored, followed by Poland and countries formerly allied with the Axis powers such as Rumania, Bulgaria, and Hungary. The following year revealed a kind of contrary movement, with Iran witnessing a first confrontation between the former allies. In 1941, Britain and Russia had partitioned the country into spheres of influence in a manner analogous to their 1907 compromise in the Great Game, while the Americans supplied the Soviets with war matériel via Iran as part of the lend-lease accord. At the beginning of March 1946, the Soviet Union refused to withdraw its troops from northern Iran, violating an agreement it had reached in 1942. Instead, the troops were used to reinforce efforts at forming an autonomous government in Iranian Azerbaijan. Moscow also decided to once again raise the Kurdish issue, thus calling into question the borders drawn up after World War I.[52] In the spring and summer of 1946, tensions in Iran between the Soviets and the Anglo-Americans intensified when it became known that the Soviets had dispatched tanks into Tabriz and the border zone between Iran and Turkey. It was against this backdrop that Churchill, with President Truman on the rostrum, delivered his famous address in Fulton, Missouri, in which he referred to an "iron curtain" that had descended across the Continent from Stettin to Trieste. It had also emerged that Soviet troops in Bulgaria had been reinforced and that the hospitals there and in Rumania had been equipped for treating casualties resulting from possible military action.[53]

These signs attested not only to enhanced Soviet influence in Iran but, above all, to a maneuver directed against Turkey. In the West, it was believed that the Soviets were exploiting the situation in pursuit of their interest in the Straits and "south of Baku and Batumi" (an interest already raised in 1940 in their negotiations with Germany). In intimidating fashion, Molotov had demanded that Turkey agree to both a revision of the Montreux Straits Treaty that would guarantee Soviet security and the establishment of a Soviet military base in the Straits. This demand had been accompanied by another that created panic in Ankara: that Turkey transfers its eastern Transcaucasian regions around Kars and Ardahan to the Soviet Union.[54] More than almost anywhere else, the checkered history of the areas in question mirrored the conflict-ridden relations between Russia and the former Ottoman Empire. In raising questions about Kars and Ardahan, the Soviet

Union seemed bent on realizing the aspirations of its imperial Russian heritage. Throughout the nineteenth century, Russia had repeatedly conquered these areas in the course of wars with the Ottomans—in 1806, 1828, 1855, and 1877. Except for the last venture, the czar had always been forced by the nations protecting the balance of power to relinquish the disputed territories. Since 1877 and the Treaty of San Stefano, they had remained under Russian control until finally, in 1921, they were restored to Turkey in the border agreement negotiated by Stalin.[55] But 1946 witnessed a renewed attempt by Russia to raise territorial demands on Turkey in the Transcaucasus region. After rejecting the Russian call for revision in August, Ankara, fearing attack by twenty-five Soviet divisions massed in the southern Caucasus, felt forced to maintain its army on alert at full strength (600,000 men). This effort put further strains on its precarious budget, heated up inflation, and left the country dependent on British financial aid.[56]

The accumulation of conflicts in the region of the former Eastern Question and the Great Game alarmed the West. After all, in the words of the American secretary of war Patterson, this area was the "crossroads of the world." And the American ambassador in Athens, McVeagh, informed Washington uneasily that by pushing south, Russia was threatening to break open "the lock of world domination." Dean Acheson, one of the architects of American foreign policy and later secretary of state, saw any Soviet attack in the region as having grave repercussions for Western Europe, especially Italy and France with their strong Communist parties. He described the events being played out as of "pivotal" importance.[57] In this context of looming danger, Greece served as a final barrier.

In his talks with Churchill at Potsdam, Stalin proposed a revision of the agreement concerning the Dardanelles. The Soviet Union required a fortified harbor in the northern Aegean, that is, Dede Agach (present-day Alexandroúpolis) on the Thracian coast of Greece, not far from the Turkish border.[58] By circumventing the Bosporus, this demand was designed to allay Turkey's anxieties. It evoked Molotov's effort to gain permission from Berlin in 1940 for Soviet-protected Bulgarian access to the Aegean. Such access would only have been possible through Bulgarian territorial expansion at Greece's expense. And in fact, in December 1946 the new Bulgarian premier and former Comintern chief Georgi Dimitrov directly presented Athens with territorial demands.[59] At the same time, Yugoslavia was increasing its pressure regarding the question of Trieste. Given this constellation of demands, it appeared that the newly established people's democracies in the Balkans were not acting on their own initiative. The West suspected the guiding hand of the Soviets behind the scenes.

The British and Americans thus viewed Greece as a "soft spot,"[60] a possible gateway for Soviet expansion into the eastern Mediterranean, North Africa, the Near East, and possibly also Southern Europe—Italy and France. After 1945, Greece appeared highly vulnerable; the war's aftereffects weighed heavily on the country, wedged as it was between the Balkans and the Aegean.[61] While other countries were gradually showing signs of recovery, Greece still showed the full effects of the harsh requisitions and reprisals by its German, Italian, and Bulgarian occupiers. Its transportation system was practically nonexistent. Indeed, there were only five locomotives and forty automobiles left in the entire country.[62] Of the seven million Greeks before the war, half a million had died of starvation, disease, and executions. Thousands had starved to death on the streets of Athens during the winter of 1941–42. After consultations with the Allies and the Axis powers, the Swedish Red Cross had attempted to alleviate the misery by shipping wheat.[63] The poorer people in the cities were the most severely affected, but the rural populace was also exposed to extreme deprivation. The worst off were those Greeks who, after having fled Asia Minor in 1922, had been resettled in northern Greece, in the areas conquered in 1912–13 in Macedonia and Thrace. A substantial portion of the partisans in the Greek resistance had been recruited from their ranks.

This resistance was led by the Greek Communist Party (the KKE)[64]—a role that in 1942 brought the party out of its shadowy existence during the interwar period, transforming it into a mass movement that included the National Liberation Front (EAM) and its paramilitary organization, the ELAS; about a third of the Greek population were active members.[65] The dramatic rise of the Greek Communists was due not only to conspiratorial skill but above all to the paralysis of the bourgeois parties: the Liberals and the Popular Party. These parties represented the two dominant political camps of the interwar era, the republicans and the royalists; both camps had made accommodations with the German occupiers out of a hope for leniency. The resulting political vacuum was filled by the KKE. Through its resistance, the party attracted republican elements while drawing on an antimonarchical mood with roots in the 1930s.[66] For it had been the monarchy (restored in 1935) that had paved the way for the unpopular dictator Metaxas. The circumstances of the prewar period continued into the war, making it easier for the EAM, born in resistance against the occupation, to mobilize remaining political resources on its own behalf.[67] The question of the king's return helped spark the civil war's decisive phase. Emerging in 1917, a sharp opposition between republicans and royalists would come to stamp Greece's political life as a "national schism"—the *ethnikos dichasmos*. The charismatic republican Elefthérios Venizelos, a visionary of Greater Greece and the architect of Greek expansion in the Balkan Wars, had been pitted against King Constantin I.[68] Their dispute concerned whether to enter World War I. While Venizelos saw such a step as a chance for Greece to expand its territories in Macedonia and Asia Minor at the expense of its traditional adversaries Bulgaria and the Ottoman Empire (who were allied with the Central Powers), Constantin, who was sympathetic to the Germans and related to the Prussian House of Hohenzollern, rejected such designs. When against expectations Constantin declined to ask Venizelos to form a government after the 1916 elections, the latter proclaimed a revolutionary government in Salonika, calling on England and France to intervene and banish the king from the country. After Venizelos was voted out of office in 1920, Constantin returned, only to be held accountable for the rout of the Greek expeditionary force in Anatolia in 1922.[69] He abdicated in favor of his son, George II, and went into exile—cursed by the million and a half refugees and expellees from Asia Minor, who blamed him for their fate. The "national schism" now had its blood-soaked founding event. From this point onward, the most diverse conflicts, social antagonisms, and political idiosyncrasies—whether between new and old elites, old Greeks and new Greeks, indigenous and resettled citizens, north and south—were rationalized in terms of the republican-royalist split.[70]

The split widened in 1944 when it became known that King George II intended to return. He had been encouraged by the British government, more specifically by Churchill, who believed the monarchy would serve as a pillar of stability in postwar Greece. Britain viewed Greece's strategic position as a cornerstone of its imperial policies. Also, the king's restoration would presumably help prevent the country from falling under Communist rule. Hence rather than opting to alienate ordinary Greeks from the Communists, the British insisted on the king's return, contributing not inconsiderably toward plunging Greece into civil war.[71] The resurgent antagonism between royalists and republicans now became tied to the ideological conflict between left and right, which proved highly convenient for the EAM.

In any event, the expectations of the Communist left regarding establishment of a people's democracy in Greece would be disappointed from the start. In November 1944, Greece was the only Balkan country included in Great Britain's sphere of influence through the notorious "percentage agreement" between Churchill and Stalin.[72] The Soviet dictator intended to keep this agreement, especially since it afforded him a free hand in Rumania and Bulgaria. The British presence in Greece after the country's liberation from the Germans was so strong that it suggested comparisons with Lord Cromer's turn-of-the-century rule in Egypt; people actually spoke of a protectorate. The British appointed governments and dismissed ministers. They controlled the budget, which they also largely covered; they determined economic and monetary policy; in practice, they were in charge of the Greek army.[73] And they had become partisans in Greece's civil war, turning the left into their enemies. In view of the resurgence after 1945 of a universal civil war between protagonists of freedom and protagonists of equality, it seemed inevitable that ties would form between the parties active on one or the other sides of the Greek schism and the parallel parties active in the emerging global dualism.

The Soviets were not actively engaged in the Greek Civil War, although they also made no efforts to hide their sympathies. Stalin was well aware of the dangers of interceding in this conflict. Relations between the former wartime allies had been severely tested by the Polish question. Meanwhile, the Truman Doctrine had been declared, in large measure as a response to the civil war raging in Greece; it involved massive economic and financial assistance for the right-wing government in Athens. In April 1948, in view of the worsening conflict between East and West, Stalin tried to dissuade the Yugoslavian and Bulgarian Communists from continuing to intervene in Greece through support of the KKE and units of the Democratic Army associated with it.[74] But his advice was ignored, since these states' solidarity with the Greek Communists was largely bound up with their own national aspirations.[75] Both Yugoslavia and Bulgaria hoped to expand their borders at the expense of their southern neighbor—a hope once again reflecting historical continuities. Couched in Communist rhetoric, the territorial claims voiced in Sofia and Belgrade were hinged to the vexing Macedonian question.[76]

The Greek Civil War, ostensibly a conflict between social classes, increasingly displayed ethnic and territorial components.[77] Thus, for example, the Communists in Greek Macedonia enjoyed considerable prestige among the local Slavic-speaking populace for the simple reason that in the 1920s they had championed the notion of an independent Macedonia. Here they were following the Comintern's directives—a deference that earned them few friends in Greece.[78] The situation was especially aggrieving to the seven-hundred-thousand-odd Greek refugees from Asia Minor who had resettled in Macedonia; they had already lost a homeland once. In December 1935, after the resolutions of the Seventh Comintern "Brussels conference," the individual parties were given a free hand in their alliance policies. This autonomy furnished the Greek Communists with at least the possibility of renouncing the Comintern's "internationalist" support for Macedonian independence in favor of championing Slavic and other minority rights.

The Greek Communists and the Slavo-Greeks had already forged closer ties during the war. The Slavo-Greeks had played a key role in the anti-German struggle; also, they had served as a link between the Greek and the Yugoslav partisans. During the civil war, they formed an independent Slavic-Macedonian National Liberation Front that fought together with the ELAS against the Athens government.[79] Especially in the struggle's final phase, the Slavo-Greeks in the north comprised a large proportion of the units in the Democratic Army, and their cadres maintain the vital connection with Belgrade. Yugoslavia had emerged from the war as the major power in the Balkans, and the help of the South Slavic Federation was crucial for the Greek Communists, whose fighters could cross the border without problems. Furthermore, there were Democratic Army training camps and supply depots in Yugoslavia, Albania, and Bulgaria.[80] Above all, Communist Yugoslavia offered the Greek Communists a hinterland essential for their operations. All told, without Yugoslav help the Greek Communists would have been hopelessly outclassed by the Greek government troops, which were well equipped by the West.

All internationalist proclamations to the contrary, Yugoslav involvement in the Greek Civil War was hardly altruistic. Rather, it was integral to the Yugoslav Communists' comprehensive strategy in the region. The South Slavic Federation under Tito was seeking to enhance the leading position in the Balkans that it had gained through its own hard efforts. Predictably, Yugoslavia's developing power led to ill feeling among neighboring comrades and provoked Stalin's opposition.[81] The relationship between the Yugoslav and the Albanian Communists was reminiscent of colonial subjugation. In the Yugoslav view, minuscule Albania was best off contenting itself with the role of supplying raw materials for its more powerful neighbor.[82] In the north, in Carinthia and around Trieste, ethnic and territorial tensions were rising. In the south, the Macedonian question was to prove ruinous for the Greek Communists in the Greek Civil War.

Yugoslavia and Bulgaria made no effort to conceal their territorial demands vis-à-vis Greece. It was even suspected that as the monarchy's heir Tito was seeking control over Salonika.[83] But what would have politically fatal consequences for the Greek Communists were the expectations of their fraternal parties in Yugoslavia and Bulgaria in the event of a KKE victory and the transformation of Greece into a people's democracy, namely, that the Greeks would relinquish both Aegean Macedonia and Thrace. To be sure, the territorial ambitions of Bulgaria and Yugoslavia were not in harmony, and the Macedonian question was also an issue between them. Tito claimed all of Macedonia for Yugoslavia; Dimitrov, for that very reason, was in favor of an independent Macedonia. Correspondingly, Belgrade was trying to pressure Sofia into surrendering its own portion of Macedonia.[84] The August 1947 Treaty of Bled then revealed the hopes of Belgrade and Sofia to resolve their differences over the Macedonian question at

Greece's expense.[85] Tito and Dimitrov agreed that in the event of a Communist victory in the Greek Civil War, Yugoslavia would absorb Greece's Aegean Macedonia while the Greek portion of Thrace would be transferred to Bulgaria. (The rulers also envisaged the eventual unification of their two states in the framework of a larger South Slavic Federation, a proposal that had been broached in 1944 but was opposed by the Soviets.)

These plans for Greek territorial surrender presented the Greek Communists with a serious dilemma. The vexing Macedonian question had overtaken them again, and they were being asked in effect to square a circle. If they wanted to assert their identity as part of the international Communist movement, they had to endorse the sacrifice of certain areas of Greek territory, thus committing treason—a plunge into a political abyss.[86] If, in contrast, they wished to preserve the national prestige they had gained so arduously through wartime resistance, then they had to oppose their fellow Communists in Bulgaria and Yugoslavia. But this would jeopardize their prospects in the civil war, especially since without Yugoslav support and the Slavo-Greek formations fighting at their side, they would be unable to stabilize their worsening military situation.

Hence as a result of the Macedonian question, the Greek Communists risked falling into the same political isolation that had plagued them during the interwar period.[87] In the civil war's final phase, the old constellation had reappeared: the Greek Communists were now ready to surrender parts of Greece to their traditionally despised Slavic neighbors or intervene in support of an independent Macedonia. This development deprived them of any backing they had still enjoyed in Greece, while contributing to an intensified ethnicization of the civil war.[88] The "reaction" portrayed itself as Greek, while the "revolution" assumed a Slavic hue. Nowhere else in Greece did the right gain more new adherents than in Macedonia.[89] In March 1949, KKE radio, broadcasting from Rumania, confirmed that the party was now calling for an independent Macedonia.[90] This sealed a defeat that at least preserved the Communists from the stigma of treason. But the direct source of the defeat was closely tied to the emergence of another schism, already visible in February 1948: that in the Communist bloc between Stalin and Tito. In response to the KKE's aligning itself with Stalin, the Yugoslavs closed their border with Greece, an action severing the Democratic Army from its hinterland and its supply of essential matériel.[91] With the Greek Civil War thus over, thousands of Greek Communists, especially the many Slavo-Macedonians in their ranks, embarked on the long trek into exile.[92]

The events in Greece confirmed many of the Western powers' old fears. In particular, Sofia's demand, supported by Moscow, for a revision of the border in Thrace pointed to persisting, traditional aspirations in the question of the Straits. Direct Bulgarian access to the Aegean would have compromised Turkey's role as sole guardian of the Bosporus and the Dardanelles. The thrust of such a demand recalled the Treaty of San Stefano in 1878, as well as the Soviet offer to Sofia in the spring of 1941 to support Bulgarian expansion to the Aegean in return for permission to station Soviet troops on its soil. What had been promoted in the nineteenth century through Pan-Slavic arguments was now simply being couched in another idiom: that of the ideological antithesis between East and West.

The transfer to the United States of Great Britain's traditional role in the Eastern Question was followed by a universalizing of the British-Russian tension that had reemerged after the Second World War. The conflict between East and West over Iran, Turkey, and especially Greece now led to a reformulated diction, with that reflecting traditional diplomatic constellations making way for abstract principles manifest in the Truman Doctrine, rightly termed the "first shot in the cold war."[93] The doctrine was, in fact, a direct response to the dramatic situation in Greece; a definitive globalization of the opposition between freedom and equality, that is, a universal civil war of values and ideologies, only became apparent with the outbreak of the Korean War.[94] Still, the dire situation in Greece would be repeatedly cited whenever it was perceived as necessary to justify Washington's engagement in similar situations, "Greece" thus emerging as a metaphor for the transition from local civil wars to the universal civil war. When North Korean forces invaded South Korea in June 1950, Truman referred to the latter country as the "Greece of the Far East."[95] Likewise, President Eisenhower used the Greek example to describe the situation in Vietnam in 1957.[96]

In an age of ideologies, the world had become united in its division. The various conflicts, however diverse and deep-rooted their origins, had fused into one conflict over values and principles. This fusion was no superficial ploy; the conflict was all-embracing because by its very nature it could only be universal. Hence even tangential conflicts were rationalized along the ideological lines of a modern war of faith; in the end, the war's codes, signs, and other tokens were absorbed into numerous constellations not tied to it in any obvious way.

The Cold War's first hot battle was fought in Korea. That it happened here is remarkable, since Europe, and not Asia, was the confrontation's real locus.[97] In 1948–49 both the Soviet Union and the United States had withdrawn their troops from the Korean peninsula, which had been divided between North and South at the thirty-eighth parallel. To be sure, with their antithetical worldviews the regimes in P'yŏngyang and Seoul had been tirelessly proclaiming their desire to unite the country by destroying the foe.[98] There had been repeated skirmishes along the partition boundary; sabotage and military diversion had become a daily routine. Kim Il Sung, North Korea's totalitarian ruler, constantly strove to harm Syngman Rhee, his dictatorial counterpart in the South, and vice versa. But it seemed a long way from this policy of pinpricks to a veritable war. Also, it could be assumed that the United States would intervene on the battlefield should the North try to take over the South by force of arms, and it was imperative to avoid such intervention at all costs.[99]

However, the North Koreans considered American intervention in the event of war improbable, and Kim Il Sung tried to convince Stalin and Mao that this assessment was sound; the Korean peninsula was, after all, at the furthest periphery of American interest. In January 1950, the U.S. secretary of state, Dean Acheson, had carelessly remarked that Washington considered neither Korea nor Taiwan to be part of its western Pacific "defensive perimeter"—as opposed to Japan or the Philippines.[100] Perhaps this comment misled Kim into believing that the risk incurred by an attack on the South was smaller than it actually was. In any event, P'yŏngyang solicited Moscow's support for its plan to unite Korea by force. The North Korean army command had developed a highly optimistic scenario for concluding operations in a few days: the American's would not get involved in an "internal" Korean affair, and the South Korean populace would itself rise up to oust the hated Rhee regime. But despite P'yŏngyang's repeated assurances that Washington would not be drawn into a domestic conflict between the two Koreas, Stalin remained skeptical. The Soviets refused to commit themselves, instead referring the North Koreans to Beijing.

Mao Zedong had just concluded a successful revolution on the Chinese mainland, forcing his nationalist opponent, Chiang Kaishek, to flee with his supporters to Taiwan. While Mao was skeptical of the North Korean plan, he was less inclined than Stalin to dismiss the enthusiasm of his Korean comrades.[101] For his own goal was the military unification of Taiwan with the Communist mainland, and for this he required Soviet backing just as much as the North Koreans did. So despite his misgivings, Mao was unwilling to reject their notion out of hand. The impression created by his ambivalence, namely, that the Chinese would not turn down P'yŏngyang's request for aid (regarded as highly unlikely in any case), was critical for the North Korean decision to attack. The North Koreans were also able to use this ambiguity to convince the Soviets that China would indeed stand by them in the event of hostilities. Still, until North Korea's June 1950 assault on the South, neither the Soviets nor the Chinese were clear about the exact extent of their commitments to P'yŏngyang.[102] After MacArthur's landing at Inch'ŏn, the North Koreans' situation turned desperate; in November, despite his reservations, Mao felt it necessary to support them with "volunteers."

Mao's decision to risk a confrontation with America may have been a result of Soviet pressure, with Stalin reminding him of the obligation he had incurred to North Korea; on the other hand, it may have resulted from an apparent Soviet willingness to accept the loss of North Korea under certain conditions. Also, the prevailing view in Beijing was that a confrontation with "imperialism" was inevitable, and better now than later. The Chinese saw this view confirmed when on 27 July Washington sent the Seventh Fleet into the Formosa Straits to prevent the Korean conflict from developing into one between the two Chinas, which were already poised for battle.[103] The Red Chinese construed this preventive act as a blatant provocation: as they saw things, the "imperialist" Americans would stop at nothing to topple their revolution, the product of so much effort and sacrifice. Since Washington had already come to France's aid in February 1950 in its struggle against the Communist Vietminh, Mao believed he was facing a coordinated action by the American imperialists—a "U.S. invasion of Asia,"[104] perhaps culminating in a campaign against China. Such fears seemed confirmed when U.N. troops under MacArthur advanced north from Inch'ŏn, crossing the thirty-eighth parallel; by November 1950 they were nearing the Yalu River frontier, which bordered China's industrial center in Manchuria.[105] The Chinese "volunteers" who had been prepared for this possibility intervened massively, driving the Americans back. In this way, the

Korean War had expanded from a territorial civil war between the two Koreas into a Sino-American confrontation.[106]

The hostility between Red China and the United States characterizing the 1950s did not have deep roots. Throughout World War II, the Americans and the Chinese Communists were inclined toward mutual cooperation.[107] In the summer of 1944, a delegation of American experts paid a visit to Yan'an, the center of Mao's revolutionary forces. At the invitation of Zhou Enlai, they had been sent into rebel territory by General Stilwell and the Office of Strategic Services to take a closer look at the Chinese Communist partisan army. The so-called Dixie Mission was deeply impressed by Mao's troops, which they believed represented an especially dynamic variant of Chinese nationalism:[108] linking patriotic aspirations with the social-revolutionary concerns of the long-suffering peasantry, the Communists had succeeded in organizing the struggle against the Japanese in areas relinquished by Chiang Kai-shek's corrupt and incompetent Kuomintang. The legendary American journalists Edgar Snow and Anna Louise Strong reported this with barely concealed sympathy for the cause of the Chinese revolution. And indeed, the triumph of the Chinese Communists and later defeat of the Kuomintang were based on this combination of patriotic struggle against external foes and internal social-revolutionary measures.

During and after the Second World War, the Americans would have been quite content with a Chinese coalition government composed of Nationalists and Communists. In the summer of 1944, at the height of the war in Asia, the United States tried to secure massive participation by Chinese troops in an invasion of the Japanese islands.[109] In the summer of 1945, especially after the Japanese surrender on 14 August, there was great American concern about the vulnerability to Soviet machinations of a China torn by civil strife, especially in Manchuria. On the other hand, while undesirable, a Communist takeover in Beijing did not seem all that threatening. To foil any Soviet ventures, George C. Marshall, then chairman of the Joint Chiefs of Staff, was dispatched to work out a compromise between Mao and Chiang.[110] But his efforts were fruitless, for the civil war parties proved unwilling to compromise: Mao saw Chiang's demands as an invitation to capitulate, and for their part the Kuomintang refused to accept the Communists as equal partners in a coalition government. In keeping with the conventions of civil war, the antagonism persisted until the bitter end. General Marshall, appointed secretary of state by Truman after his return, now concentrated his energies on the incipient Cold War's European theater.

Despite growing fears that a Communist victory in China would in fact deliver the country to the Soviets, the Americans maintained hopes for some time that Mao Zedong's Chinese nationalism would prove more potent than international Communist solidarity, and that differences between the Soviets and the Chinese would soon come to the fore. Drawing an analogy with the Balkans in 1948, Washington thus counted on Mao to be an "Asian Tito."[111] In this vein George Kennan, then chief of planning in the State Department, expected tensions to emerge between the Soviets and the nationalist, independent-minded Chinese Communists; Kennan was convinced of the priority of Europe when it came to Western security. The tensions he anticipated did, of course, emerge, but much later. With Nixon's visit to Beijing in 1972, the prevailing structure of two opposing, purely ideological blocs would split apart, to be superseded by a form of geopolitical multipolarity. This development would be catalyzed by Nixon's trusted foreign-policy advisor Henry Kissinger, a statesman of German-Jewish origin who diverged from America's dominant ideological confession, trusting more in the grand traditions and patterns of nineteenth-century European power politics.[112]

Several decades before this turn of affairs unfolded, the Communists emerged victorious from China's civil war. This turn of events was especially surprising to Stalin, who in Teheran and Yalta had agreed with Roosevelt that the Kuomintang held the stronger cards. When the Americans granted the Soviets special concessions in Manchuria, to be negotiated with the Chinese Nationalists, this reflected Soviet regard for the Nationalists as amenable partners. This was based on a background of mutual trust; at the end of the 1930s, Moscow had supplied the Kuomintang with ammunition and other matériel in its struggle against the Japanese invaders. Stalin, moreover, was suspicious of the Chinese Communists. And he had little inclination to affront the Americans, who unlike the Soviets were militarily active in Asia. For such reasons, the Soviet strongman had called on Mao to reach an agreement with Chiang Kai-shek.[113]

The Americans incurred the irreconcilable enmity of the Chinese Communists by intervening, intentionally or not, in the civil war that had flared up again after the surrender of Japan. To disarm the Japanese in northeastern China and secure railways, harbors, and airports in Manchuria, the United States employed all the formidable naval and air capabilities at its disposal to transport hundreds of thousands of Kuomintang troops from southern China north.[114] With this logistical support for Chiang, the Americans found themselves at odds with the Communists, who had launched a plan to gain control over this economically crucial region. Also, Truman's call to the Japanese troops in China to surrender to the Kuomintang was denounced by the Communists as a brazen intervention in the civil war. Later Mao would repeatedly refer to the events in northeastern China when speaking about both the break with Washington and America's position against the revolution he led. Despite the close ties that had actually been formed between the United States and Chinese Communists, Mao here reflected his allegiance to a historical narrative grounded in the conceptual vocabulary of the universal civil war. Within this narrative, the "imperialist" United States was assigned the role of paramount rogue.

The victory of the Chinese Communists in October 1949 and Chiang's expulsion from the mainland to Taiwan gave rise to a wide range of world-revolutionary expectations. Even Stalin, whose assessment of situations was generally guided by realpolitik, was carried away by these events. A revolution proceeding in Europe solely because of Soviet rule appeared to be advancing in Asia by its own impetus. Revolutionary romanticism aside, these developments were highly advantageous for the Soviets: the Chinese revolution had dramatically transformed political relations between West and East. The friendship treaty concluded in 1950 between Beijing and Moscow ratified a slogan proclaimed by Mao that summer: "Lean to one side!"[115] A not insubstantial portion of the globe was now "red." In this manner, the Chinese Communists played their part in the world's division, emerging as a party in the universal civil war. Correspondingly, the images and analogies he used continued to adhere to a polarized narrative schema: imperialism on the one side, Communist-oriented national liberation on the other side. Everywhere, he detected the machinations of the imperialists, with America at the fore. He recalled the early American interventions in China, such as during the Boxer uprising of 1900 and earlier the Taiping Rebellion of 1851–64, quelled with the help of American adventurers. These episodes of Chinese history were tied, in turn, to American participation in the Entente's intervention in the Russian Civil War.[116] Mao was so convinced of American hostility that he was astounded at the absence of imperialist intervention after Communist forces crossed the Yangtze River in April 1949 and took Shanghai a month later. To the bewilderment of the Communist Chinese, the hasty fortification of the coastal region proved superfluous: the Americans did not appear. Mao failed to understand that Washington wished to remain aloof from the civil war's final phase[117] and in fact felt no obligation to defend Taiwan. Hence when at the start of the Korean conflict in 1950 the U.S. Seventh Fleet was dispatched to the Straits of Formosa to draw a cordon between the Nationalists and the Chinese Communists, the Chinese Communists saw their fears as about to finally come true: American "imperialism" was now poised to strike. But it seemed more prudent not to confront it directly, with regular troops; rather, it could be confronted on the Korean front with "volunteers."

The surprise attack by North Korean forces on the South brought America into the fray. If the P'yŏngyang regime had contented itself with trying to destabilize the Rhee government through subversion, it is unlikely this would have occurred. The North Korean incursion awakened memories in Washington of the Japanese invasion of Manchuria in 1931 and of the proceedings in Munich in 1938.[118] Such analogies and accompanying rhetoric spurred a swift and direct American response. Its initiative under U.N. auspices imposed certain restrictions on the campaign; the United States had to take its allies into consideration.

The transition to a universal civil war had already been implicit in the Truman Doctrine.[119] The transition unfolded in a series of steps. Presented with the rhetoric of global intervention, Congress had been persuaded to provide support for Greece and Turkey; but as yet there was no generally recognized policy. Presidential directive NSC-68, which envisioned a tripling of the military budget to confront real or imagined Soviet machinations everywhere, was certainly a qualitative leap. As a fiscal conservative, Truman had hesitated to give final approval to the recommendations of the National Security Council, which he had solicited after the "loss" of China and the detonation of the first Soviet nuclear bomb in 1949. But North Korea's wanton attack on the South seemed to confirm the assessment that the United States was facing a global and coordinated Communist conspiracy, guided by Moscow. Setting aside his reservations, Truman adopted the National Security Council recommendations in September, incorporating them into a presidential directive—a veritable call to arms. From now on the confrontation between the "free world" and Communism would encircle the globe.[120] Gray zones were thus colored black, the case, for instance, with various nationalist movements against traditional colonial powers. American troops were stationed permanently in Europe; West Germany was rearmed.[121]

A political paradox was playing itself out on the Korean peninsula. While in Europe the universal civil war's antagonists avoided direct confrontation while standing face to face, the military vacuum created by the withdrawal of American and Soviet forces from the peninsula in 1948–49 opened up a space for both Kim Il Sung and Syngman Rhee to become active, producing a hot war.[122] The Korean peninsula now became a substitute zone for the East-West conflict, since by 1950 clear dividing lines had already been drawn at the conflict's epicenter, Europe.[123] The Truman Doctrine and the Marshall Plan had achieved their purpose. In Germany in 1948, the currency reform had passed its first test in relation to the crisis sparked by the Berlin blockade. In 1949, two ideologically stamped German states had been established whose mutual relations were not dissimilar to those between the two Koreas. NATO had been founded. In the West, the Soviets had encountered barriers erected against their expansionist ambitions. In Asia the confrontation was less clear-cut and seemed remote from the situation in Europe; the United States had yet to take a definite stand. For precisely these reasons— potently supplemented, as revealed in both the Chinese Civil War and the confrontation in Indochina, by a characteristic fusion of anticolonialism and Communist nationalism—Asia emerged as eminently suited for military conflict.

From the beginning, with the disarming of the Japanese in Indochina by Chinese troops advancing from the north and the British army arriving from the south, Southeast Asia appeared to follow a distinct line of development. But the symbolism of Ho Chi Minh's citations from the American Declaration of Independence in his proclamation of Vietnam's independence in September 1945 would turn out to have been deceptive.[124] The Vietnamese Communists, once in the vanguard of a national resistance to Japanese occupation, soon emerged as America's bitter enemy—a development that from our perspective does not seem self-evident. The peoples of Asia and others under colonial rule had placed great hope in the United States and President Roosevelt, who was, as suggested, ill-disposed toward colonialism. Had he not adopted the promises of the Atlantic Charter and sung the praises of self-determination? Harry Truman, who became president at Roosevelt's death in April 1945, also stood firmly in this tradition. Washington thus now tried to persuade Britain to relinquish India and a reluctant Netherlands to grant independence to Indonesia.[125] But history took a different turn in Indochina, drawing an anticolonial America to the side of colonial France. By degrees, Washington would become entangled in a drawn-out conflict. Robert S. McNamara, secretary of defense under President Kennedy and one of the key architects of this second Indochina war, would confess decades later that it had been a terrible mistake.[126]

America acted against the standards set by its own tradition as a result of a particular mutation characterizing nearly all the relevant conflicts of the 1950s, 1960s, and 1970s: the mutation of national liberation movements against colonial powers into social-revolutionary confrontations. Solely on account of the ideological rationalization accompanying these conflicts, they were readily conflated with the conflict between East and West. The drama in Indochina illustrates this conflation.[127] By the end of 1946, Indochina had probably become the most important arena in the struggle between France and a colonized population resisting its subjugation. Together with Korea, Indochina would become the stage for an increasingly global contest between East and West—a contest in which the traditional colonial powers increasingly receded behind an America rapidly distancing itself from its anti-colonial heritage. More than any other conflict, the struggle in

Indochina thus bore both of the era's hallmarks: colonialism and the Cold War.[128] Its conclusion was also epoch making: the defeat of French troops at Dien Bien Phu in May 1954, a conventional battle forced on the colonizing power by the indigenous population, was more than the defeat of France and its empire. It was understood as the historic defeat of the white man per se. Dien Bien Phu was the beacon signaling the end of the French colonial empire and the historical event that accelerated France's withdrawal to Europe.

In February 1950, the United States came to the aid of France in its "dirty war"[129] in Indochina. America's support for the French colonial power thus preceded the North Korean attack on South Korea and became the turning point in relations between East and West in Asia.[130] The American readiness to become engaged in Indochina on the side of France, which by all accounts was sparing no effort in ignoring the signs of the times, was based on weightier reasons than Washington's general determination, in the sense of the Truman Doctrine, to confront the Communist threat *everywhere*. Hints of an approaching clash in Indochina between the universal civil war's protagonists, a clash going beyond the colonial struggle of the past four years between French troops and the Vietminh, had begun to multiply after the Communist victory in the Chinese Civil War and the proclamation of the People's Republic of China in October 1949. It soon became known that the Red Chinese, whose troops were massed on the frontier with Indochina, were training its soldiers and providing the Vietminh with all manner of assistance, a development the French naturally found troubling. Yet the Chinese support was also convenient for the French, since their untimely colonial war could now be inscribed with the insignia of anti-Communism. Hoping to stress the national character of his struggle, Ho Chi Minh had just begun to distance himself from Mao Zedong's revolution when the Democratic Republic of Vietnam was formally recognized by both Moscow and Beijing in January 1950.[131] The outbreak of the Korean War in June 1950 lent further credibility to the anti-Communist rhetoric that France had resorted to for years in regard to Indochina. When the high commissioner and commanding general of the French Union Forces in Indochina, Jean de Lattre de Tassigny, hurried to Washington in September 1951 to plead for increased assistance, he spoke of France's difficult role as "foot soldier of the Free World."[132] France was trying to persuade Washington to share this responsibility. The situation shared some similarities with that of Britain in 1946–47, when the British found it necessary to press the Americans, oriented toward the present, to accept the yoke of history. A "Greek" constellation had also formed in Indochina.[133] In the Levant, in the eastern Mediterranean, American had supplanted Britain; in Asia, in Indochina, it seemed obliged to assume France's onerous burden. The transfer of the power insignia was successful. After 1950, France no longer stood alone in Indochina; its colonial war had been subsumed into the universal civil war.[134]

It did not really require great persuasive skills to convince the United States to support the French in Indochina with financial and material aid.[135] Washington by itself had come to realize the strategic importance of the Indochinese region, which far exceeded that of Korea or Taiwan. As already noted, in January 1950 Dean Acheson had described both countries as lying outside the American defensive perimeter in the western Pacific. In an analogy with Japan's effort in World War II to gain control over Southeast Asia's raw materials by invading Indochina and preemptively attacking Pearl Harbor, the Americans viewed the region as a corridor for the possible conquest of the Philippines and Thailand from the north. Also, Indochina lay along the path to the British possessions in Southeast Asia, especially the resource-rich colony of Malaya, where the British, parallel to the French in Indochina, were successfully quelling a Communist guerrilla insurrection.[136] Furthermore, in the context of Japan's reconstruction,

Washington had selected Indochina as a substitute for the "lost" Chinese mainland; economic exchange—Japanese industrial products and services for Indochina's raw materials—would help restore the economy of America's former enemy in East Asia and, in view of the worsening antagonism between East and West, bind it to the United States on a long-term basis.[137] Hence in contrast to the approach taken toward Korea, the strategic and geopolitical importance of Indochina induced the Americans to forget their traditional anticolonialism, so that at the end of 1949, after the Communist triumph in China, they came to the aid of the embattled French.

Despite the American support that now began to flow to the troops of the Union Française, amounting at the height of the war to some 70 percent of its total costs, friction between Paris and Washington was constantly apparent.[138] In the end, two unequal partners with divergent motives were waging differing wars in Indochina. Beneath the umbrella of the Union Française, France was stubbornly trying to preserve its colonial empire. Washington was mainly buttressing the French for strategic reasons, in line with a domino theory steadily winning adherents; the United States thus urged Paris to grant full independence to the associated states of the union in Indochina: Vietnam, Laos, and Cambodia.[139] Consequently, it is not surprising that France's colonial motives came into conflict with Washington's anti-Communist policies. The French republic's jealous colonial egoism affected nearly all transactions, from the conduct of the war to the distribution of American funds to local authorities. France steadfastly refused to permit the creation of truly independent Vietnamese combat units. Instead, the French troops were subjected to a largely ineffective process of "yellowing" through recruitment of local soldiers.[140] There were no plans for a genuine transfer of power to the Vietnamese. Ngo Dinh Diem, who as an anti-French nationalist and staunch anti-Communist was favored by the

Americans, could be named prime minister of South Vietnam by Emperor Bao Dai only when the end of French involvement in Indochina was already in sight.[141]

Tensions between America and France only increased in the war's final phase. At home, more and more voices were calling for Paris to end its "dirty war." But the Americans were now urging the French to stand fast. Washington feared that negotiations would not only validate the Vietminh's military triumphs but also lead to recognition of both the Democratic Republic of Vietnam and the People's Republic of China, which was still scorned as Red China and under a kind of diplomatic quarantine.[142] In order to conclude the war, France had no option but to approach China, since without Chinese influence being brought to bear on the Vietminh the war would drag on indefinitely. In May 1953, a French economic delegation paid an official visit to Beijing and its Maoist government.[143] Great Britain, cochairman (together with the Soviet Union) of the Geneva Conference on Indochina in the summer of 1954, espoused a more moderate position; in any event, it had already established diplomatic relations with Mao's regime. In this way, while Washington's European allies made conciliatory moves toward China to enhance their maneuvering room in the region, the United States stuck with its ideological campaign. China's entry into the world political arena had to be thwarted. The estrangement between America and its European allies, already palpable at Geneva, culminated in a genuine crisis in autumn 1956 when President Eisenhower forced Britain and France, acting in collusion with Israel, to halt their late-colonial Suez adventure. Under sharp censure by the world community, they withdrew from Egypt without having achieved their aims.[144]

French tenacity in Indochina and American anti-Communism were difficult to reconcile. The tensions, exacerbated by differing traditions and mentalities, surfaced especially in relation to the conduct of the war.[145] The Americans construed the unaggressive and diffuse French approach, deriving from the colonial strategy of pacification developed by Marshal Lyautey in North Africa around the turn of the century, as an expression of the timorous Maginot Line posture that had led France to catastrophe in 1940.[146] France, determined to offset that historical debacle with victory in Asia, perceived American interference as haughty and humiliating. The French were suffering in any case from a sense of being in Washington's pay. Not only were their weapons and materiel from U.S. Army stocks, but even their uniforms were American. France was fighting with borrowed power. The bitterness reached its acme when the French requested massive American aerial support to relieve their fortress at Dien Bien Phu, which was encircled by the Vietminh, and Washington declined. As long as France refused to internationalize the Indochina war, the Americans avoided anything that might draw them directly into combat.[147] But France's chief concern was not struggling against Communism but maintaining control over a substantial portion of its colonial empire. If Indochina were lost, the possessions in North Africa might well also break free.[148] And in fact, the French defeat at Dien Bien Phu would lead directly to the Algerian revolt in November 1954.

Washington decisively rebuffed France's repeated calls for the deployment of American troops in Indochina. The Korean conflict had already involved thousands upon thousands of casualties. And while the United States government was sending draftees to Korea and thus risking public discontent, the French army in Indochina was largely made up of colonial troops; Paris was averse to mobilizing French regulars.[149] Its request that the Americans threaten to use nuclear weapons, as they had done in Korea to accelerate the signing of an armistice agreement, was ignored. The French undoubtedly drew conclusions from Washington's refusal to provide them with the aegis of its absolute weapon. It was probably shortly after the Geneva Indochina conference that Prime Minister Pierre Mendès-France, otherwise conciliatory in his stance and engaged in dismantling the empire, ordered the development of a French bomb.[150]

The Americans had various reasons for not getting directly involved in the French war in Indochina. President Eisenhower had remarked early on, albeit in a private conversation, that the war was unwinnable, at least the way France was conducting it.[151] But the true reasons for America's distance lay deeper; they were connected with the role it had assumed after 1945 as a superpower in the universal civil war.[152] Each time it directly entered a conflict, its full global prestige was on the line, its efforts to wage limited wars consistently thwarted. Extreme situations were thus to be avoided.[153] That the United States found itself mired in Vietnam less than a decade after the Geneva conference was due to the erroneous policy that McNamara would deplore more than thirty years later. The war against North Vietnam and the Vietcong was truly not winnable; the ends and means were totally disproportionate. America would withdraw from Vietnam in defeat in April 1975.[154] But its retreat was accompanied by a relatively small loss of prestige, since American policy had successfully exploited the burgeoning antagonism between Beijing and Moscow. France, for its part, had distanced itself from Washington since Dien Bien Phu. In 1966, under de Gaulle, it had left the military framework of NATO to seek its own way in the Western alliance.[155]

The Indochina war was an Asian war, but it had major implications for France's role in Europe. France, determined to halt the steady slide in its international standing, was equally present in both the Asian and the European arena. The dilemmas accompanying this double engagement and were soon transferred to the United States, which now had to assimilate tensions in Asia and Europe both politically *and* financially. America increasingly worried whether France, overtaxed by its colonial responsibilities, was capable of sustaining the burden of being Europe's major Continental power in the Western alliance.[156] For despite its engagement in Asia, Washington was pursuing a policy of "Europe first": it was essential that Western Europe be protected from a possible Soviet attack, French troops in Europe here being irreplaceable.

Also, the Americans were actively arming the new Federal Republic of Germany and integrating it into NATO—a project tenaciously opposed by the French. In any event, America's guarantee of West European security was only practicable if its Western allies jettisoned colonial empires siphoning off their urgently needed reserves.[157]

Hence the funds France received from the Marshall Plan were being dissipated in the jungles of Indochina. But for the sake of Europe's security, the United States had no choice but to supply France with whatever support it needed for its colonial war there.[158] The Americans feared, not unjustly, that if forced to choose between maintaining its empire and European security, France might be guided not by reason, not by Cold War logic, but by traditional considerations of prestige. It had maneuvered itself into a hopeless impasse, between the claims of the past and the exigencies of the present. The preservation of its colonial empire was incompatible with its obligation to promote European integration—an integration furthermore, that stipulated reconciliation with Germany and the fact of its rearmament.[159]

Wedged between the needs of the European present and the draining demands of its colonies, France sought leeway for action. This was furnished by the project of European security—here as a traditional Continental power, France was certain of being indispensable for the British and the Americans. The French trump card was ratification of the treaty establishing a European Defense Community (EDC) comprising a West German contingent: with the Korean War's outbreak in June 1950, the deployment of additional conventional forces in Europe had become unavoidable; in view of France's colonial commitments in Asia, Germany alone seemed able to fill the breach. By degrees, the British and the Americans thus came to the conclusion that Germany had to be rearmed, but this required French agreement.[160] Under duress, Washington was ready to indulge any demand. For its part, Paris was adept at converting this inclination into support for its Indochina venture. At the NATO conference in Lisbon in April 1952, Prime Minister Edgar Faure thus made clear that France would be unable to sign the EDC treaty as long as it had to sustain the total burden of the war in Indochina. Washington immediately hastened to offer further pledges to the French.[161]

The American administration, particularly Secretary of State Dulles, saw itself faced with a necessary "deal": support for France in Indochina in turn for French ratification of the EDC treaty. It was imperative to avoid affronting the sole remaining Western European Continental power. For such reasons, France had already managed to obtain the Western defense community's protection for Algeria, recognized in Article 5 of the NATO treaty as part of French national territory. Now the problem seemed even thornier: the fewer troops France maintained in Europe because of its colonial obligations, the less it would be inclined to agree to German rearmament.[162] This coupling of European security with French colonial policy, and a closely interconnected political paralysis that was undermining the Fourth Republic, could finally be overcome after the defeat at Dien Bien Phu in May 1954.[163] The Laniel-Bidault government, which itself had basically supported the EDC treaty, now collapsed, opening the way for Pierre Mendès-France. With the signing of the Geneva Indochina accords in July 1954, Mendès-France ended the French Asian war; in August he brought the irksome EDC treaty to a vote—but without the cabinet's recommendation. Although Mendès-France came to power as the grand liquidator of the French colonial empire, he would be unable to fulfill his historical mission, for he was toppled in February 1955 through a vendetta carried out by adherents of the EDC. But before this happened, he initiated the crucial process leading to Tunisian and Moroccan independence from French rule.[164]

Dulles' concerns would turn out to be well founded: with the end of the war in Indochina, French interest in the EDC,

doubtful in any case, dissolved. Moreover, the Americans suspected Mendès-France of being an inveterate neutralist. He had
been supported by the Communists in the chamber of deputies,
even though he deftly eluded their advances. Rumors that he
and Molotov had arranged a pact in Geneva—a *marchandage
planétaire*[165]—fit this image. The Americans understood the putative pact as follows: a favorable accord would emerge for France in
Indochina, for which France in turn would foil the EDC treaty,
hence the formation of a European army with West German
participation.

As it turned out, the results of the Geneva agreement on Indochina were less onerous for France than had been feared. This relatively favorable outcome was due to the negotiating skills of the
liquidateur, Mendès-France. He had threatened to expand the war
if the negotiations failed to reach an immediate conclusion satis-
factory to all. He had not hesitated to contact both the Vietminh
and representatives of the Beijing regime, thus granting Communist China de facto recognition. For their part, Moscow and
Beijing had pressured Ho Chi Minh to scale down his demands,
which were generally thought excessive.[166] The division of Vietnam at the seventeenth parallel was thus the territorial expression
of a compromise. Demarcating the border further north than the
North Vietnamese had wanted was actually in line with American
concerns—the greatest American fear had been fluid, indefinite
fronts. In any case, South Vietnam had been saved for the West;
with all the social-technical means at their disposal, the Americans were now determined to make it a showcase for the "free
world." Hence all told, the French defeat and withdrawal from
Indochina were convenient for the United States, as they removed
the colonial component from the central confrontation: the ideological confrontation between Western freedom and the Communist ideal of literal equality. Washington was convinced that it
could decide the struggle in its favor by pursuing policies based on
the better example. When Dulles stated that the United States
now faced a clear-cut situation in Vietnam, devoid of any trace of

colonialism, he was taunting the cunning of history. Dien Bien Phu, he declared, had been a "blessing in disguise."[167] As it turned out, this "blessing" would become America's curse.

The loss of Indochina was a key factor contributing to the final French rejection of the EDC treaty in August 1954. With the end of the war in Asia, the French believed they no longer needed America. Paris had not succeeded in drawing NATO into its colonial war in Asia through clamorous anti-Communist rhetoric. The North Atlantic alliance had remained faithful to its regional mission. When France had been forced to reveal its military destitution, neither the Americans nor the British had made their air forces available for a strike against the Vietminh.[168] After France's defeat, America pursued its plans to create a Western alliance, analogous to NATO, for Southeast Asia. SEATO's primary purpose was to combat Communism. The establishment of a regional alliance calibrated to the requirements of the universal civil war prompted the postcolonial states of Asia and Africa, who wished to eschew the East-West conflict, to reach an understanding among themselves. Meeting in April 1955 in Bandung, Indonesia, with the participation of the People's Republic of China (internationally legitimated through the Geneva Conference on Indochina), they formulated the principle of nonalignment, which soon led to the notion of "positive neutrality" between East and West.[169]

The French National Assembly's rejection of the EDC treaty had been carried out through a procedural ploy—a qualified majority arguing that the issue should not even be raised[170]—that was humiliating to that body's "Europeans." The rejection prepared the way for West Germany's entry into NATO, thus affording the Federal Republic a considerable gain in sovereignty.[171] Such a turn of events was extremely surprising: the Pleven Plan, proposed by the French in light of both the Korean conflict and rising fears of a new war in Europe, had been designed to deny West Germany an independent military force within the NATO framework, thus thwarting the country's "rearmament."[172] But shortly after the National Assembly rejected the EDC treaty, it met again to pass the Paris Treaties, which not only ended the Allied occupation of West Germany and formally approved a German-French compromise on the question of the Saar but also anticipated West Germany's admission into NATO, hence the creation of an independent West German military force.

What explains France's volte-face, its decision to act against its notion, developed in 1950, of an integrated European army and finally accept a rearmed Germany into the Western alliance, an option it had initially opposed? What had changed in France's relations with Germany over those four dramatic years? What path had France been forced to travel since 1944–45 until it was finally prepared, in 1954, to come to terms with the inevitable—a new power constellation in Europe and the world? Although politically speaking this development unfolded over barely a decade, historically speaking it represents a considerable journey. It took France out of the nineteenth and into the twentieth century.

France needed that decade to abandon the traditional political patterns of its relationship with Germany, its historical rival on the Continent, to seek a new "European" understanding with its eastern neighbor, against the backdrop of the nascent Cold War. At the end of the Second World War, France's double agenda of preserving its colonial empire and confirming its status as the dominant Continental power had impeded any such understanding. Especially among its allies, the defeat of 1940 and ensuing years of collaboration had damaged French repute. Free France under de Gaulle had not even been invited to the wartime Allied conferences—for the first time in its centuries-old history, France had not been included in the consultations of the great. It had played no part in the establishment of the new order—not in Casablanca, not in Teheran, not at Yalta, not in Potsdam. But following their maritime tradition, the British had been interested in confirming France's Continental role after the war; at Great

Britain's request, the French had thus been granted an occupation zone in Germany, as a kind of trophy they hardly deserved. For its part Russia, having achieved unprecedented power in Europe after 1945, had scant esteem for France, although Stalin and de Gaulle had concluded a pact in 1944 directed—like the pact between England and France signed at Dunkirk in March 1947—against possible German expansionism.[173] In actuality, such pacts mirrored past constellations, and in view of ongoing changes and challenges would soon prove worthless. Because of its in-between status as both an occupied, collaborating nation and a formally resisting nation, France had not been truly destroyed by the war. Now it sought to exploit the moment, bidding to extend past patterns into the future: Germany was prostrate and should never be allowed to regain hegemony in Europe.[174] As it had after 1918, France planned Germany's dismemberment. It raised the idea of a Rhenish Confederation in the Napoleonic tradition; the Rhine was in any case to be reaffirmed as Germany's western border. But against the opposition of wartime allies who wished to preserve Germany's unity, such ambitious demands could not be enacted; that being the case, then at least the potential economic power of France's historical rival was to be curtailed: the Ruhr and the Saar, coal and steel, it was hoped, would be completely removed from German control.

France resisted the policies of the other victorious powers. In the joint committees pondering Germany's present and future situation, the French delegates, still bound to *fin de siècle* and interwar patterns of political thinking, pursued obstructionist tactics. After 1945, France, the homeland of revolution, was oblivious to nascent ideological confrontation between the world powers. For a while, it could maintain such a stance. But a shift began to occur in 1947, owing not least of all to the dismal state of the French economy. France in fact depended on massive infusions of American aid beyond that provided through the Marshall Plan and soon found itself unable to escape the Cold War's political undercurrents. With the Communists' couplike seizure of power in Prague in February 1948, Western Europe was overtaken by a profound sense of foreboding. Nevertheless France continued to seek a special role for itself in the emerging institutions of the Western alliance, since, along with the East-West antagonism gripping Europe and the rest of the world, two questions from the past continued to absorb the republic: the question of its colonial empire and that of its relationship with Germany. In characteristic fashion, against the background of the unfolding ideological conflict, these questions coalesced.

Like France's colonial expansion in the last third of the nineteenth century, its "return" to Europe in the 1950s and 1960s was in many respects connected to its relations with Germany. After all, its intensified expansion abroad after both the founding of the German Empire at Versailles in 1871 and the accompanying loss of Alsace and Lorraine had partly served as compensation for having forfeited the Continental hegemony to which it had customarily laid claim. Pushed to the western periphery of Europe, it dedicated itself to constructing a colonial empire. Its orientation toward Africa in the early phase of the Third Republic had even been welcomed by Bismarck; he encouraged it as a kind of diversion from revanchism on the part of the recently defeated archenemy. In this respect, Bismarck was in basic harmony with leading politicians of the Third Republic. For example, Eugène Etienne, the statesman and proponent of colonial expansion, proclaimed in a campaign speech in Oran in 1885 that France had to gain respect overseas in order to be esteemed in Europe. Similarly, Léon Gambetta congratulated Jules Ferry on his occupation of Tunis by declaring that once again France was a great power.[175] But France's energetic expansion in Africa generated ill will and conflicts with England, culminating in 1898 with the confrontation at Fashoda, which led to the brink of war. Paradoxically, the Fashoda affair ended in a compromise paving the way for the entente cordiale and the wartime alliance between Europe's Western powers.

After 1945 France had no choice but to liquidate its colonial empire, closing a historical circle whose starting point was 1870–71. The circle was closed at a time when the emerging East-West conflict made it imperative to shore up and rearm the western half of a totally defeated Germany. In light of Russia's overwhelming might, the return of France — a traditional Continental power — to Europe and its finally reconciliation with West Germany were being pushed forward insistently by the West's two maritime powers: the American masters, together with the British, their tutors in European affairs. To be sure, this new constellation on the old Continent created a dilemma for France.[176] Following traditional patterns, it was seeking to realize an impossible configuration: Germany was to be stronger than Russia but weaker than France; France aspired to strength both with Germany and against it.[177] This wish could be fulfilled only by the permanent military presence on the Continent of France's Anglo-American allies. But they refused. Washington hoped to reduce its forces in Europe, while London, economically weakened and tired of its global responsibilities, saw itself as unable to enter into long-term commitments on the Continent in peacetime. It was generally assumed that only the newly founded Federal Republic could provide the military divisions lacking in Europe. France, however, was still not ready to accept an independent West German army in NATO. This is why, in view of the Korean War, it took refuge in defense minister René Pleven's plan:[178] the creation of a supranational European army including West German contingents but denying the Federal Republic any access to command. Until Pleven's fall in 1954, his plan — France's ceding of sovereignty over its own armed forces for the sake of a German defense contribution exceeding its own — weighed heavily on French domestic policy.[179]

The Pleven Plan and the ensuing EDC agreement were basically modeled on a proposal by French foreign minister Robert

Schuman. In the spring of 1950, the French government, adopting the proposal, laid out plans for a supranational common market for coal and steel.[180] The Montan Union (European Coal and Steel Community) of 1952 was the first step in the direction of European integration. Concluded between West Germany, France, Italy, and the Benelux countries, it seemed to fulfill Churchill's vision of a federated Europe, presented in Zurich in 1946. However, Britain's absence from the arrangement dampened the euphoria. At their inception, the plans for a supranational administration of coal and steel were in fact meant more as a provisional and preventive measure taken to domesticate an ever-stronger West Germany than as an altruistic step toward an integrated European future. But the denationalization of strategically important industries was, of course, not imposed on a defeated Germany alone: with the cancellation of the international Ruhr statute of 1948, which regulated coal and steel production, and the establishment of a high authority under Jean Monnet's direction, all the signatories to the treaty gave up effective national control over strategic resources. From a restrained punitive action against Germany, an authentic program of European integration had emerged. The key Western European players in 1950 thus sought to avoid the errors of 1919.

The generation of European politicians emerging after the war had come of age in the interwar era.[181] Above all, the events of 1923, when French and Belgian troops invaded the Ruhr in accordance with French prime minister Raymond Poincaré's "policy of productive pawns," comprised one of their key experiences. Their pursuit of a policy of European unification after World War II was in part a delayed reaction to the destructive nationalism of the past. It is striking that these leading "Europeans" were individuals who tended to belong to the cultural and geographical margins of their different polities: the Rhinelander Adenauer was suspected after World War I of separatist leanings; Robert Schuman, the scion of a Lorraine family, had been born in Luxembourg, raised

in German Alsace, and served during WWI in the German Imperial Army; and Alcide de Gasperi, from the irredentist region of
Trentino, has been formerly a deputy to the Austrian imperial
chamber in Vienna. Perhaps their particular origins and historical
experiences were reflected in their strong espousal of supranational European policies; in any event, in the Montan Union they
sought to defuse Franco-German discord through administrative
and economic measures.[182] The French had first introduced the
code word "Europeanization" to neutralize Germany's key industries, but with the membership of Italy and the Benelux countries,
it was generalized and linked conceptually with the idea of Europe.

While France was prepared to accept a certain loss of control over coal and steel, any forfeiture of its military prerogative
infringed on the heart of its sense of sovereignty. Since the 1951
election, the Gaullists, guardians of the nation and its colonial empire, had enjoyed massive representation in the National Assembly. In a rash of issues, European integration and considerations
of military security came into conflict. The very distinction between the French Republic and the Union Française raised the
problem of a command divided between troops stationed in
Europe and troops deployed in the colonies. De Gaulle cautioned
that the EDC project would split the French army and undermine
the French Union.[183] Because of its overseas commitments, France
would be unable to match German troop strength in Europe, that
is, to achieve a balance within the balance. But since the deployment of German forces was indispensable for the Americans, they
threatened Paris with an alternative strategy: the peripheral defense of Europe by means of an external ring, well suited to a
naval and air power, in the eastern Atlantic.[184] Furthermore, since
1953 the United States had been seeking to offset the lack of conventional forces on the Continent by developing and deploying
tactical nuclear weapons.

Ironically enough, the resort to atomic weaponry would later
afford France an escape from its dilemma vis-à-vis Germany. With

the signing of a decree on the establishment of the Commission supérieure des applications militaires by Mendès-France in October 1954 and a decision, probably reached earlier, in favor of nuclear arms, France seemingly eased its consent to West Germany's admission to NATO, as stipulated by the Paris treaties.[185] Since the Federal Republic had forsworn incorporation of nonconventional weapons into its arsenal on its own initiative, France's nuclear armament neutralized the conventional strength of its historical rival, at least symbolically. France's return to Europe and its accord with Germany in the framework of European institutions and the Western alliance were thus reinforced by nuclear means.[186]

In 1954, far fewer obstacles impeded West Germany's admission into NATO than in 1950. France had come to terms with the idea of a German defense contribution and felt more secure in NATO together with the United States and Britain than alone with West Germany in a European Defense Community. Britain's previous refusal to join a European army had been a crucial hindrance to French participation.[187] Also, France now had greater trust in the German state. The nationalist silver lining contained in the so-called Stalin Note of 10 March 1952, in which the dictator proposed a unified—and fully neutral—Germany nearly forty years before unification would actually occur had not seduced the West Germans; they seemed much more strongly attracted by the prospect of Western integration under an aegis of freedom than by that of national unification in an uncertain future. Moreover, they were reacting to imposed political and national restrictions as more of a blessing than a burden. The boom triggered by the war in Korea propelled West German's economy to new heights, laying the foundations of what in retrospect can be viewed as a "golden age" for its citizens.[188]

From a historical perspective, the Cold War era was, paradoxically, an age of great neutralizations. The ideological confrontation between East and West and the distinction between friend and foe based on social values and principles—so similar to civil war—annulled the traditional political meaning of national memories inherited from the late nineteenth century and the interwar period. Long-standing conflicts, rivalries, and animosities were crushed beneath the opposition between blocs. Residues of old European particularism in the various national political cultures were neutralized by the Soviet threat, the presence of the United States, and the European institutions germinating in the biotope of the Cold War. In contrast to the interwar years, when America withdrew and left the Europeans to their own devices, the United States now attempted to preserve Europe not only from freedom's ideological antithesis—the ideal of literal equality promoted by Soviet-style Communism—but also from itself. Washington had promoted the EDC project in considerable measure to effect a historical compromise between (West) Germany and France. A fundamental transformation had been imposed on the polities of Western Europe by the Soviet threat, the impact of America's protective shield, and the paradigm of European integration. Its results show that the Cold War was a powerful historical accelerator. From being a cauldron of nationalism and war, Western Europe became a domain of international compromise and prosperity. Such success was probably due to the Atlantic Revolution and its universal republican sponsor—the United States. Atlantic values and ways of life thus took possession of the Continental European polities, civilizing their institutions. Of these, the Federal Republic of Germany was certainly the most profoundly altered. Simply by virtue of its division, Germany was denied the possibility of constituting itself as a *nation*. It found itself in the altogether providential situation of being exclusively a *society*. It was precisely this feature of the old Federal Republic that allowed the West German polity, more than any other in Europe, to internalize the structural and institutional effects of the external neutralization process.

The great neutralizing of previous history through the agency of the Cold War was brought about by the language and organizations of economics. It was much easier to regulate differences, enmities, and conflicts in an integrative process grounded in *quantifying* semantics and symbolism than in questions of grand politics and national security, which involved fundamental principles and existential motives. In this manner, the European Economic Community, set up in Rome in 1957, provided a far more solid and durable foundation for Europe's gradual unification than the admirable but abortive EDC. The neutralization of Europe's differences probably took the only viable course: it emigrated from the center—from politics, which had been contaminated by the legacy of history—to the periphery, the realm of economics. There, for decades, it practiced that forgetting of diverse pasts that makes politics possible in the first place. Having now crossed the threshold into another century, Europe will probably have urgent need of the reserves accrued from the successes of an era that itself has become history.

Acknowledgments

This book is obliged to many. When it saw light in German in the year 1999, it was by and large the outcome of my teaching on the twentieth century at the history departments of the universities of Essen and of Tel Aviv in the mid-1990s. To a wider academic audience the subject matter was presented during my stay as a visiting professor at the Ludwig-Maximilians-University, Munich, in early 1997. The book was written during a sabbatical in 1997–98 at the Internationales Forschungszentrum Kulturwissenschaften in Vienna. Concerning the original version I owe a dept of gratitude to Dirk Blasius, John Bunzl, Detlev Claussen, Justus Cobet, Saul Friedländer, Avi Glezerman, Liliane Granierer, Andreas Heldrich, Markus Kirchhoff, Paul Mendes-Flohr, Lutz Musner, Iris Nahum, Susan Neiman, Moshe Postone, Anson Rabinbach, Florian Riedler, Christiane Schmidt, Bruno Schoch, Paola Traverso, Gotthard Wunberg, Zvi Yavetz, and Moshe Zimmermann.

The translation from German to English was not an easy task. I am particularly thankful to William Templer, and owe my gratitude as well to Carl Ebert and George Williamson. Special thanks to Joel Golb for his deep understanding of the cultural complexities with languages. Much appreciation goes to John Tortorice of the George L. Mosse Program, who made the publication possible with the University of Wisconsin Press.

This publication was supported by the Simon Dubnow Institute for Jewish History and Culture at Leipzig University and the

Franz Rosenzweig Research Centre for German-Jewish Literature and Cultural History at the Hebrew University of Jerusalem. Last but not least I would like to thank Robert Zwarg for his support in the final preparation of the manuscript and proofreading assistance.

Notes

Introduction

1. Niel Ascherson, *Black Sea* (London: Cape, 1995).

2. John H. Clapham, ed., *John Brunton's Book: Being the Memories of John Brunton Engineer* (Cambridge: University Press, 1939), 68–69, quoted in Justus Cobet, "Troja vor Schliemann," in *Heinrich Schliemann nach hundert Jahren,* ed. William M. Calder and Justus Cobet (Frankfurt am Main: Klostermann, 1990), 143–44.

3. Egmont Zechlin, "Die türkischen Meerengen—ein Brennpunkt der Weltgeschichte," *Geschichte in Wissenschaft und Unterricht* 17 (1966): 1–31.

4. Halford J. Mackinder, "The Geographical Pivot of History," *Geographical Journal* 23 (1904): 421–37.

5. Christoph V. Albrecht, *Geopolitik und Geschichtsphilosophie* (Berlin: Akademie-Verlag, 1998), 3.

6. François Hartog, *Le miroir d'Hérodote: Essai sur la représentation de l'autre* (Paris: Gallimard, 1980).

7. Gerhard Schulz, *Revolutionen und Friedensschlüsse 1917–1920* (Munich: Deutscher Taschenbuch Verlag, 1967).

8. Ivan T. Berend, *The Crisis Zone of Europe: An Interpretation of East-Central European History in the First Half of the Twentieth Century* (Cambridge: Cambridge University Press, 1986).

9. Albert Sorel, *The Eastern Question in the Eighteenth Century: The Partition of Poland and the Treaty of Kainardji* (1889; repr., New York: Fertig, 1969).

10. Michael Geyer, "Das Stigma der Gewalt und das Problem der nationalen Identität in Deutschland," in *Von der Aufgabe der Freiheit: Politische Verantwortung und bürgerliche Gesellschaft im 19. und 20. Jahrhundert. Festschrift für Hans Mommsen zum 5. November 1995,* ed. Christian Jansen, Lutz

Niethammer, and Bernd Weisbrod, 673–98 (Berlin: Akademie-Verlag, 1995), 692–93.

Chapter 1. Interpretations: Two Varieties of Universal Civil War

1. Ernst Jünger, *Tagebücher*, in his *Werke*, vol. 2 (Stuttgart: Klett, 1962), 433.

2. On the history of the concept, see Hanno Kesting, *Geschichtsphilosophie und Weltbürgerkrieg* (Heidelberg: Winter, 1959); Reinhart Koselleck, *Critique and Crisis: Enlightenment and the Pathogenesis of Modern Society* (Oxford: Berg, 1988); Emile M. Ciorcan, *Histoire et Utopie* (Paris: Gallimard, 1960); Ernst Nolte, "Weltbürgerkrieg 1917–1989," in *Totalitarismus im 20. Jahrhundert: Eine Bilanz der internationalen Forschung*, ed. Eckhard Jesse, 357–69 (Baden-Baden: Nomos, 1996).

3. Lothar Kettenacker, "'Unconditional Surrender' als Grundlage der angelsächsischen Nachkriegsplanung," in *Der Zweite Weltkrieg: Analysen, Grundzüge, Forschungsbilanz*, ed. Wolfgang Michalka, 174–88 (Munich: Piper, 1989); Alfred Vagts, "Unconditional Surrender—vor und nach 1945," *Vierteljahrshefte für Zeitgeschichte* 7 (1959): 280–309.

4. Franklin D. Roosevelt, *Complete Presidential Press Conferences*, vols. 21–22 (New York: Da Capo Press, 1972), 88.

5. Carl Schmitt, *Der Nomos der Erde im Völkerrecht des Jus Publicum Europaeum* (Cologne: Greven, 1950), 215.

6. Roman Schnur, "Weltfriedensidee und Weltbürgerkrieg 1791/92," in his *Revolution und Weltbürgerkrieg: Studien zur Ouverture nach 1789*, 11–32 (Berlin: Duncker & Humblot, 1983).

7. For a different perspective, see Kesting, *Geschichtsphilosophie und Weltbürgerkrieg*, 231ff.

8. G. W. F. Hegel, *The Philosophy of History*, trans. J. Sibree (New York: Dover, 1956), 86.

9. Knud Krakau, *Missionsbewußtsein und Völkerrechtsdoktrin in den Vereinigten Staaten von Amerika* (Frankfurt am Main: Metzner, 1967).

10. See Hannah Arendt, *On Revolution* (New York: Viking, 1963), 13ff.

11. On this double concept of history, see Reinhart Koselleck, *Futures Past: On the Semantics of Historical Time* (Cambridge, Mass.: MIT Press, 1985), 92ff.

12. Walter Grab, *Ein Volk muß seine Freiheit selbst erobern: Zur Geschichte der deutschen Jakobiner* (Frankfurt am Main: Büchergilde Gutenberg, 1984), 167ff.

13. Heinz Gollwitzer, *Geschichte des weltpolitischen Denkens*, vol. 1, *Vom Zeitalter der Entdeckungen bis zum Beginn des Imperialismus* (Göttingen: Vandenhoeck & Ruprecht, 1972), 101–2.

14. Winfried Baumgart, *Vom europäischen Konzert zum Völkerbund. Friedensschlüsse und Friedenssicherung von Wien bis Versailles* (Darmstadt: Wissenschaftliche Buchgesellschaft, 1974).

15. Henry A. Kissinger, *A World Restored: Metternich, Castlereagh and the Problems of Peace 1812–22* (London: Mifflin, 1957), 41ff.

16. Arno J. Mayer, *Politics and Diplomacy of Peacemaking: Containment and Counterrevolution at Versailles 1918–1919* (London: Weidenfeld & Nicolson, 1968), 5.

17. Ludwig Dehio, *The Precarious Balance: Four Centuries of the European Power Struggle* (New York: Alfred A. Knopf, 1962), 180.

18. Carl Schmitt, "Clausewitz als politischer Denker: Bemerkungen und Hinweise," *Der Staat* 6 (1967): 479ff.

19. Geoffrey Best, *War and Society in Revolutionary Europe 1770–1870* (London: Leicester University Press, 1982).

20. John Keegan and Richard Holmes, *Soldiers: A History of Men in Battle* (London: Hamilton, 1985), 148–49.

21. James M. McPherson, *Battle Cry of Freedom: The Civil War Era* (New York: Oxford University Press, 1988); Hans Delbrück, *Geschichte der Kriegskunst* (1920; Berlin: de Gruyter, 1962).

22. Theodor Schieder, "Idee und Gestalt des übernationalen Staates seit dem 19. Jahrhundert," in *Nationalismus und Nationalstaat: Studien zum nationalen Problem im modernen Europa*, ed. Otto Dann and Hans-Ulrich Wehler, 38–64 (Göttingen: Vandenhoeck & Ruprecht, 1992).

23. Gordon A. Craig, *Europe since 1815*, 2nd ed. (New York: Holt, Rinehart & Winston, 1966) 11ff.

24. Robert Gildea, *Barricades and Borders: Europe 1800–1914* (London: Oxford University Press, 1987), 96ff.

25. Robert A. Kann, *The Multinational Empire: Nationalism and National Reform in the Habsburg Monarchy, 1848–1918*, vol. 2, *Empire Reform* (New York: Octagon Books, 1950), 3ff.

26. Eric Hobsbawm, *The Age of Capital, 1848–1875* (New York: Scribner, 1975), 9ff.

27. Dehio, *Precarious Balance*, 202ff.

28. Matthew S. Anderson, *The Eastern Question, 1774–1923: A Study in International Relations* (London: Macmillan, 1966); Rostislav Andreyevich Fadeyev, *Die Entwicklung der orientalischen Frage* (Leipzig: Prochaska, 1871);

Edouard Driault, *La question d'Orient depuis ses origines jusqu'à nos jours* (Paris: F. Alcan, 1898).

29. Leopold von Ranke, "Geschichte Serbiens bis 1842" (3rd ed. of *Die Serbische Revolution*, 1829), in *Serbien und die Türkei im neunzehnten Jahrhundert: Leopold von Rankes sämtliche Werke*, vols. 43–44 (Leipzig: Duncker & Humblot, 1879).

30. Ernst Flachbarth, *System des internationalen Minderheitenschutzes* (Budapest: Gergely, 1937), 12.

31. R. Cromer, "Die Sonderrechte der Polen in Preußen in der ersten Hälfte des 19. Jahrhunderts," *Nation und Staat* 6 (1922/23): 613; Klaus Zernack, *Polen und Rußland: Zwei Wege in der europäischen Geschichte* (Berlin: Propyläen, 1994), 316; *Recueil des traités, conventions et actes diplomatiques concernant la Pologne 1762–1782 par le comte d'Angeberg* [pseudonym for Leonard Chodzko] (Paris: Amyot, 1862), 688–89, 693.

32. Kissinger, *World Restored*, 286ff.

33. Dietrich Beyrau, *Russische Orientpolitik und die Entstehung des deutschen Kaiserreiches 1866–1870/71* (Wiesbaden: Harrassowitz, 1974).

34. Francis R. Bridge, *From Sadowa to Sarajevo: The Foreign Policy of Austro-Hungary, 1866–1914* (London: Routledge & Kegan Paul, 1972).

35. Robert William Seton-Watson, *The Southern Slav Question and the Habsburg Monarchy* (London: Constable, 1911).

36. Charles Jelavich, *Tsarist Russia and Balkan Nationalism* (Berkeley: University of California Press, 1958).

37. Charles Jelavich and Barbara Jelavich, *The Establishment of the Balkan National States, 1804–1920* (Seattle: University of Washington Press, 1977).

38. Baumgart, *Vom europäischen Konzert*, 27–28.

39. The Carnegie Commission of Investigation, *Report of the International Commission to Inquire into the Causes and Conduct of the Balkan Wars* (Washington, 1914), is still impressive for its wealth of material.

40. Immanuel Geiss, *German Foreign Policy, 1871–1914* (London: Routledge & Kegan Paul, 1976); Johannes Burkhardt et al., eds., *Lange und kurze Wege in den Ersten Weltkrieg: Vier Augsburger Beiträge zur Kriegsursachenforschung* (Munich: Vögel, 1996).

41. Anderson, *Eastern Question*, 287ff.

42. Richard von Kühlmann, *Erinnerungen* (Heidelberg: Schneider, 1948), 565.

43. Jehuda L. Wallach, *The Dogma of the Battle of Annihilation: The Theories of Clausewitz and Schlieffen and Their Impact on the German Conduct of Two World Wars* (Westport, Conn.: Greenwood Press, 1986), 56.

44. Gerald D. Feldman, *Army, Industry and Labor in Germany, 1914–1918* (Princeton, N.J.: Princeton University Press, 1966), 168ff.; on the social impact of the war, see Jürgen Kocka, *Klassengesellschaft im Krieg: Deutsche Sozialgeschichte 1914–1918* (Göttingen: Vandenhoeck & Ruprecht, 1973), 21–22, 105–6.

45. On the concept of civil war, see Reinhart Koselleck, "Revolution, Rebellion, Aufruhr, Bürgerkrieg," in *Geschichtliche Grundbegriffe: Historisches Lexikon zur politisch-sozialen Sprache in Deutschland*, vol. 5 (Stuttgart: Klett, 1984), 653–788.

46. Karl Dietrich Bracher, *Europa in der Krise: Innengeschichte und Weltpolitik seit 1917* (Frankfurt am Main: Ullstein, 1979), 127–28.

47. Peter Grupp, "Deutsche Schriftsteller im Ersten Weltkrieg," in *Der Erste Weltkrieg: Wirkung, Wahrnehmung, Analyse,* ed. Wolfgang Michalka, 825–48 (Munich: Piper, 1994).

48. Modris Eksteins, *Rites of Spring: The Great War and the Birth of the Modern Age* (Boston: Houghton Mifflin, 1989), 90ff.

49. On Franco-German relations, see Michael Jeismann, *Das Vaterland der Feinde: Studien zum nationalen Feindbegriff und Selbstverständnis in Deutschland und Frankreich, 1792–1918* (Stuttgart: Klett-Cotta, 1992), 299ff.

50. Rolf Peter Sieferle, "Der deutsch-englische Gegensatz und die 'Ideen von 1914,'" in *Das kontinentale Europa und die britischen Inseln,* ed. Gottfried Niedhart, 139–60 (Mannheim: Palatium-Verlag, 1993).

51. Eksteins, *Rites of Spring,* 88–89.

52. Ernst Stenzel, *Die Kriegsführung des deutschen Imperialismus und das Völkerrecht* (Berlin: Militärverlag der DDR, 1973), 32.

53. Werner Hahlweg, *Lenins Rückkehr nach Rußland* (Leiden: Brill, 1957), 10; Winfried B. Scharlau and Zbynek A. Zeman, *The Merchant of Revolution: The Life of Alexander Israel Helphand (Parvus) 1867–1924* (London: Oxford University Press, 1965), 207–8.

54. Eksteins, *Rites of Spring,* 132.

55. Ibid., 94.

56. Reinhard Rürup, "Der Geist von 1914 in Deutschland: Kriegsbegeisterung und Ideologisierung des Krieges im Ersten Weltkrieg," in *Ansichten vom Krieg. Vergleichende Studien zum Ersten Weltkrieg in Literatur und Gesellschaft,* ed. Bernd Hüppauf, 4ff. (Königstein im Taunus: Forum Academicum, 1984).

57. On the cultural presence of the war and each side's perception of the other, see Paul Fussel, *The Great War in Modern Memory* (London: Oxford University Press, 1975), 75ff.; George L. Mosse, *Fallen Soldiers: Reshaping the Memory of the World Wars* (New York: Oxford University Press,

1990), 70ff.; Jay Winter, *Sites of Memory, Sites of Mourning: The Great War in European Cultural History* (Cambridge: Cambridge University Press, 1995), 204–5.

58. Eksteins, *Rites of Spring*, 185.

59. Jost Dülffer, "Kriegserwartung und Kriegsbild in Deutschland vor 1914," in *Der Erste Weltkrieg*, ed. Michalka, 778–98; Marc Ferro, *The Great War, 1914–1918* (Boston: Routledge & Kegan Paul, 1982), 26; Ivan S. Bloch, *The Future of War in Its Economic and Political Relations: Is War Now Possible?* (New York: Doubleday & McClure, 1899).

60. Hoffmann Nickerson, "Nineteenth-Century Military Techniques," *Cahiers d'histoire mondiale* 4 (1958): 348–58.

61. Ferro, *Great War*, 85ff.

62. Alfred Vagts, *A History of Militarism: Civilian and Military* (New York: Free Press, 1967), 224–25.

63. P. G. Razzall, "Social Origins of Army Officers," *British Journal of Sociology* 14 (1963): 253; Paul-Marie de la Gore, *The French Army: A Military Political History* (London: Weidenfeld & Nicolson, 1963), 35.

64. Michael Howard, "Men against Fire: The Doctrine of the Offensive in 1914," in *Makers of Modern Strategy: From Machiavelli to the Nuclear Age*, ed. Peter Paret, 510–26 (Princeton, N.J.: Princeton University Press, 1986).

65. Anthony Farrar-Hockley, *The Somme* (London: Pan, 1966), 122–23.

66. Werner Sombart, *Händler und Helden: Patriotische Besinnungen* (Munich: Duncker & Humblot, 1915), 48.

67. Michael Geyer, "German Strategy in the Age of Machine Warfare, 1914–1945," in Paret, *Makers of Modern Strategy*, 527–97.

68. David Jones, *In Parenthesis* (London: Faber & Faber, 1982), 9, quoted in Eksteins, *Rites of Spring*, 211.

69. Ernst Jünger, *The Storm of Steel: From the Diary of a German Storm-Troop Officer on the Western Front* (1929; repr., London: Constable, 1994), 110.

70. John Ellis, *The Social History of the Machine Gun* (London: Croom Helm, 1975), 111ff.; William H. McNeill, *The Pursuit of Power: Technology, Armed Force and Society since A.D. 1000* (Oxford: Blackwell, 1983).

71. In his book treating the war, *Geschichte als Sinngebung des Sinnlosen* (Munich: Beck, 1919), 98ff., Theodor Lessing describes the effects of a novel spatial distance between the soldier at the front, aware only of the immediate site of combat, and war reporting, furnishing him with a view of his situation.

72. Ferro, *Great War*, 75ff.

73. Ellis, *Social History of the Machine Gun*, 142.

74. Ibid., 120.

75. Basil H. Liddell-Hart, *Foch: Man of Orleans* (Harmondsworth: Penguin, 1937), 1:76, quoted in Ellis, *Social History of the Machine Gun*, 54–55.

76. Barbara Tuchman, *August 1914* (London: New English Library, 1964), 216.

77. Ellis, *Social History of the Machine Gun*, 17.

78. Ibid., 113ff.

79. Rolf Wirtgen, "Zur Geschichte und Technik der automatischen Waffen im 19. Jahrhundert," in *Militär und Technik: Wechselbeziehungen zu Staat, Gesellschaft und Industrie im 19. und 20. Jahrhundert,* ed. Roland-Götz Foerster and Heinrich Walle, 99–120 (Herford: Mittler, 1992); Manfred Lachmann, "Zur Entwicklung und zum Einsatz des Maschinengewehrs," *Militärgeschichte* 12 (1973): 720–30.

80. Ellis, *Social History of the Machine Gun*, 74.

81. Graham Seton Hutchison, *Machine Guns: Their History and Tactical Employment* (London: Macmillan, 1938), 41ff.

82. Ellis, *Social History of the Machine Gun*, 79ff.

83. Ferro, *Great War*, 75ff.

84. Ellis, *Social History of the Machine Gun*, 85–86.

85. Ibid., 94.

86. On the problem of equality, see Albert Memmi, *The Colonizer and the Colonized* (1957; Boston: Beacon Press, 1991).

87. Detlev Claussen, *Die List der Gewalt: Soziale Revolutionen und ihre Theorien* (Frankfurt am Main: Campus, 1982), 135ff., 194ff.

88. Omer Bartov, "Man and Mass: Reality and the Heroic Image of War," *History & Memory* 1 (1989): 99–122.

89. Ferro, *Great War*, 93ff.

90. Walther von Schultzendorff, *Proletarier und Prätorianer: Bürgerkriegssituation aus der Frühzeit der Weimarer Republik* (Cologne: Markus-Verlag, 1966).

91. Hagen Schulze, *Freikorps und Republik, 1918–1920* (Boppard: Boldt, 1969).

92. "Wanderers into the void" is the title of a novel by Friedrich Freksa, *Wanderer ins Nichts* (Munich: Müller, 1920).

93. Gabriele Krüger, *Die Brigade Ehrhardt* (Hamburg: Leibniz-Verlag, 1971), 28ff.

94. Dominik Venner, *Ein deutscher Heldenkampf: Die Geschichte der Frei-korps, 1918–1923. Söldner ohne Sold* (Kiel: Arndt, 1989), 123.

95. Claus Grimm, *Jahre deutscher Entscheidung im Baltikum, 1918/1919* (Essen: Essener Verlagsanstalt, 1939), 341–42.

96. Ernst von Salomon, *Die Geächteten* (Berlin: Rowohlt, 1930), 167.

97. Edgar Anderson, "Die baltische Frage und die internationale Politik der alliierten und assoziierten Mächte 1918–1921," in *Von den baltischen Provinzen zu den baltischen Staaten: Beiträge zur Entstehungsgeschichte der Republiken Estland und Lettland 1918–1920*, ed. Jürgen von Hehn, Hans von Rismscha, and Hellmuth Weiss, 327–77 (Marburg: Herder-Institut, 1977); Stanley W. Page, *The Formation of the Baltic States: A Study of the Effects of Great Power Politics upon the Emergence of Lithuania, Latvia, and Estonia* (Cambridge, Mass.: Harvard University Press, 1959).

98. Georg von Rauch, *Geschichte der baltischen Staaten* (Stuttgart: Kohlhammer, 1970), 50ff.

99. Sigmar Stopinski, *Das Baltikum im Patt der Mächte* (Berlin: Berlin-Verlag Spitz, 1997), 181ff.

100. Fritz Fischer, *Germany's Aims in the First World War* (London: Chatto & Windus, 1967), 460ff.

101. Helmut Altrichter, *Rußland 1917: Ein Land auf der Suche nach sich selbst* (Paderborn: Schöningh, 1997), 421.

102. Walter Laqueur, *Russia and Germany: A Century of Conflict* (London: Weidenfeld & Nicolson, 1965), 56ff.

103. Ernst Nolte, *Der europäische Bürgerkrieg, 1917–1945: Nationalsozialismus und Bolschewismus* (Frankfurt am Main: Propyläen, 1987), 106ff.

104. Schulze, *Freikorps und Republik*, 332.

105. On the ethnic tenor of the term "Bolshevism" in the Baltic region, see Rauch, *Geschichte der baltischen Staaten*, 55–56.

106. Schulze, *Freikorps und Republik*, 329.

107. Krüger, *Die Brigade Ehrhardt*, 38ff.

108. Laqueur, *Russia and Germany*, 176–77.

109. "Freiheit," in *Geschichtliche Grundbegriffe*, 2:425–542; on freedom and equality, cf. 531ff. (Christoph Dipper).

110. "Gleichheit," in *Geschichtliche Grundbegriffe*, 997–1046 (Otto Dahn).

111. Heinz Gollwitzer, *Geschichte des weltpolitischen Denkens*, vol. 2, *Zeitalter des Imperialismus und der Weltkriege* (Göttingen: Vandenhoeck & Ruprecht, 1982), 83ff.

112. Alfred Th. Mahan, *Der Einfluss der Seemacht auf die Geschichte*, vol. 2, *1783–1912: Die Zeit der Französischen Revolution und des Kaiserreichs* (1899; repr., Kassel: Hamecher, 1974), 25–26.

113. Dehio, *Precarious Balance*, 93ff.

114. Carl Schmitt, *Land and Sea* (Washington, D.C.: Plutarch Press, 1997); Roman Schnur, "Land und Meer—Napoleon gegen England: Ein Kapitel der Geschichte internationaler Politik," in his *Revolution und Weltbürgerkrieg*, 33–58.

115. Giulio Douhet, *Luftherrschaft* (Berlin: Drei Masken-Verlag, 1935); John Bucklez, *Air Power in the Age of Total War* (Bloomington: Indiana University Press, 1999).

116. Jörg Friedrich, *Das Gesetz des Krieges: Das deutsche Heer in Rußland, 1941 bis 1945* (Munich: Piper, 1995), 883ff.

117. Ernst Fraenkel, "Martial Law und Staatsnotstand in England und USA," in his *Der Staatsnotstand* (Berlin: Colloquium Verlag, 1965), 138ff.; Hans Boldt, "Der Ausnahmezustand in historischer Perspektive," *Der Staat* 6 (1967): 409ff.

118. Robert R. Palmer, *The Age of Democratic Revolution*, vol. 1 (Princeton, N.J.: Princeton University Press, 1959), 5–6.

119. Erwin Hölzle, "Formverwandlung der Geschichte: Das Jahr 1917," *Saeculum* 6 (1955): 329–44.

120. Henry A. Kissinger, *Diplomacy* (New York: Simon & Schuster, 1994), 78ff.

121. Dehio, *Precarious Balance*, 183ff.

122. Richard Pipes, *Russia under the Bolshevik Regime, 1919–1924* (London: Harvill, 1994), 63ff.

123. John L. Gaddis, *Russia, the Soviet Union, and the United States: An Interpretative History* (New York: McGraw-Hill, 1990), 51–52.

124. W. Wilson, "Speech to Congress, April 1917," in *American Perspectives: The United States in the Modern Age*, ed. Carl Bode, 52–53 (Washington, D.C.: United States Information Agency, 1990).

125. Thomas Knock, *To End All Wars: Woodrow Wilson and the Quest for a New World Order* (New York: Oxford University Press, 1992), 140–41.

126. Dietrich Geyer, "Wilson und Lenin: Ideologie und Friedenssicherung in Osteuropa 1917–1919," *Jahrbücher für Geschichte Osteuropas* 3 (1955): 431–41.

127. Thomas Masaryk, *The Making of a State: Memories and Observations, 1914–1918* (London: Allen & Unwin, 1927).

128. Point 13 called for an independent Poland, "which should include the territories inhabited by indisputably Polish populations."

129. Paul Kluke, *Selbstbestimmung: Vom Weg der Idee durch die Geschichte* (Göttingen: Vandenhoeck & Ruprecht, 1963), 73.

130. Erwin Viefhaus, *Die Minderheitenfrage und die Entstehung der Minderheitenschutzverträge auf der Pariser Friedenskonferenz: Eine Studie zur Geschichte des Nationalitätenproblems im 19. und 20. Jahrhundert* (Würzburg: Holzner, 1960).

131. Ibid., 193ff.; Kluke, *Selbstbestimmung*, 90.

132. Pawel Korzec, "Polen und der Minderheitenschutzvertrag 1919–1934," *Jahrbücher für Geschichte Osteuropas* 22 (1974): 515–55.

133. Cf. the statement by the Brazilian representative at a council meeting of the League of Nations in December 1925, which was endorsed by representatives of other Western countries. On this, see Viefhaus, *Die Minderheitenfrage und die Entstehung der Minderheitenschutzverträge*, 204.

134. W. Roger Louis, *Imperialism at Bay 1941–1945: The United States and the Decolonization of the British Empire* (Oxford: Clarendon Press, 1977), 121ff. The Atlantic Charter would form the basis for the 1945 charter of the United Nations.

135. "Atlantic Charter," Dept. of State Executive Agreement Series, no. 236.

136. Jürgen Lütt, "'Übertragung der Macht' oder 'Sieg im Freiheitskampf'? Der Weg zur indischen Unabhängigkeit," in *Das Ende der Kolonialreiche: Dekolonisation und die Politik der Großmächte*, ed. Wolfgang J. Mommsen (Frankfurt am Main: Fischer Taschenbuch Verlag, 1990), 47–66.

137. Detlef Junker, *Der unteilbare Weltmarkt: Die ökonomischen Interessen in der Außenpolitik der USA 1933–1941* (Stuttgart: Klett, 1975). Specifically, the charter speaks of "the enjoyment by all States, great or small, victor or vanquished, of access, on equal terms, to the trade and to the raw materials of the world which are needed for their economic prosperity."

138. Warren F. Kimball, "The Atlantic Charter: 'With All Deliberate Speed,'" in *The Atlantic Charter*, ed. Douglas Brinkley, 83–114 (London: Macmillan, 1994).

139. Gabriel Gorodetsky, *The Precarious Truce: Anglo-Soviet Relations, 1924–1927* (Cambridge: Cambridge University Press, 1977), 247.

140. Francis Fukuyama, *The End of History and the Last Man* (New York: Macmillan, 1992).

141. Margret Boveri, *Treason in the Twentieth Century* (New York: Putnam, 1963), 51ff.

142. *Raum*, or "space," is a key category in National Socialist cultural-geographic, geopolitical, and economic-geographic theory.

143. Hermann Graml, *Europa zwischen den Kriegen* (Munich: Deutscher Taschenbuch Verlag, 1982), 307ff. At Stresa in April 1935, Mussolini joined France and Britain in condemning breaches of the Versailles treaty; the general message of the Stresa agreements was that these three powers constituted an anti-German front. See Peter Calvocoressi, Guy Wint, and John Pritchard, *Total War: The Causes and Courses of the Second World War*, vol. 1 (London: Viking, 1989), 72.

144. Teddy J. Uldricks, "Soviet Security Policy in the 1930s," in *Soviet Foreign Policy, 1917–1991: A Retrospective*, ed. Gabriel Gorodetsky, 65–74 (London: Cass, 1994), 66ff.

145. Gerald Howson, *Arms for Spain: The Untold Story of the Spanish Civil War* (London: Murray, 1998).

146. Walther L. Bernecker, *Krieg in Spanien 1936–1939* (Darmstadt: Wissenschaftliche Buchgesellschaft, 1991), 49–50.

147. Hugh D. Ford, *A Poet's War: British Poets and the Spanish Civil War* (Philadelphia: University of Pennsylvania Press, 1965).

148. Hans-Henning Abendroth, "Hitlers Entscheidung," in *Der Spanische Bürgerkrieg in der internationalen Politik 1936–1939*, ed. Wolfgang Schieder and Christoph Dipper, 76–128 (Munich: Nymphenburger Verlagshandlung, 1976), 98ff.

149. Hans-Henning Abendroth, *Hitler in der spanischen Arena: Die deutsch-spanischen Beziehungen im Spannungsfeld der europäischen Interessenpolitik vom Ausbruch des Bürgerkrieges bis zum Ausbruch des Weltkrieges 1936–1939* (Paderborn: Schöningh, 1973), 41.

150. Robert H. Whealey, *Hitler and Spain: The Nazi Role in the Spanish Civil War, 1936–1939* (Lexington: University Press of Kentucky, 1989), 26ff.

151. Bernecker, *Krieg in Spanien*, 70.

152. W. Schieder and C. Dipper, "Einleitung," in *Der Spanische Bürgerkrieg*, ed. Schieder and Dipper, 7–52, see esp. 13ff.

153. Hugh Thomas, *The Spanish Civil War* (London: Eyre & Spottiswoode 1961), 612ff.

154. Nathanael Greene, *Crisis and Decline: The French Socialist Party in the Popular Front Era* (Ithaca, N.Y.: Cornell Univeristy Press, 1969), 78–79.

155. Maurice Agulhon, *The French Republic, 1879–1992* (Oxford: Blackwell, 1995), 232–33.

156. Adam B. Ulam, *Expansion and Coexistence: The History of Soviet Foreign Policy, 1917–1967* (London: Secker & Warburg, 1968), 209ff.

157. Gottfried Niedhardt, "Britisch-sowjetische Gegensätze 1936/37," in *Der Spanische Bürgerkrieg*, ed. Schieder and Dipper, 275–89.

158. Thomas, *Spanish Civil War*, 214ff.

159. François Furet, *The Passing of an Illusion: The Idea of Communism in the Twentieth Century* (Chicago: University of Chicago Press, 1999), 35.

Chapter 2. Conversions: Nation and Revolution

1. Still useful is Arno J. Mayer's copiously documented *Politics and Diplomacy of Peacemaking: Containment and Counterrevolution at Versailles, 1918–1919* (London: Weidenfeld & Nicolson, 1968), 23.

2. Eric Hobsbawm, *The Age of Extremes: A History of the World, 1914–1991* (New York: Vintage Books, 1996), 8.

3. François Furet, *The Passing of an Illusion: The Idea of Communism in the Twentieth Century* (Chicago: University of Chicago Press, 1999), 60–61.

4. Recently esp. Helmut Altrichter, *Rußland 1917: Ein Land auf der Suche nach sich selbst* (Paderborn: Schöningh 1997), 25ff.; an overview is provided in Dietrich Geyer, *Die Russische Revolution: Historische Probleme und Perspektiven* (Göttingen: Vandenhoeck & Ruprecht, 1985).

5. Werner Hahlweg, *Der Diktatfrieden von Brest-Litowsk* (Münster: Aschendorff, 1960), 51.

6. Richard Pipes, *The Russian Revolution* (New York: Knopf, 1990), 278–79.

7. Altrichter, *Rußland 1917*, 325–26.

8. Pipes, *Russian Revolution*, 588–89.

9. Fritz Fischer, *Germany's Aims in the First World War* (London: Chatto & Windus, 1967), 477; Winfried Baumgart, *Deutsche Ostpolitik 1918* (Vienna: Oldenbourg, 1966).

10. John F. N. Bradley, *Allied Intervention in Russia [1917–1920]* (London: Weidenfeld & Nicolson, 1968), 25.

11. Pipes, *Russian Revolution*, 598.

12. Bradley, *Allied Intervention in Russia*, 24ff.; Fischer, *Germany's Aims in the First World War*, 484–85.

13. Pipes, *Russian Revolution*, 612ff.

14. George F. Kennan, *Soviet-American Relations, 1917–1920*, vol. 1, *Russia Leaves the War* (Princeton, N.J.: Princeton University Press, 1956), 92–93.

15. Bradley, *Allied Intervention in Russia*, 9.

16. Richard Ullman, *Anglo-Soviet Relations, 1917–1921*, vol. 1, *Intervention and the War* (Princeton, N.J.: Princeton University Press, 1961), 74.

17. Altrichter, *Rußland 1917*, 399ff.

18. Richard Pipes, *Russia under the Bolshevik Regime, 1919–1924* (London: Harvill, 1994), 146ff.

19. The Allies were certainly cognizant of the nexus between defeat and revolution. See, for example, Ferdinand Foch, *Mémoires pour servir a l'histoire de la guerre de 1914–1918*, vol. 1 (Paris: Plon, 1931), 295.

20. Gerhard Schulz, *Revolutionen und Friedensschlüsse 1917–1920* (Munich: Deutscher Taschenbuch Verlag, 1967), 233ff.

21. Robert A. Kann, *The Multinational Empire: Nationalism and National Reform in the Habsburg Monarchy, 1848–1918*, vol. 2, *Empire Reform* (New York: Octagon Books, 1950), 286ff.

22. Mayer, *Politics and Diplomacy of Peacemaking*, 90ff.

23. Schulz, *Revolutionen und Friedensschlüsse*, 233ff.

24. Helen Gabor, "The Hungarian Revolution and Austria," in *Revolutions and Interventions in Hungary and Its Neighbor States, 1918–1919*, ed. Peter Pastor, 201–10 (New York: Columbia University Press, 1988), 205ff.

25. Matthias Erzberger, *Erlebnisse im Weltkrieg* (Stuttgart: Deutsche Verlags-Anstalt, 1920), 132–33; General Weygand, *Le 11 Novembre* (Paris: Flammarion, 1932), 61–62.

26. John Maynard Keynes, *The Economic Consequences of the Peace* (New York: Duncker & Humblot, 1920), 38.

27. Mayer, *Politics and Diplomacy of Peacemaking*, 9.

28. Ray Stannard Baker, *Woodrow Wilson and World Settlement: Written from His Unpublished and Personal Material*, vol. 2 (London: Heinemann, 1923), 64, quoted in Mayer, *Politics and Diplomacy of Peacemaking*, 29.

29. David Lloyd George, *The Truth about the Peace Treaties*, vol. 1 (London: Gollancz, 1938), 407–8.

30. Peter Lösche, *Der Bolschewismus im Urteil der deutschen Sozialdemokratie 1903–1920* (Berlin: Colloquium Verlag, 1967), 116ff.

31. Hermann Graml, *Europa zwischen den Kriegen* (Munich: Deutscher Taschenbuch Verlag, 1982).

32. Jean Bernachot, *Les armées françaises en Orient après l'armistice de 1918: L'armée du Danube, l'armée française d'Orient, 28 Octobre 1918–25 Janvier 1920* (Paris: Impr. Nationale, 1970).

33. *Le Figaro*, 25 and 28 March 1919, quoted in Mayer, *Politics and Diplomacy of Peacemaking*, 58.

34. Peter Pastor, *Hungary between Wilson and Lenin: The Hungarian Revolution of 1918–1919 and the Big Three* (Boulder, Colo.: East European Quarterly; distributed by Columbia University Press, 1976), 132–33.

35. Glenn E. Torrey, "General Henri Berthelot and the Army of the Danube, 1918–1919," in *Revolutions and Interventions in Hungary and Its Neighbor States*, ed. Pastor, 277–92.

36. Peter Pastor, "The French Military Mission in Hungary, 1918–1919," in his *Revolutions and Interventions in Hungary and Its Neighbor States*, 251–60; see esp. 256ff.

37. George A. Brinkley, *The Volunteer Army and Allied Intervention in South Russia, 1917–1921* (Notre Dame, Ind.: University of Notre Dame Press, 1966); Michael Jabara Carley, *Revolution and Intervention: The French Government and the Russian Civil War, 1917–1919* (Kingston, Ont.: McGill-Queen's University Press, 1983); Theofanis G. Stavrou, "Greek Participation and the French Army Intervention in the Ukraine," in *Revolutions and Interventions in Hungary and Its Neighbor States*, ed. Pastor, 321–34.

38. Stavrou, "Greek Participation and the French Army Intervention," 323.

39. N. Petsalis-Diomidis, "Hellenism in Southern Russia and the Ukrainian Campaign," *Balkan Studies* 13 (1972): 221–58; see esp. 228–29.

40. Ibid., 230.

41. Stavrou, "Greek Participation and the French Army Intervention," 323.

42. Kim Munholland, "The French Army Intervention in the Ukraine," in *Revolutions and Interventions in Hungary and Its Neighbor States*, ed. Pastor, 335–56.

43. Ibid., 342.

44. Ibid., 348.

45. Petsalis-Diomidis, "Hellenism in Southern Russia and the Ukrainian Campaign," 241–42.

46. Vujica Kovacev, "The Yugoslav Government and the Counterrevolution in Hungary, 1919–1920," in *Revolutions and Interventions in Hungary and Its Neighbor States*, ed. Pastor, 221–30; see esp. 226ff.; Sherman D. Spector, *Rumania at the Peace Conference* (New York: Bookman, 1962), 110.

47. Zsuzsa L. Nagy, "The Hungarian Democratic Republic and the Paris Peace Conference, 1918–1919," in *Revolutions and Interventions in Hungary and Its Neighbor States*, ed. Pastor, 261–75; see esp. 272ff.

48. See Frank J. Coppa, "The Hungarian Communist Revolution and the Partito Socialista Italiano," in *Revolutions and Interventions in Hungary and Its Neighbor States*, ed. Pastor, 231–48; see esp. 238ff.

49. Mayer, *Politics and Diplomacy of Peacemaking*, 575, 717.

50. *Az Ujsag*, 22 March 1919, quoted in Mayer, *Politics and Diplomacy of Peacemaking*, 555.

51. Mihály Károlyi, *Memoirs: Faith without Illusion* (New York: Dutton, 1957), 125–26.

52. Mayer, *Politics and Diplomacy of Peacemaking*, 547.

53. Arpád Szépal, *Les 133 jours de Béla Kun* (Paris: Fayard, 1959).

54. *Arbeiter-Zeitung* (Vienna), 22/24 March 1919, quoted in Mayer, *Politics and Diplomacy of Peacemaking*, 591.

55. Pastor, *Hungary between Wilson and Lenin*, 140–41.

56. Torrey, "General Henri Berthelot and the Army of the Danube," 288.

57. Mayer, *Politics and Diplomacy of Peacemaking*, 601.

58. On the role of Rumania in the French strategy, see Kalervo Hovi, *Cordon Sanitaire or Barrière de l'Est? The Emergence of the New French Eastern European Alliance Policy, 1917–1919* (Turku, Finland: Turun yliopisto, 1975), 176–77; Glenn E. Torrey, "The Romanian Intervention in Hungary, 1919," in *Revolutions and Interventions in Hungary and Its Neighbor States*, ed. Pastor, 301–20.

59. Andrew C. Janos, *The Politics of Backwardness in Hungary, 1825–1945* (Princeton, N.J.: Princeton University Press, 1982), 152–53.

60. Béla Rasky, "Nationale Frage und Arbeiterbewegung in Ungarn," in *Arbeiterbewegung und Nationale Frage in den Nachfolgestaaten der Habsburgermonarchie*, ed. Helmut Konrad, 70 (Vienna: Europaverlag, 1993).

61. Peter Hanak, *Ungarn in der Donaumonarchie: Probleme der bürgerlichen Umgestaltung eines Vielvölkerstaates* (Vienna: Verlag für Geschichte und Politik, 1984), 138ff.

62. Eva S. Balogh, "Nationality Problems of the Hungarian Soviet Republic," in *Hungary in Revolution*, ed. Ian Völgyes, 89–120 (Lincoln: University of Nebraska Press, 1971).

63. Wilhelm Böhm, *Im Kreuzfeuer zweier Revolutionen* (Munich: Verlag für Kulturpolitik, 1924), 357–58.

64. Sándor Szakoly, "The Officer Corps of the Hungarian Red Army," in *Revolutions and Interventions in Hungary and Its Neighbor States,* ed. Pastor, 169–78; see esp. 172ff.

65. Balogh, "Nationality Problems of the Hungarian Soviet Republic," 109.

66. Peter Pastor, "One Step Forward, Two Steps Back: The Rise and Fall of the First Hungarian Communist Party, 1918–1922," in *The Effects of World War I: The Class War after the Great War: The Rise of the Communist Parties in East Central Europe, 1918–1921,* ed. Ivo Banac, 85–126 (New York: Brooklyn College Press, 1983).

67. Mayer, *Politics and Diplomacy of Peacemaking,* 736.

68. Böhm, *Im Kreuzfeuer zweier Revolutionen,* 407–8.

69. Mária Ormos, "The Foreign Policy of the Hungarian Soviet Republic," in *Revolutions and Interventions in Hungary and Its Neighbor States,* ed. Pastor, 357–65.

70. Tibor Hadju, "Plans of Strategic Cooperation between the Russian and Hungarian Red Armies," in *Revolutions and Interventions in Hungary and Its Neighbor States,* ed. Pastor, 367–75; see esp. 368ff.

71. Ibid., 371.

72. Pipes, *Russia under the Bolshevik Regime,* 80–81.

73. Hadju, "Plans of Strategic Cooperation," 371.

74. Viscount D'Abernon, *The Eighteenth Decisive Battle of World History* (London: Hodder & Stoughton, 1931), 8–9.

75. The following is based on the now classic study by Norman Davies, *White Eagle, Red Star: The Polish-Soviet War, 1919–20* (London: Orbis, 1972); and Thomas C. Fiddick, *Russia's Retreat from Poland, 1920: From Permanent Revolution to Peaceful Coexistence* (London: Macmillan, 1990).

76. Pipes, *Russia under the Bolshevik Regime,* 369–70.

77. On the extensive consequences of the war, see Davies, *White Eagle, Red Star,* 274–75.

78. Christoph Klessmann, "Der polnisch-sowjetische Krieg von 1920 als europäisches Problem," in *Ostmitteleuropa: Berichte und Forschungen,* ed. Ulrich Haustein et al., 310–34 (Stuttgart: Klett-Cotta, 1981).

79. Pipes, *Russia under the Bolshevik Regime,* 217ff.

80. Horst Günther Linke, *Deutsch-sowjetische Beziehungen bis Rapallo* (Cologne: Verlag Wissenschaft und Politik, 1970), 106ff.

81. For an overview, see Klaus Zernack, "Deutschland und Rußland: Die Klammer um Polen," *Tel Aviver Jahrbuch für deutsche Geschichte* 24 (1995): 1–14; Gottfried Schramm, "Grundmuster deutscher Ostpolitik,"

in *Zwei Wege nach Moskau: Vom Hitler-Stalin-Pakt bis zum "Unternehmen Barbarossa,"* ed. Bernd Wegner, 3–18 (Munich: Piper, 1991).

82. Stefan Kieniewicz, "Le développement de la conscience nationale polonaise au XIX siècle," *Acta Poloniae Historica* 19 (1968): 37–48.

83. Bradley, *Allied Intervention in Russia*, 184ff.

84. Davies, *White Eagle, Red Star*, 115.

85. Ibid., 135.

86. Adam Zamoyski, *The Battle for the Marchland* (New York: Columbia University Press, 1981).

87. Davies, *White Eagle, Red Star*, 42, 38.

88. Fiddick, *Russia's Retreat from Poland*, 211.

89. Jerzy T. Lukawski, *Liberty's Folly: The Polish-Lithuanian Commonwealth in the Eighteenth Century* (London: Routledge, 1991).

90. Gotthold Rhode, "Staatenunion und Adelstaat: Zur Entwicklung von Staatsdenken und Staatsgestaltung in Osteuropa, vor allem in Polen und Litauen im 16. Jahrhundert," *Zeitschrift für Osteuropaforschung* 9 (1960): 185–215; Stanislaw Russocki, "Structures politiques dans l'Europe des Jagellons," *Acta Poloniae Historica* 39 (1979): 101–42.

91. Stephan Horak, *Poland and Her National Minorities, 1919–1939: A Case Study* (New York: Vantage Press, 1961).

92. Johann Wolfgang Brügel, "Neues zur Entstehungsgeschichte der Curzon-Linie," *Osteuropa* 10 (1960): 181–84; Gotthold Rhode, "Die Entstehung der Curzon-Linie," *Osteuropa* 5 (1955): 81–92.

93. Pawel Korzec, "Polen und der Minderheitenschutzvertrag 1919–1934," *Jahrbücher für Geschichte Osteuropas* 22 (1974): 515–55.

94. For a detailed discussion, see John Rothschild, *East Central Europe between the Two World Wars* (Seattle: University of Washington Press, 1974).

95. Hans Roos, *Polen und Europa: Studien zur polnischen Außenpolitik 1931–1939* (Tübingen: Mohr, 1965).

96. Wacław Jędrzejewicz, *Piłsudski: A Life for Poland* (New York: Hippocrene Books, 1982); Marian K. Dziewanowski, *Joseph Piłsudski: A European Federalist, 1918–1922* (Stanford, Calif.: Hoover Institute Press, 1969).

97. Semen Chromov, *Feliks Dzierzynski: Biographie* (Berlin: Dietz, 1980).

98. Jędrzejewicz, *Piłsudski*, 54ff.

99. Pipes, *Russian Revolution*, 800ff.; see also David Shub, *Lenin* (London: Penguin, 1966), 347ff.

100. Davies, *White Eagle, Red Star,* 41–42.

101. Ibid., 163.

102. On the dilemma of the Polish Communists between class and nation, see Piotr S. Wandycz, *Soviet-Polish Relations, 1917–1921* (Cambridge, Mass.: Harvard University Press, 1969), 65ff.

103. Marian K. Dziewanowski, *The Communist Party of Poland: An Outline of History* (Cambridge, Mass.: Harvard University Press, 1959).

104. Fiddick, *Russia's Retreat from Poland,* 53ff.

105. Davies, *White Eagle, Red Star,* 266.

106. Ibid., 22.

107. Ibid., 130ff.

108. Fiddick, *Russia's Retreat from Poland,* 125–26.

109. Pipes has another view, suggesting the invasion of Poland was planned long beforehand, independent of Piłsudski's march on Kiev; see Pipes, *Russia under the Bolshevik Regime,* 177ff.

110. Norbert H. Gaworek, "From Blockade to Trade: Allied Economic Warfare against Soviet Russia, June 1919 to January 1920," *Jahrbücher für Geschichte Osteuropas* 23 (1975): 39–69; Pipes, *Russia under the Bolshevik Regime,* 217ff.

111. Richard Ullman, *Anglo-Soviet Relations, 1917–1921,* vol. 3, *The Anglo-Soviet Accord* (Princeton, N.J.: Princeton University Press, 1972), 107.

112. Randolph S. Churchill and Martin Gilbert, *Winston S. Churchill,* vol. 4, *1916–1922* (Boston: Heinemann, 1975), 379.

113. F. Russel Bryant, "Lord D'Abernon, the Anglo-French Mission, and the Battle of Warsaw, 1920," *Jahrbücher für Geschichte Osteuropas* 38 (1990): 526–47; Bryant considers the military role of the mission more important than is generally assumed in the literature.

114. Fiddick, *Russia's Retreat from Poland,* 218ff.; Isaak Babel, *Tagebuch 1920* (Berlin: Friedenauer Press, 1990).

115. Leon Trotsky, *Stalin: An Appraisal of the Man and His Influence* (London: Hollis & Charter, 1947), 328ff.

116. Fiddick, *Russia's Retreat from Poland,* 235.

117. Ibid., 271.

118. Edgar O'Ballance, *The Red Army* (New York: Faber & Faber, 1964), 87.

119. Davies, *White Eagle, Red Star,* 275.

120. Jaroslav Valenta, "Die Tschechoslowakei am Vorabend des Zweiten Weltkrieges," in *1939, An der Schwelle zum Weltkrieg: Die Entfesselung des Zweiten Weltkrieges und das internationale System,* ed. Klaus Hildebrand et

al., 150–60 (Berlin and New York: de Gruyter, 1990). Cieszyn remains located in Poland, on the border with the Czech Republic.

121. Manfred Zeidler, *Reichswehr und Rote Armee, 1920–1933: Wege und Stationen einer ungewöhnlichen Zusammenarbeit* (Munich: Oldenbourg, 1994), 301ff.

122. Davies, *White Eagle, Red Star,* 185.

123. See Gerhard Wagner, *Deutschland und der polnisch-sowjetische Krieg 1920* (Wiesbaden: Steiner, 1979), 168–69. During the Soviet advance on the Vistula, German refugees near the East Prussian–Polish frontier and in other areas near the common border cherished hopes of a possible return after a Polish defeat.

124. Linke, *Deutsch-sowjetische Beziehungen bis Rapallo,* 106ff.; Wagner, *Deutschland und der polnisch-sowjetische Krieg 1920,* 101ff.; Aleksandr M. Nekrich, *Pariahs, Partners, Predators: German-Soviet Relations, 1922–1941* (New York: Columbia University Press, 1997), 1ff.

125. Nekrich, *Pariahs, Partners, Predators,* 3–4.

126. Ibid., 6.

127. Otto-Ernst Schüddekopf, "Karl Radek in Berlin: Ein Kapitel deutsch-russischer Beziehungen im Jahre 1919," *Archiv für Sozialgeschichte* 2 (1962): 87–166; Marie-Luise Goldbach, *Karl Radek und die deutsch-sowjetischen Beziehungen 1918–1923* (Bonn-Bad Godesberg: Neue Gesellschaft, 1973), 43ff.

128. Karl Radek, *Die auswärtige Politik Sowjet-Rußlands* (Hamburg: Hoym, 1921), 73.

129. Christian Höltje, *Die Weimarer Republik und das Ostlocarno-Problem, 1919–1934: Revision oder Garantie der deutschen Ostgrenze von 1919* (Würzburg: Holzner, 1958), 90–91.

130. Ibid., 83ff.

131. Heinrich August Winkler, *Weimar, 1918–1933: Die Geschichte der ersten deutschen Demokratie* (Munich: Beck, 1993), 566.

132. Nekrich, *Pariahs, Partners, Predators,* 41.

133. Ibid., 87.

134. J. Calvitt Clarke III, *Russia and Italy against Hitler: The Bolshevik-Fascist Rapprochement of the 1930s* (New York: Greenwood Press, 1991), 77ff.

135. Donald C. Watt, *How War Came: The Immediate Origins of the Second World War, 1938–1939* (London: Heinemann, 1989), 109ff.

136. Arnold J. Toynbee, introduction to *The Eve of War, 1939,* ed. Arnold Toynbee and Veronica M. Toynbee, 1–60 (London: Oxford University Press, 1958), see esp. 17ff.

137. Nekrich, *Pariahs, Partners, Predators,* 157.

138. Gabriel Gorodetsky, "Russian 'Appeasement' of Germany, Spring 1941," *Tel Aviver Jahrbuch für deutsche Geschichte* 24 (1995): 257–82; see esp. 265ff.

139. Nekrich, *Pariahs, Partners, Predators,* 110.

140. Ibid., 93.

141. Olaf Groehler, *Selbstmörderische Allianz: Deutsch-sowjetische Militär-beziehungen 1920–1941* (Berlin: Vision-Verlag, 1992), 122–23.

142. Nekrich, *Pariahs, Partners, Predators,* 104ff.

143. Gerhard L. Weinberg, *Germany and the Soviet Union, 1939–1941* (Leiden: Brill, 1972), 46, 87ff.

144. Gerhard L. Weinberg, *A World at Arms: A Global History of World War II* (Cambridge: Cambridge University Press, 1994), 72–73; Hans-Joachim Lorbeer, *Westmächte gegen die Sowjetunion: 1939–1941* (Freiburg: Rombach, 1975).

145. Nekrich, *Pariahs, Partners, Predators,* 163–64.

146. Adam B. Ulam, *Expansion and Coexistence: The History of Soviet Foreign Policy, 1917–1967* (London: Secker & Warburg, 1968), 297–98.

147. Gorodetsky, "Russian 'Appeasement' of Germany," 262.

148. On Hitler's subordinating of his political timetable to his own life expectancy, see Sebastian Haffner, *The Meaning of Hitler* (London: Phoenix Giant, 1999), 7–8; for a philosophical treatment of the broader topic, see Hans Blumenberg, *Lebenszeit und Weltzeit* (Frankfurt am Main: Suhrkamp, 1986), 64.

149. Jörg Friedrich, *Das Gesetz des Krieges: Das deutsche Heer in Rußland, 1941 bis 1945* (Munich: Piper, 1995); Theo Schulte, *The German Army and Nazi Policies in Occupied Russia* (Oxford: Berg, 1989); Christian Streit, *Keine Kameraden: Die Wehrmacht und die sowjetischen Kriegsgefangenen 1941–1945* (Stuttgart: Deutsche Verlags-Anstalt, 1978); Omer Bartov, *The Eastern Front, 1941–45: German Troops and the Barbarisation of Warfare* (New York: Macmillan, 1985).

150. Weinberg, *World at Arms,* 187ff.

151. Nekrich, *Pariahs, Partners, Predators,* 184–85.

152. Martin van Creveld, *Hitler's Strategy 1940–1941: The Balkan Clue* (Cambridge: Cambridge University Press, 1973).

153. Nekrich, *Pariahs, Partners, Predators,* 201.

154. Ibid. 203.

155. Peter Calvocoressi et al., *Total War: Causes and Courses of the Second World War* (London: Allen Lane, 1972), 174ff.

156. Klaus Hildebrand, *Das vergangene Reich: Deutsche Außenpolitik von Bismarck bis Hitler 1871–1945* (Stuttgart: Deutsche Verlags-Anstalt, 1995), 729ff.

157. Gorodetsky, "Russian 'Appeasement' of Germany," 264.

158. Jürgen Förster, *Stalingrad: Risse im Bündnis 1942/43* (Freiburg: Rombach, 1975).

159. Karl Marx, *Manuskripte über die polnische Frage (1863–1864)*, ed. Werner Conze and Dieter Hertz-Eichenrode (The Hague: Mouton, 1961).

Chapter 3. Regimes: Democracy and Dictatorship

1. Heinrich August Winkler, "Deutschland vor Hitler: Der historische Ort der Weimarer Republik," in *Der historische Ort des Nationalsozialismus,* ed. Walter H. Pehle, 11–30 (Frankfurt am Main: Fischer Taschenbuch Verlag, 1990).

2. Detlev Junker, "Die letzte Alternative zu Hitler: Verfassungsbruch und Militärdiktatur: Die machtpolitische Situation in Deutschland im Jahre 1932," in *Das Ende der Weimarer Republik und die nationalsozialistische Machtergreifung,* ed. Christoph Gradmann and Oliver von Mengersen, 67–85 (Heidelberg: Manutius, 1994).

3. Horst Möller, "Die Weimarer Republik in der zeitgeschichtlichen Perspektive der Bundesrepublik Deutschland während der fünfziger und frühen sechziger Jahre: Demokratische Tradition und NS-Ursachenforschung," in *Deutsche Geschichtswissenschaft nach dem Zweiten Weltkrieg: 1945–1965,* ed. Ernst Schulin, 157–80 (Munich: Oldenbourg 1989).

4. Thomas Nipperdey, "1933 und die Kontinuität der deutschen Geschichte," *Historische Zeitschrift* 227 (1978): 86–111; Dirk Blasius, "Von Bismarck zu Hitler: Kontinuität und Kontinuitätsbegehren in der deutschen Geschichte," *Aus Politik und Zeitgeschichte* 51 (1998): 3–10.

5. Henry A. Turner, *Hitler's Thirty Days to Power: January 1933* (London: Bloomsbury, 1997), 163–87.

6. Hans-Ulrich Wehler, *The German Empire, 1871–1918* (Leamington Spa, Warwickshire: Berg, 1985); Geoff Eley and David Blackbourn, *The Peculiarities of German History: Bourgeois Society and Politics in Nineteenth Century Germany* (Oxford: Oxford University Press, 1984); for a summary, see Helga Grebing, *Der "deutsche Sonderweg" in Europa 1806–1945: Eine Kritik* (Stuttgart: Kohlhammer, 1986).

7. Eberhard Jäckel, in *Das deutsche Jahrhundert: Eine historische Bilanz* (Stuttgart: Deutsche Verlagsanstalt, 1996), titles his chapter on Weimar "The Greatest Conceivable Mishap" ("Der größte anzunehmende Unfall"), 151ff.

8. Heinrich August Winkler, *Der Schein der Normalität: Arbeiter und Arbeiterbewegung in der Weimarer Republik, 1924 bis 1930* (Berlin: Dietz, 1985), 736ff.

9. Ilse Maurer, *Reichsfinanzen und große Koalition: Zur Geschichte des Reichskabinetts Müller (1928–1930)* (Bern: Lang, 1973).

10. Helga Timm, *Die deutsche Sozialpolitik und der Bruch der Großen Koalition im März 1930* (1952; repr., Düsseldorf: Droste, 1982).

11. Winkler, *Der Schein der Normalität*, 805ff.

12. Ibid., 759ff.

13. Charles S. Maier, *Recasting Bourgeois Europe: Stabilization in France, Germany, and Italy in the Decade after World War I* (Princeton, N.J.: Princeton University Press, 1975), 53ff.

14. Gerald D. Feldman, "The Origins of the Stinnes-Legien Agreement: A Documentation," *Internationale Wissenschaftliche Korrespondenz zur Geschichte der deutschen Arbeiterbewegung* 9 (1973): 45–103.

15. Knut Borchardt, *Wachstum, Krisen, Handlungsspielräume der Wirtschaftspolitik* (Göttingen: Vandenhoeck & Ruprecht, 1982), 165–82.

16. Ernst Fraenkel, "Der Ruhreisenstreit 1928–1929 in historisch-politischer Sicht," in *Staat, Wirtschaft und Politik in der Weimarer Republik: Festschrift für Heinrich Brüning*, ed. Ferdinand A. Hermens and Theodor Schieder, 97–117 (Berlin: Duncker & Humblot, 1967); Bernd Weisbrod, *Die Schwerindustrie in der Weimarer Republik* (Wuppertal: Hammer, 1978), 415ff.

17. Harold James, *The German Slump: Politics and Economics, 1924–1936* (Oxford: Clarendon Press, 1986).

18. Gerhard A. Ritter, *Der Sozialstaat: Entstehung und Entwicklung im internationalen Vergleich* (Munich: Oldenbourg, 1991), 109.

19. Gilbert Ziebura, *World Economy and World Politics, 1924–1931: From Reconstruction to Collapse* (Oxford: Berg, 1990); Dietmar Petzina, "Was There a Crisis before the Crisis? The State of the German Economy in the 1920s," in *Economic Crisis and Political Collapse: The Weimar Republic, 1924–1933*, ed. Jürgen Baron von Kruedener, 1–19 (New York: Berg, 1990).

20. Hugh Armstrong Clegg, *A History of British Trade Unions since 1889*, vol. 2, *1911–1933* (Oxford: Clarendon Press, 1985), 512ff.

21. Trevor O. Lloyd, *Empire, Welfare State, Europe: English History 1906–1992* (Oxford: Oxford University Press, 1993), 177ff.

22. James Joll, "National History and National Historians: Some German and English Views of the Past," in *The 1984 Annual Lecture* (London: German Historical Institute London, 1985), 3–25.

23. Noreen Branson, *Britain in the Nineteen Twenties* (London: Weidenfeld & Nicolson, 1975), 166–67.

24. Clegg, *1911–1933*, 403–4.

25. Eric Hobsbawm, *Industry and Empire: An Economic History of Britain since 1750* (London: Weidenfeld & Nicolson, 1968).

26. Adolf M. Birke, "Die englische Krankheit: Tarifautonomie als Verfassungsproblem in Geschichte und Gegenwart," *Vierteljahrshefte für Zeitgeschichte* 30 (1982): 621–45.

27. R. A. C. Parker, *Europe, 1918–1945* (London: Weidenfeld & Nicolson, 1969), 129.

28. Peter Dorey, *The Conservative Party and the Trade Unions* (London: Routledge 1995), 25–26.

29. Branson, *Britain in the Nineteen Twenties*, 103–4.

30. Thomas F. Lindsay and Michael Harrington, *The Conservative Party, 1918–1970* (London: Macmillan, 1974).

31. Richard Biernacki, *The Fabrication of Labor: Germany and Britain, 1640–1914* (Berkeley: University of California Press, 1995), 255ff.

32. Clive Behagg, "Controlling the Product: Work, Time, and the Early Industrial Workforce in Britain, 1800–1850," in *Worktime and Industrialization: An International History*, ed. Gary Cross (Philadelphia: Temple University Press, 1988).

33. John Saville, "The British State, the Business Community and Trade Unions," in *The Development of Trade Unionism in Great Britain and Germany, 1880–1914*, ed. Wolfgang Mommsen and Hans-Gerhard Husung, 315–24 (London: Allen & Unwin, 1985).

34. Clegg, *1911–1933*, 357–58.

35. Alan Bullock, *The Life and Times of Ernest Bevin*, vol. 1, *Trade Union Leader, 1881–1940* (London: Heinemann, 1969).

36. Michael Kitchen, *Europe between the Wars: A Political History* (London: Longman, 1988), 188.

37. Lloyd, *Empire, Welfare State, Europe*, 91ff.

38. Hermann Graml, *Europa zwischen den Kriegen* (Munich: Deutscher Taschenbuch Verlag, 1969), 126ff.

39. Ian M. Drummond, *The Gold Standard and the International Monetary System, 1900–1939* (Basingstoke, Hampshire: Macmillan, 1987).

40. Maier, *Recasting Bourgeois Europe*, 276.

41. A. J. P. Taylor, *English History, 1914–1945* (London: Penguin Books, 1975), 285–86.

42. Parker, *Europe, 1918–1945*, 121.

43. Clegg, *1911–1933*, 393ff.

44. Philip Williamson, *National Crisis and National Government: British Politics, the Economy, and Empire, 1926–1932* (Cambridge: Cambridge University Press, 1992), 12.

45. Fritz Blaich, *Der Schwarze Freitag: Inflation und Wirtschaftskrise* (Munich: Deutscher Taschenbuch Verlag, 1985), 91ff.

46. Rudolf Hilferding, *Finance Capital: A Study of the Latest Phase of Capitalist Development* (London: Routledge & Kegan Paul, 1985), 297.

47. Jürgen Falter, "Unemployment and the Radicalization of the German Electorate, 1928–1933: An Aggregate Data Analysis with Special Emphasis on the Rise of National Socialism," in *Unemployment and the Great Depression in Weimar Germany*, ed. Peter D. Stachura, 187–208 (London: Macmillan, 1986).

48. Michael Schneider, *Das Arbeitsbeschaffungsprogramm des ADGB: Zur Gewerkschaftspolitik in der Endphase der Weimarer Republik* (Bonn-Bad Godesberg: Verlag Neue Gesellschaft, 1975).

49. Kitchen, *Europe between the Wars*, 197.

50. Peter Alter, "Der britische Generalstreik von 1926 als politische Wende," in *Beiträge zur britischen Geschichte im 20. Jahrhundert*, ed. Theodor Schieder, 89–116 (Munich: Oldenbourg, 1983).

51. Roy Douglas, *World Crisis and British Decline, 1929–56* (London: Macmillan, 1986), 11ff.

52. Williamson, *National Crisis and National Government*, 523.

53. Karl Rohe and Gustav Schmidt, eds., *Krise in Großbritannien? Studien zu Strukturproblemen der britischen Gesellschaft und Politik im 20. Jahrhundert* (Bochum: Brockmeyer, 1987).

54. Patricia Clavin, *The Failure of Economic Diplomacy: Britain, Germany, France and the United States, 1931–1936* (London: Macmillan, 1996), 19–20, 23–24.

55. Lloyd, *Empire, Welfare State, Europe*, 173–74.

56. Williamson, *National Crisis and National Government*, 530.

57. David. E. Butler, *The Electoral System in Britain since 1918* (1963; repr., Westport, Conn.: Greenwood Press, 1986).

58. Jane Lewis, "Class against Class: The Political Culture of the Communist Party of Great Britain, 1930–1935," in *Class, Culture and Social Change: A New View of the 1930s*, ed. Frank Gloversmith, 208–39 (Brighton, Sussex: Harvester Press, 1980).

59. Karl J. Newman, *European Democracy between the Wars* (London: Allen & Unwin, 1970), 87.

60. Carl-Ludwig Holfterisch, "Alternativen zu Brünings Wirtschaftspolitik in der Weltwirtschaftskrise?" *Historische Zeitschrift* 235 (1982): 605–31; Knut Borchardt, "Noch einmal: Alternativen zu Brünings Wirtschaftspolitik?" *Historische Zeitschrift* 237 (1983): 67–83.

61. Dolf Sternberger and Bernhard Vogel, eds., *Die Wahl der Parlamente und anderer Staatsorgane: Ein Handbuch*, vol. 1, *Europa* (Berlin: de Gruyter, 1969), 240ff.

62. Ferdinand A. Hermens, *Demokratie oder Anarchie* (Frankfurt am Main: Metzner 1951), 167, quoted in Newman, *European Democracy between the Wars*, 88.

63. Philippe Bernard and Henri Dubief, *The Decline of the Third Republic, 1914–1938* (Cambridge: Cambridge University Press, 1988), 128ff.

64. Charles Bloch, *Die Dritte Französische Republik: Entwicklung und Kampf einer Parlamentarischen Demokratie (1870–1940)* (Stuttgart: Koehler, 1972), 368–69.

65. Julian Jackson, *The Politics of Depression in France, 1932–1936* (Cambridge: Cambridge University Press, 1985), 23–26, 29; Bernard and Dubief, *Decline of the Third Republic*, 23f.

66. Jackson, *Politics of Depression in France*, 29; Bernard and Dubief, *Decline of the Third Republic*, 233–34.

67. Rudolf V. Albertini, "Parteiorganisation und Parteibegriff in Frankreich 1789–1940," *Historische Zeitschrift* 193 (1961): 529–600.

68. Sternberger and Vogel, *Europa*, 240ff.

69. Heinz-Gerhard Haupt, "Frankreich: Langsame Industrialisierung und republikanische Tradition," in *Europäische Arbeiterbewegung im 19. Jahrhundert*, ed. Jürgen Kocka, 39–76 (Göttingen: Vandenhoeck & Ruprecht, 1983).

70. Wilfried Loth, *Geschichte Frankreichs im 20. Jahrhundert* (Stuttgart: Kohlhammer, 1987), 74–75.

71. Eduard Bonnefous, *Histoire politique de la Troisième République*, vol. 6, *Vers la guerre: Du Front Populaire à la conférence de Munich 1936–1938* (Paris: Presses Universitaires de France, 1965), 336ff., 362ff.

72. Newman, *European Democracy between the Wars*, 94ff.

73. Robert Soucy, *French Fascism: The Second Wave, 1933–1939* (New Haven, Conn.: Yale University Press, 1995), 26ff., 167–68.

74. Newman, *European Democracy between the Wars,* 96ff.; Bloch, *Die Dritte Französische Republik,* 390.

75. Serge Berstein, *Histoire du parti radical,* vol. 1, *La recherche de l'age d'or, 1919–1926* (Paris: Fondation Nationale des Sciences Politiques, 1980), 23ff.

76. Serge Berstein, *Histoire du parti radical,* vol. 2, *Le temps des crises et des mutations, 1926–1939* (Paris: Fondation Nationale des Sciences Politiques, 1982), 591–92.

77. Parker, *Europe, 1918–1945,* 179.

78. Ibid., 186.

79. Bruno Schoch, *Marxismus in Frankreich seit 1945* (Frankfurt am Main: Campus, 1980), 35–36.

80. Kitchen, *Europe between the Wars,* 226.

81. Berstein, *Le temps des crises et des mutations,* 519.

82. On the nineteenth-century background of the republic's split between proletarian and bourgeois democracy, see Gustav Mayer's 1912 essay "Die Trennung der proletarischen von der bürgerlichen Demokratie 1863–1870," in *Radikalismus, Sozialismus und bürgerliche Demokratie,* ed. Hans-Ulrich Wehler, 108–78 (Frankfurt am Main: Suhrkamp, 1969).

83. Susanne Miller, *Die Bürde der Macht: Die deutsche Sozialdemokratie 1918–1920* (Düsseldorf: Droste, 1978).

84. Hans Mommsen, "Die Sozialdemokratie in der Defensive: Der Immobilismus der SPD und der Aufstieg des Nationalsozialismus," in his *Sozialdemokratie zwischen Klassenbewegung und Volkspartei,* 106–33 (Frankfurt am Main: Athenäum Fischer Taschenbuch Verlag, 1974).

85. Hagen Schulze, "Die sozialdemokratische Parlamentsfraktion im Reich und in Preußen 1918–1933," *Vierteljahrshefte für Zeitgeschichte* 26 (1978): 419–32

86. Winkler, *Der Schein der Normalität,* 812–13.

87. Hagen Schulze, *Otto Braun oder Preußens demokratische Sendung: Eine Biographie* (Frankfurt am Main: Ullstein, 1977).

88. Antony Polonsky, *The Little Dictators: The History of Eastern Europe since 1918* (London: Routledge & Kegan Paul, 1975).

89. Joseph Rothschild, *East Central Europe between the Two World Wars* (Seattle: University of Washington Press, 1974).

90. Theodor Eschenburg, "Der Zerfall der demokratischen Ordnung zwischen dem Ersten und dem Zweiten Weltkrieg," in his *Der Weg in die Diktatur, 1918 bis 1933,* 7–28 (Munich: Piper, 1962), 15.

91. Reinhard Rürup, "Demokratische Revolution und 'dritter Weg': Die deutsche Revolution von 1918/19 in der neuen wissenschaftlichen Diskussion," *Geschichte und Gesellschaft* 9 (1983): 278–301.

92. Hans Mommsen, *The Rise and Fall of Weimar Democracy* (Chapel Hill: University of North Carolina Press, 1996), 12–13.

93. Heinrich August Winkler, *Weimar, 1918–1933: Die Geschichte der ersten deutschen Demokratie* (Munich: Beck, 1993), 27.

94. H. Mommsen, *Rise and Fall of Weimar Democracy*, 13–14.

95. Wolfgang Sauer, "Das Scheitern der parlamentarischen Monarchie," in *Vom Kaiserreich zur Weimarer Republik*, ed. Eberhard Kolb, 77–99 (Cologne: Kiepenheuer & Witsch, 1972).

96. Eberhard Kolb, *The Weimar Republic* (London: Unwin Hyman, 1988), 3.

97. Blaich, *Der Schwarze Freitag*, 58ff.

98. Gerhard Schulz, "Bemerkungen zur Wegscheide zwischen parlamentarischer und autoritärer Entwicklung in der Geschichte der Weimarer Republik," in *Die deutsche Staatskrise 1930–1933*, ed. Heinrich August Winkler, 39–47 (Munich: Oldenbourg, 1992).

99. Karl Dietrich Bracher, *Die Auflösung der Weimarer Republik: Eine Studie zum Problem des Machtverfalls in der Demokratie* (Stuttgart: Ring-Verlag, 1957), 51ff.

100. Rudolf Morsey, "Die deutsche Zentrumspartei," in *Das Ende der Parteien*, ed. Rudolf Morsey and Erich Matthias, 281–453 (1960; repr., Königstein: Athenäum-Verlag, 1979).

101. Karl Dietrich Bracher, "Brünings unpolitische Politik und die Auflösung der Weimarer Republik," *Vierteljahrshefte für Zeitgeschichte* 19 (1971): 113–23.

102. Originally meant to be used for states of civil unrest and similar emergencies, Article 48 allowed presidential rule by decree. In 1933, Article 48 would serve as Hitler's vehicle to absolute power and the Third Reich.

103. Turner, *Hitler's Thirty Days to Power*, 150–51.

104. Thilo Vogelsang, *Kurt von Schleicher: Ein General als Politiker* (Göttingen: Musterschmidt, 1965).

105. Winkler, *Der Schein der Normalität*, 806.

106. Ibid., 802.

107. Heinrich August Winkler, *Der Weg in die Katastrophe: Arbeiter und Arbeiterbewegung in der Weimarer Republik*, 2nd ed. (Bonn: Dietz, 1990), 244–45.

108. Thilo Vogelsang, "Zur Politik Schleichers gegenüber der NSDAP 1932," *Vierteljahrshefte für Zeitgeschichte* 6 (1958): 86–118.

109. Gotthard Jasper, *Die gescheiterte Zähmung: Wege zur Machtergreifung Hitlers, 1930–1934* (Frankfurt am Main: Suhrkamp, 1986), 88–125.

110. Axel Schildt, *Militärdiktatur mit Massenbasis? Die Querfrontkonzeption der Reichswehrführung um General von Schleicher am Ende der Weimarer Republik* (Frankfurt am Main: Campus, 1981), 97ff.

111. Eberhard Kolb and Wolfram Pyta, "Die Staatsnotstandsplanung unter den Regierungen Papen und Schleicher," in *Die deutsche Staatskrise 1930–1933*, ed. Winkler, 155–182.

112. Richard Breitman, "On German Social Democracy and General Schleicher 1932/33," *Central European History* 9 (1976): 352–78.

113. Winkler, *Der Weg in die Katastrophe*, 746–47, 794.

114. Dietmar Petzina, "Elemente der Wirtschaftspolitik in der Spätphase der Weimarer Republik," *Vierteljahrshefte für Zeitgeschichte* 21 (1973): 127–33.

115. Schildt, *Militärdiktatur mit Massenbasis?* 7.

116. Martin Fiederlei, "Der deutsche Osten und die Regierungen Brüning, Papen, Schleicher" (PhD diss., University of Würzburg, 1966).

117. Reinhard Neebe, *Großindustrie, Staat und NSDAP 1930–1933: Paul Silverberg und der Reichsverband der Deutschen Industrie in der Krise der Weimarer Republik* (Göttingen: Vandenhoeck & Ruprecht, 1981), 201.

118. Michael Geyer, *Aufrüstung oder Sicherheit: Die Reichswehr in der Krise der Machtpolitik 1924–1936* (Wiesbaden: Steiner, 1980), 302–3.

119. H. Mommsen, *Rise and Fall of Weimar Democracy*, 490.

120. Peter Hayes, "'A Question Mark with Epaulettes?' Kurt von Schleicher and Weimar Politics," *Journal of Modern History* 52 (1980): 35–65.

121. Henry M. Adams and Robin K. Adams, *Rebel Patriot: A Biography of Franz von Papen* (Santa Barbara, Calif.: McNally & Loftin, 1987).

122. For a different view, see Fritz Arndt, "Vorbereitungen der Reichswehr für den militärischen Ausnahmezustand," *Zeitschrift für Militärgeschichte* 4 (1965): 195–203.

123. Carl Schmitt, *Gespräch über die Macht und den Zugang zum Machthaber: Gespräch über den Neuen Raum* (1954; repr., Berlin: Akademie, 1994), 7–34.

124. Turner, *Hitler's Thirty Days to Power*, 121–22.

125. Detlev Junker, *Die deutsche Zentrumspartei und Hitler 1932/33: Ein Beitrag zur Problematik des deutschen Katholizismus* (Stuttgart: Klett, 1969).

126. Turner, *Hitler's Thirty Days to Power*, 145–46.

127. Ibid., 150–51.

128. Rudolf Morsey, "Hitlers Verhandlungen mit der Zentrumspartei am 31. Januar 1933: Dokumentation," *Vierteljahrshefte für Zeitgeschichte* 9 (1961): 182–94.

129. Immanuel Geiss, "Die Rolle der Persönlichkeiten in der Geschichte: Zwischen Überwerten und Verdrängen," in *Persönlichkeit und Struktur in der Geschichte*, ed. Michael Bosch, 10–24 (Düsseldorf: Schwann, 1977).

130. Norbert Frei, "'Machtergreifung': Anmerkungen zu einem historischen Begriff," *Vierteljahrshefte für Zeitgeschichte* 31 (1983): 136–45.

131. Carl Schmitt, *Verfassungslehre* (1928; repr., Berlin: Duncker & Humblot, 1957), 345; Heinrich Muth, "Carl Schmitt in der deutschen Innenpolitik des Sommers 1932," in *Beiträge zur Geschichte der Weimarer Republik*, ed. Theodor Schieder, 75–147 (Munich: R. Oldenburg, 1971).

132. Wolfgang J. Mommsen, "1933: Die Flucht in den Führerstaat," in *Wendepunkte deutscher Geschichte, 1848–1990*, ed. Carola Stern and Heinrich August Winkler, 127–58 (Frankfurt am Main: Fischer Taschenbuch Verlag, 1994).

133. Winkler, *Weimar, 1918–1933*, 541.

134. Klaus Schönhoven, "Zwischen Anpassung und Ausschaltung: Die Bayerische Volkspartei in der Endphase der Weimarer Republik 1932/33," *Historische Zeitschrift* 224 (1977): 340–78.

135. Richard Breitman, "On German Socialism and General Schleicher 1932/33," *Central European History* 9 (1976): 352–78.

136. Winkler, *Weimar, 1918–1933*, 582.

137. Ibid., 589.

138. Ibid., 587.

139. Wolfram Pyta, *Gegen Hitler und für die Republik: Die Auseinandersetzung der deutschen Sozialdemokratie mit der NSDAP in der Weimarer Republik* (Bonn: Droste, 1989).

140. Rainer Schaefer, *SPD in der Ära Brüning: Tolerierung oder Mobilisierung? Handlungsspielräume und Strategien sozialdemokratischer Politik 1930–1932* (Frankfurt am Main: Campus, 1990).

141. Klaus Schönhoven, "Strategie des Nichtstuns? Sozialdemokratischer Legalismus und kommunistischer Attentismus in der Ära der Präsidialkabinette," in *Die deutsche Staatskrise 1930–1933*, ed. Winkler, 59–76; see esp. 74.

142. Turner, *Hitler's Thirty Days to Power*, 53–78.

143. Winkler, *Weimar, 1918–1933*, 583.

144. Turner, *Hitler's Thirty Days to Power*, 29.

145. Ibid., 163–83.
146. Bracher, *Die Auflösung der Weimarer Republik,* 728.
147. Hans Mommsen, "Regierung ohne Parteien: Konservative Pläne zum Verfassungsumbau am Ende der Weimarer Republik," in *Die deutsche Staatskrise 1930–1933,* ed. Winkler, 1–18; see esp. 1.

Chapter 4. Cataclysms: Genocide and Memory

1. Matthew S. Anderson, *The Eastern Question, 1774–1923: A Study in International Relations* (London: Macmillan, 1966), 364.
2. Harry J. Psomiades, *The Eastern Question—the Last Phase: A Study in Greek-Turkish Diplomacy* (Thessaloniki: Institute for Balkan Studies, 1969); Marjorie H. Dobkin, *Smyrna 1922: The Destruction of a City* (London: Faber 1972).
3. P. Risal, *La ville convoitée Salonique* (Paris: Perrin, 1914), 338.
4. Arnold J. Toynbee, *The Western Question in Greece and Turkey: A Study in the Contact of Civilizations* (1922; repr., New York: Fertig, 1970), 272; Justine McCarthy, *Death and Exile: The Ethnic Cleansing of Ottoman Muslims, 1821–1922* (Princeton, N.J.: Darwin Press, 1995), 262–63.
5. Toynbee, *Western Question,* 275.
6. Barbara Jelavich and Charles Jelavich, *The Establishment of the Balkan National States, 1804–1920* (Seattle: University of Washington Press, 1977), 216ff.
7. Karl Pauli, *Kriegsgreuel: Erlebnisse im türkisch-bulgarischen Kriege 1912: Nach den Berichten von Mitkämpfern und Augenzeugen bearbeitet von Carl Pauli* (Minden: Köhler, 1913).
8. Carnegie Commission of Investigation, *Report of the International Commission to Inquire into the Causes and Conduct of the Balkan Wars* (Washington, D.C.: Carnegie Endowment for International Peace, 1914), 155–56.
9. Fikret Adanir, *Die makedonische Frage: Ihre Entstehung und Entwicklung bis 1908* (Wiesbaden: Steiner, 1979).
10. Feroz Ahmad, "Unionist Relations with the Greek, Armenian, and Jewish Communities of the Ottoman Empire 1908–1914," in *Christians and Jews in the Ottoman Empire: The Functioning of a Plural Society,* vol. 1, *The Central Lands,* ed. Benjamin Braude and Bernard Lewis, 401–37 (New York: Holmes & Meier, 1982).
11. Malcolm E. Yapp, *The Making of the Modern Near East, 1792–1923* (London: Longman, 1987), 189–90.
12. Anderson, *Eastern Question,* 273.

13. Ibid., 275.

14. McCarthy, *Death and Exile*, 156–57.

15. Katrin Boeckh, *Von den Balkankriegen zum Ersten Weltkrieg: Kleinstaatenpolitik und ethnische Selbstbestimmung auf dem Balkan* (Munich: Oldenbourg, 1996), 270.

16. Stephan P. Ladas, *The Exchange of Minorities: Bulgaria, Greece and Turkey* (New York: Macmillan, 1932), 19.

17. Dimitri Pentzopoulos, *The Balkan Exchange of Minorities and Its Impact upon Greece* (Paris: Mouton, 1962), 57; John A. Petropulos, "The Compulsory Exchange of Populations: Greek-Turkish Peacemaking, 1922–1930," *Byzantine and Modern Greek Studies* 2 (1976): 135–60.

18. Michael R. Marrus, *The Unwanted: European Refugees in the Twentieth Century* (New York: Oxford University Press, 1985), 61–62.

19. Carol Iancu, *Jews in Romania, 1866–1919: From Expulsion to Emancipation* (New York: Columbia University Press, 1996), 178.

20. Robert Coonrod, "The Duma's Attitude towards Wartime Problems of Minority Groups," *American Slavic and East European Review* 13 (1954): 34; Dan Brower, "Kyrgiz Nomads and Russian Pioneers: Colonization and Ethnic Conflict in the Turkestan Revolt of 1916," *Jahrbücher für die Geschichte Osteuropas* 44 (1996): 52.

21. General C. Korganoff, *La participation des Arméniens à la guerre mondiale sur le front du Caucase (1914–1918)* (Paris: Massis, 1927).

22. On the historiographical controversy, see Gwynne Dyer, "Turkish 'Falsifiers' and Armenian 'Deceivers': Historiography and the Armenian Massacres," *Middle Eastern Studies* 12 (1976): 99–107.

23. Robert Melson, *Revolution and Genocide: On the Origins of the Armenian Genocide and the Holocaust* (Chicago: University of Chicago Press, 1992), 143–44.

24. Kemal Karpat, "Millets and Nationality: The Roots of the Incongruity of Nation and State in the Post-Ottoman Era," in *Central Lands*, ed. Braude and Lewis, 141–70.

25. Roderic H. Davison, *Reform in the Ottoman Empire, 1856–1876* (Princeton, N.J.: Princeton University Press, 1963).

26. Richard Clogg, "The Greek Millet in the Ottoman Empire," in *Central Lands*, ed. Braude and Lewis, 185–201.

27. Johannes Lepsius, *Armenia and Europe* (London: Hodder & Stoughton, 1897), 35, 76.

28. Stanford Shaw and Ezel K. Shaw, *History of the Ottoman Empire and Modern Turkey*, vol. 2 (Cambridge: Cambridge University Press, 1977), 302.

29. Anderson, *Eastern Question,* 271.

30. McCarthy, *Death and Exile,* 193ff.

31. Yapp, *Making of the Modern Near East,* 47–96.

32. Melson, *Revolution and Genocide,* 161.

33. Henry Morgenthau, *Ambassador Morgenthau's Story* (Garden City, N.Y.: Doubleday, 1918), 351–52; concerning documentation, see Vahakn N. Dadrian, "The Naim-Andonian Documents on the World War I Destruction of Ottoman Armenians: The Anatomy of a Genocide," *International Journal of Middle Eastern Studies* 18 (1986): 311–60.

34. Joseph Rothschild, *East Central Europe between the Two World Wars* (Seattle: University of Washington Press, 1974), 3ff.

35. Eugene M. Kulischer, *Europe on the Move: War and Population Changes, 1917–1947* (New York: Columbia University Press, 1948); Heinz Fassmann and Rainer Münz, "European East-West Migration 1945–1992," *International Migration Review* 4 (1994): 520–38.

36. Jacob Robinson, *Were the Minorities Treaties a Failure?* (New York: Institute for Jewish Affairs, 1943).

37. Rothschild, *East Central Europe between the Two World Wars,* 29–30.

38. Emanuel Melzer, *No Way Out: The Politics of Polish Jewry, 1935–1939* (Cincinnati: Hebrew Union College Press, 1997), 39–53.

39. Ezra Mendelsohn, *The Jews of East Central Europe between the Two World Wars* (Bloomington: Indiana University Press, 1983).

40. Marrus, *Unwanted,* 141ff.

41. William Hagen, "Before the 'Final Solution': Towards a Comparative Analysis of Political Anti-Semitism in Interwar Germany and Poland," *Journal of Modern History* 68 (1996): 351–81.

42. Pawel Korzec, "Antisemitism in Poland as an Intellectual, Social and Political Movement," in *Studies on Polish Jewry, 1919–1939,* ed. Joshua A. Fishman, 12–104 (New York: Yivo Institute for Jewish Research, 1974).

43. Saul Friedländer, *Nazi Germany and the Jews,* vol. 1, *The Years of Persecution, 1933–1939* (New York: HarperCollins, 1997), 244–45.

44. Oskar Mendelsohn, "Norwegen," in *Dimension des Völkermords: Die Zahl der jüdischen Opfer des Nationalsozialismus,* ed. Wolfgang Benz, 187–98 (Munich: Oldenbourg, 1991).

45. Liliane Picciotto Fargion, "Italien," in *Dimension des Völkermords,* ed. Benz, 199–228; see esp. 213–14.

46. Norbert Frei, *Der Führerstaat: Nationalsozialistische Herrschaft 1933 bis 1945* (Munich: Deutscher Taschenbuch Verlag, 1987), 130ff.; Raphael

Gross, "Politische Polykratie 1936: Die legendenumwobene SD-Akte Carl Schmitt," *Tel Aviver Jahrbuch für deutsche Geschichte* 23 (1994): 115–43.

47. Hans Mommsen, "Die Realisierung des Utopischen: Die 'Endlösung der Judenfrage' im 'Dritten Reich,'" *Geschichte und Gesellschaft* 9 (1983): 381–420.

48. S. Friedländer, *Years of Persecution,* 72ff.

49. Götz Aly and Susanne Heim, *Architects of Annihilation: Auschwitz and the Logic of Destruction* (Princeton, N.J.: Princeton University Press, 2003).

50. Kurt Jakob Ball-Kaduri, "Die illegale Einwanderung der deutschen Juden in Palästina," *Jahrbuch des Instituts für deutsche Geschichte* 4 (1975): 387–422.

51. Abraham Margalijot, "The Problem of the Rescue of German Jewry during the Years 1938–45: The Reasons for the Delay in the Emigration from the Third Reich," in *Rescue Attempts during the Holocaust: Proceedings of the Second Yad Vashem International Historical Conference, Jerusalem, April 8–11, 1974,* ed. Yisrael Gutman and Efraim Zuroff, 247–66 (Jerusalem: Yad Vashem, 1977).

52. Herbert Rosenkranz, *Verfolgung und Selbstbehauptung: Die Juden in Österreich 1938–1945* (Vienna: Herold, 1978).

53. Michael Mashberg, "American Diplomacy and the Jewish Refugees 1938/39," *Yivo Annual* (1974): 339–65.

54. Marrus, *Unwanted,* 203–4.

55. Götz Aly, *"The Final Solution": Nazi Population Policy and the Murder of European Jewry* (London: Oxford University Press, 1999), 18.

56. Yisrael Gutman and Shmuel Krakowski, *Unequal Victims: Poles and Jews during World War Two* (New York: Holocaust Library, 1986).

57. Quoted in Philippe Burrin, *Hitler and the Jews: The Genesis of the Holocaust* (London: Arnold, 1994), 69; Seev Goshem, "Eichmann und die Nisko-Aktion im Oktober 1939: Eine Fallstudie zur NS-Judenpolitik in der letzten Etappe vor den 'Endlösung,'" *Vierteljahrshefte für Zeitgeschichte* 27 (1981): 74–96.

58. Christopher R. Browning, "Nazi Ghettoization Policy in Poland 1939–1941," in his *Path to Genocide: Essays on Launching the Final Solution,* 28–56 (Cambridge: Cambridge University Press, 1992).

59. Raul Hilberg, *The Destruction of the European Jews* (New York: Holmes & Meier, 1985), 162.

60. Leni Yahil, "Madagascar—Phantom of a Solution for the Jewish Question," in *Jews and Non-Jews in Eastern Europe, 1918–1945,* ed. Bela

Vago and George Mosse, 315–34 (Jerusalem: Israel Universities Press, 1974).

61. Magnus Brechtken, *"Madagaskar für die Juden": Antisemitische Idee und politische Praxis 1885–1945* (Munich: Oldenbourg, 1997), 270–71.

62. Hilberg, *Destruction of the European Jews*, 162.

63. Henry Friedlander, *The Origins of Nazi Genocide: From Euthanasia to the Final Solution* (Chapel Hill: University of North Carolina Press, 1995), 22.

64. Reiner Pommerin, *"Sterilisierung der Rheinlandbastarde": Das Schicksal einer farbigen deutschen Minderheit 1918–1937* (Düsseldorf: Droste, 1979).

65. S. Friedländer, *Years of Persecution*, 152–53.

66. For a different view, see H. Friedlander, *Origins of Nazi Genocide*, 1.

67. Ludolf Herbst, *Das nationalsozialistische Deutschland 1933–1945: Die Entfesselung der Gewalt—Rassismus und Krieg* (Frankfurt am Main: Suhrkamp, 1996), 381.

68. Christian Streit, "Ostkrieg, Antibolschewismus und 'Endlösung,'" *Geschichte und Gesellschaft* 17 (1991): 242–55.

69. Walter Laqueur, *Russia and Germany: A Century of Conflict* (London: Weidenfeld & Nicolson, 1965).

70. Klaus Hildebrand, *1933–1945: Kalkül oder Dogma* (Stuttgart: Kohlhammer, 1980), 115.

71. Hans Buchheim, ed., *Anatomie des SS-Staates*, vol. 2, Martin Broszat, H.-A. Jacobsen, and H. Krausnick , eds. *Konzentrationslager, Kommissarbefehl, Judenverfolgung* (Olten: Walter-Verlag, 1965), 200ff.

72. Peter Longerich, "Vom Massenmord zur 'Endlösung': Die Erschießungen von jüdischen Zivilisten in den ersten Monaten des Ostfeldzuges im Kontext des nationalsozialistischen Judenmordes," in *Zwei Wege nach Moskau: Vom Hitler-Stalin-Pakt zum "Unternehmen Barbarossa,"* ed. Bernd Wegner, 251–74 (Munich: Piper, 1991).

73. Omer Bartov, *Hitler's Army: Soldiers, Nazis, and War in the Third Reich* (New York: Oxford University Press, 1991), 129–30.

74. Christian Streit, *Keine Kameraden: Die Wehrmacht und die sowjetischen Kriegsgefangenen 1941–1945* (Stuttgart: Deutsche Verlags-Anstalt, 1978).

75. Andreas Hillgruber, "Die 'Endlösung' und das deutsche Ostimperium als Kernstück des rassistischen Programms des Nationalsozialismus," *Vierteljahrshefte für Zeitgeschichte* 20 (1972): 133–53.

76. Daniel J. Goldhagen, *Hitler's Willing Executioners: Ordinary Germans and the Holocaust* (New York: Alfred A. Knopf, 1996).

77. Ralf Ogorreck, *Die Einsatzgruppen und die "Genesis der Endlösung"* (Berlin: Metropol, 1996), 191.

78. Walter Grode, *Die "Sonderbehandlung 14f 13" in den Konzentrationslagern des Dritten Reiches: Ein Beitrag zur Dynamik faschistischer Vernichtungspolitik* (Frankfurt am Main: Lang, 1994).

79. H. Friedlander, *Origins of Nazi Genocide*, 298.

80. Ulrich Herbert, ed., *National Socialist Extermination Policies: Contemporary German Perspectives and Controversies* (New York: Berghahn Books, 2000)

81. Eberhard Jäckel, "Die Konferenz am Wannsee," *Die Zeit*, 17 January 1992, 33–34.

82. Herbst, *Das nationalsozialistische Deutschland*, 374ff.

83. Kurt Pätzold and Erika Schwarz, *Tagesordnung: Judenmord: Die Wannsee-Konferenz am 20. Januar 1942: Eine Dokumentation zur Organisation der Endlösung* (Berlin: Metropol, 1992).

84. Peter Longerich, ed., *Die Ermordung der europäischen Juden: Eine umfassende Dokumentation des Holocaust 1941–1945* (Munich: Piper, 1990), 94. The German term Eichmann used was *annageln*.

85. Christian Gerlach, "Die Wannsee-Konferenz: Das Schicksal der deutschen Juden und Hitlers politische Grundsatzentscheidung, alle Juden zu ermorden," *Werkstatt Geschichte* 18 (1997): 7–44; see esp. 11–12.

86. Joseph Goebbels, *Tagebücher*, part 2, vol. 2 (Munich: Piper, 1992), 498–99, entry for 13 December 1941.

87. Leendert J. Hartog, *Der Befehl zum Judenmord: Hitler, Amerika und die Juden* (Bodenheim: Syndikat, 1997).

88. Saul Friedländer, *Auftakt zum Untergang: Hitler und die Vereinigten Staaten von Amerika, 1939–1941* (Stuttgart: Kohlhammer, 1965).

89. Quoted in Gerlach, "Die Wannsee-Konferenz," 22n92 ("Judenfrage/als Partisanen auszurotten").

90. Herbst, *Das nationalsozialistische Deutschland*, 374–75.

91. Yitzhak Arad, *Belzec, Sobibor, Treblinka: The Operation Reinhard Death Camps* (Bloomington: Indiana University Press, 1987), 23–29.

92. Pätzold and Schwarz, *Tagesordnung: Judenmord*, 56.

93. Norbert Frei, *Adenauer's Germany and the Nazi Past: The Politics of Amnesty and Integration* (New York: Columbia University Press, 2002), 235.

94. Martin Broszat, "Soziale Motivation und Führer-Bindung des Nationalsozialismus," *Vierteljahrshefte für Zeitgeschichte* 3 (1970): 392–409; see esp. 401–2.

95. Goldhagen, *Hitler's Willing Executioners.*

96. Nathan Stoltzfus, *Resistance of the Heart: Intermarriage and the Rosenstraße Protest in Nazi Germany* (New York: Norton, 1996), 258ff.

97. S. Friedländer, *Years of Persecution,* 83–84.

98. Jeremy Noakes, "The Development of the Nazi Policy towards the German-Jewish 'Mischlinge' 1933–1945," *Leo Baeck Institute Yearbook* 34 (1989): 291–354.

99. Christopher R. Browning, *Ordinary Men: Reserve Police Battalion 101 and the Final Solution in Poland* (New York: HarperCollins, 1992); cf. Goldhagen, *Hitler's Willing Executioners.*

100. Dan Diner, "Gestaute Zeit: Massenvernichtung und jüdische Erzählstruktur," in his *Kreisläufe: Nationalsozialismus und Gedächtnis,* 123–40 (Berlin: Berlin-Verlag, 1995).

101. Peter Burke, "Geschichte als soziales Gedächtnis," in *Mnemosyne: Formen und Funktionen der kulturellen Erinnerung,* ed. Aleida Assmann and Dietrich Harth, 298–304 (Frankfurt am Main: Fischer Taschenbuch Verlag, 1991).

102. Stefan Andriopoulos, *Unfall und Verbrechen: Konfigurationen zwischen juristischem und literarischem Diskurs um 1900* (Pfaffenweiler: Centaurus, 1996).

103. Uriel Tal, "On Structures of Political Theology and Myth in Germany Prior to the Holocaust," in *The Holocaust as Historical Experience: Essays and a Discussion,* ed. Yehuda Bauer and Nathan Rotenstreich, 43–74 (New York: Holmes & Meier, 1981).

104. Detlev Claussen, *Grenzen der Aufklärung: Die gesellschaftliche Genese des modernen Antisemitismus,* rev. ed. (Frankfurt am Main: Fischer Taschenbuch Verlag, 1994).

105. Max Horkheimer and Theodor W. Adorno, "Elements of Anti-Semitism: Limits of Enlightenment," in their *Dialectic of Enlightenment,* 162–208 (London: Verso, 1997).

106. H. Friedlander, *Origins of Nazi Genocide,* 198–99.

107. Ibid., 199.

108. Michael Zimmermann, *Rassenutopie und Genozid: Die nationalsozialistische "Lösung der Zigeunerfrage"* (Hamburg: Christians, 1996).

109. Eric Hobsbawm, "Introduction: Inventing Traditions," in *The Invention of Tradition,* ed. Eric Hobsbawm and Terence Ranger, 1–14 (Cambridge: Cambridge University Press, 1992).

110. Ernst Klee, *"Euthanasie" im NS-Staat: Die "Vernichtung lebensunwerten Lebens"* (Frankfurt am Main: S. Fischer, 1983).

111. Dirk Blasius, "Das Ende der Humanität: Psychiatrie und Krankenmord in der NS-Zeit," in *Der historische Ort des Nationalsozialismus: Annäherungen,* ed. Walter H. Pehle, 47–70 (Frankfurt am Main: Fischer Taschenbuch Verlag, 1990).

112. Dov B. Yaroshewski, "Political Participation and Public Memory: The Memorial Movement in the USSR 1987–1989," *History & Memory. Studies in Representation of the Past* 2 (1999): 5–31.

113. Dietrich Geyer, "Klio in Moskau und die sowjetische Geschichte," *Sitzungsberichte der Heidelberger Akademie der Wissenschaften, Philosophisch-historische Klasse* 2 (1985): 36–38.

114. Ekkehard Klug, "Das 'asiatische' Russland: Über die Entstehung eines europäischen Vorurteils," *Historische Zeitschrift* 245 (1987): 256–89.

115. Karlheinz Mack, ed., *Revolutionen in Ostmitteleuropa 1789–1989: Schwerpunkt Ungarn* (Vienna: Verlag für Geschichte und Politik, 1995).

116. Aleksandr M. Nekrich, *The Punished Peoples: The Deportations and Fate of Soviet Minorities at the End of the Second World War* (New York: Norton, 1978).

117. Nicolas Werth, "Ein Staat gegen sein Volk: Gewalt, Unterdrückung und Terror in der Sowjetunion," in *Das Schwarzbuch des Kommunismus: Unterdrückung, Verbrechen und Terror,* ed. Stéphane Courtois and Irmela Arnsperger, 51–298 (Munich: Piper, 1998), 188–89.

118. Lynee Viola, "The Second Coming: Class Enemies in the Soviet Countryside 1927–1935," in *Stalinist Terror: New Perspectives,* ed. J. Arch Getty and Roberta T. Manning, 65–98 (Cambridge: Cambridge University Press, 1993), 75–76.

119. Ibid., 77.

120. Lynne Viola, "The Campaign to Eliminate the Kulak as a Class, Winter 1929–1930: A Reevaluation of the Legislation," *Slavic Review* 45 (1986): 508–11.

121. Igal Halfin, "From Darkness to Light: Student Communist Autobiography during NEP," *Jahrbücher für die Geschichte Osteuropas* 45 (1997), 210–36.

122. Alec Nove, "Victims of Stalinism: How Many," in *Stalinist Terror,* ed. Getty and Manning, 260–74.

123. J. Arch Getty, *Origins of the Great Purges: The Soviet Communist Party Reconsidered, 1918–1938* (Cambridge: Cambridge University Press, 1985).

124. Werth, "Ein Staat gegen sein Volk," 257ff.

125. Anton Antonov-Ovseenko, *The Time of Stalin: Portrait of a Tyranny* (New York: Harper & Row, 1981), 216.

126. Hannah Arendt, *The Origins of Totalitarianism* (New York: Meridian Books, 1963), 390.

127. Borys Lewytzkyj, *Die Rote Inquisition: Die Geschichte der sowjetischen Sicherheitsdienste* (Frankfurt am Main: Societäts-Verlag, 1967).

128. Ernst Nolte, "A Past That Will Not Pass Away (A Speech It Was Possible to Write, but Not to Present)," *Yad Vashem Studies* 19 (1988): 65–74.

129. Uwe Dietrich Adam, *Judenpolitik im Dritten Reich* (Dusseldorf: Droste, 1979).

130. Ralf Stettner, *"Archipel Gulag": Stalins Zwangslager—Terrorinstrument und Wirtschaftsgigant: Entstehung, Organisation und Funktion des sowjetischen Lagersystems* (Paderborn: Schöningh, 1996), 118.

131. Ibid., 337–38.

132. Ulrich Herbert, *Hitler's Foreign Workers: Enforced Foreign Labor in Germany under the Third Reich* (Cambridge: Cambridge University Press, 1997).

133. Mechthild Rössler and Sabine Schleiermacher, eds., *Der "Generalplan Ost": Hauptlinien der nationalsozialistischen Planungs- und Vernichtungspolitik* (Berlin: Akademie-Verlag, 1993).

134. David J. Dallin and Boris I. Nicolaevski, *Forced Labor in Russia* (New Haven, Conn.: Yale University Press, 1947).

135. Dan Diner, "Nazism and Stalinism: On Memory, Arbitrariness, Labor, and Death," in his *Beyond the Conceivable: Studies on Germany, Nazism, and the Holocaust,* 187–200 (Berkeley: University of California Press, 2000).

136. Andrzej Paczkowski, "Polen, der 'Erbfeind,'" in *Das Schwarzbuch des Kommunismus,* ed. Courtois and Arnsperger, 397–429.

137. Peter P. Knoch, "Das Bild des russischen Feindes," in *Stalingrad: Mythos und Wirklichkeit einer Schlacht,* ed. Wolfram Wette and Gerd R. Ueberschär, 160–67 (Frankfurt am Main: Fischer Taschenbuch Verlag, 1992).

138. Lutz Niethammer, "Juden und Russen im Gedächtnis der Deutschen," in *Der historische Ort des Nationalsozialismus,* ed. Pehle, 114–34.

139. Norman M. Naimark, *The Russians in Germany: A History of the Zone of Occupation, 1945–1949* (Cambridge, Mass.: Belknap Press of Harvard University Press, 1995); Atina Grossmann, "A Question of Silence: The Rape of German Women by Occupation Soldiers," *October* 72 (1995): 43–63.

140. Alfred Maurice de Zayas, *Nemesis at Potsdam: The Expulsion of the*

Germans from the East (Lincoln: University of Nebraska Press, 1989), 8off.; Klaus-Dietmar Henke, "Der Weg nach Potsdam: Die Allierten und die Vertreibung," in *Die Vertreibung der Deutschen aus dem Osten: Ursachen, Ereignisse, Folgen,* ed. Wolfgang Benz, 49–69 (Frankfurt am Main: Fischer Taschenbuch Verlag, 1985).

141. Richard Matthias Müller, *Normal-Null und die Zukunft der deutschen Vergangenheitsbewältigung* (Schernfeld: SH-Verlag, 1994).

142. Dan Diner, *Der Krieg der Erinnerungen und die Ordnung der Welt* (Berlin: Rotbuch, 1991).

143. Antonia Grunenberg, *Antifaschismus—ein deutscher Mythos* (Reinbek: Rowohlt, 1993).

144. Sigrid Meuschel, *Legitimation und Parteiherrschaft in der DDR* (Frankfurt am Main: Suhrkamp, 1992), 101–2.

145. Ernst Nolte, *Lehrstücke oder Tragödie? Beiträge zur Interpretation der Geschichte des 20. Jahrhunderts* (Cologne: Böhlau, 1991).

146. See arguments in Courtois and Arnsperger, *Das Schwarzbuch des Kommunismus,* 11–50, 29–30.

147. Dan Diner, "On Guilt and Other Narratives: Epistemological Observations regarding the Holocaust," *History & Memory: Studies in Representation of the Past* 9 (1997): 301–20.

Chapter 5. Dualisms: Decolonization and the Cold War

1. Dean Acheson, *Present at the Creation* (New York: Norton, 1969), 217; Terry H. Anderson, *The United States, Great Britain and the Cold War, 1944–1947* (Columbia: University of Missouri Press, 1981), 165–66.

2. Carl Schmitt, "Raum und Großraum im Völkerrecht," in his *Staat, Großraum, Nomos: Arbeiten aus den Jahren 1916–1969,* ed. Günter Maschke, 234–68 (Berlin: Duncker & Humblot, 1995), 262.

3. Henry A. Kissinger, *Diplomacy* (New York: Simon & Schuster, 1994), 22–23.

4. Bruce R. Kuniholm, *The Origins of the Cold War in the Near East: Great Power Conflict and Diplomacy in Iran, Turkey, and Greece* (Princeton, N.J.: Princeton University Press, 1980).

5. Wilfried Loth, *Die Teilung der Welt: Geschichte des Kalten Krieges,* 8th ed. (Munich: Deutscher Taschenbuch Verlag, 1990), 163ff.

6. Gavriel Ra'anan, *International Policy Formation in the USSR: Factional "Debates" during the Zhdanovschina* (Hamden, Conn.: Archon Books, 1983), 101–2.

7. Robert V. Daniels, ed., *A Documentary History of Communism*, vol. 2 (Hanover, N.H.: University Press of New England, 1984), 148.

8. For a comprehensive but Germanocentric interpretation, see Ernst Nolte, *Deutschland und der Kalte Krieg* (Munich: Piper, 1974), 231ff.

9. Kissinger, *Diplomacy*, 470ff.

10. Carl Schmitt, "Die geschichtlichen Strukturen des heutigen Weltgegensatzes von Ost und West: Bemerkungen zu Ernst Jüngers Schrift 'Der Gordische Knoten,'" in his *Staat, Großraum, Nomos*, 523–51.

11. Tony Smith, *America's Mission: The United States and the Worldwide Struggle for Democracy in the Twentieth Century* (Princeton, N.J.: Princeton University Press, 1994).

12. William Roger Louis, *Imperialism at Bay: The United States and the Decolonization of the British Empire, 1941–1945* (New York: Oxford University Press, 1978).

13. Bernd Martin, "The Politics of Expansion of the Japanese Empire: Imperialism or Pan-Asiatic Mission?" in *Imperialism and After: Continuities and Discontinuities*, ed. Wolfgang J. Mommsen and Jürgen Osterhammel, 63–82, 71ff. (London: Allen & Unwin, 1986).

14. Jürgen Lütt, "'Übertragung der Macht' oder 'Sieg im Freiheitskampf'? Der Weg zur indischen Unabhängigkeit," in *Das Ende der Kolonialreiche: Dekolonisation und die Politik der Großmächte*, ed. Wolfgang J. Mommsen, 47–66 (Frankfurt am Main: Fischer Taschenbuch Verlag, 1990).

15. Lloyd C. Gardner, "The Atlantic Charter: Idea and Reality," in *The Atlantic Charter*, Douglas Brinkley and David Facey-Crowther, 45–81 (Basingstoke, Hampshire: Macmillan, 1994).

16. Louis, *Imperialism at Bay*, 200.

17. Lütt, "'Übertragung der Macht' oder 'Sieg im Freiheitskampf'?" 53.

18. D. H. Fieldhouse, "The Labour Governments and Empire-Commonwealth, 1945–1951," in *The Foreign Policy of the British Labour Governments, 1945–1951*, ed. Ritchie Ovendale, 83–120 (Leicester: Leicester University Press, 1984).

19. Anderson, *United States, Great Britain, and the Cold War*, 173–74; Rouhollah Ramazani, *The Northern Tier: Afghanistan, Iran, and Turkey* (Princeton, N.J.: Van Nostrand, 1966).

20. Alex J. Robertson, *The Bleak Midwinter 1947* (Manchester: Manchester University Press, 1987), 23ff.

21. Anderson, *United States, Great Britain, and the Cold War*, 165–66.

22. John L. Gaddis, *We Now Know: Rethinking Cold War History* (Oxford: Clarendon Press, 1997), 44.

23. Howard Jones, *A New Kind of War: America's Global Strategy and the Truman Doctrine in Greece* (New York: Oxford University Press, 1989), 45.

24. Scott Bills, *Empire and Cold War: The Roots of US–Third World Antagonism* (New York: St. Martin's Press, 1990), 5ff.

25. Denise Artaud, "France between the Indochina War and the European Defense Community," in *Dien Bien Phu and the Crisis of Franco-American Relations, 1954–1955,* ed. Lawrence S. Kaplan, Denise Artaud, and Mark R. Rubin, 251–67 (Wilmington, Del.: Scholarly Resources, 1990), 258.

26. Tony Smith, "A Comparative Study of French and British Decolonisation," *Comparative Studies in Society and History* 20, no.1 (1978): 70–102.

27. Alain Ruscio, *La décolonisation tragique: Une histoire de la de´colonisation francaise, 1945–1962* (Paris: Messidor, 1987).

28. Gaddis, *We Now Know,* 152–53.

29. Yonosuka Nagai and Akira Iriye, eds., *The Origins of the Cold War in Asia* (Tokyo: University of Tokyo Press, 1977).

30. Malcolm E. Yapp, *The Making of the Modern Near East* (London: Longman, 1987), 47–96.

31. Gerald D. Clayton, *Britain and the Eastern Question: Missolonghi to Gallipoli* (London: University of London Press, 1971).

32. Muriel E. Chamberlain, *British Foreign Policy in the Age of Palmerston* (London: Longman, 1980); Martin Kingsley, *The Triumph of Lord Palmerston: A Study of Public Opinion in England before the Crimean War* (1924; repr., London: Hutchinson, 1963).

33. Winfried Baumgart, *The Peace of Paris 1856: Studies in War, Diplomacy and Peacemaking* (Oxford: Clio Press, 1981).

34. Werner E. Mosse, *The Rise and Fall of the Crimean System 1855–71: The Story of the Peace Settlement* (London: St. Martin's Press, 1963).

35. Winfried Baumgart, "Der Krimkrieg in der angelsächsischen und russischen militärgeschichtlichen Literatur der 60er Jahre," *Militärgeschichtliche Mitteilungen* 8 (1970): 181–94.

36. Robert Conquest, *Power and Policy in the USSR* (New York: Harper & Row, 1967), 135.

37. Harish Kapur, *Soviet Russia and Asia, 1917–1927: A Study of Soviet Policy towards Turkey, Iran and Afghanistan* (Geneva: Chevalier, 1965), 93–94.

38. Howard M. Sachar, *The Emergence of the Middle East, 1919–1924* (New York: Knopf, 1969), 62ff.

39. David Fromkin, *A Peace to End All Peace: Creating the Modern Middle East, 1914–1922* (London: A. Deutsch, 1989), 130–31.

40. Howard M. Sachar, *Europe Leaves the Middle East, 1936–1954* (New York: Knopf, 1972), 364ff.

41. Kuniholm, *Origins of the Cold War in the Near East,* 68–69.

42. George Kirk, *The Middle East in War* (London: Oxford University Press, 1952), 443–44.

43. George Lenczowski, *The Middle East in World Affairs,* 3rd ed. (Ithaca, N.Y.: Cornell University Press, 1962), 134ff.

44. Kuniholm, *Origins of the Cold War in the Near East,* 20–21.

45. Edward Weisband, *Turkish Foreign Policy, 1943–1945* (Princeton, N.J.: Princeton University Press, 1973), 228–29.

46. William Roger Louis, *The British Empire in the Middle East, 1945–1951: Arab Nationalism, the United States and Postwar Imperialism* (Oxford: Clarendon Press, 1984), 74.

47. Weisband, *Turkish Foreign Policy,* 183.

48. Bernard Lewis, *The Emergence of Modern Turkey* (London: Oxford University Press, 1961), 477–78.

49. Albert Sorel, *The Eastern Question in the Eighteenth Century: The Partition of Poland and the Treaty of Kainardji* (1878; repr., New York: Fertig, 1969), 41ff.

50. Matthew S. Anderson, *The Eastern Question, 1774–1923: A Study in International Relations* (London: Macmillan, 1966), 388ff.

51. Weisband, *Turkish Foreign Policy,* 134.

52. Kuniholm, *Origins of the Cold War in the Near East,* 304–5.

53. Ibid., 317.

54. Ibid., 258.

55. George Kirk, *The Middle East, 1945–1950* (London: Oxford University Press, 1954), 21–22.

56. Kuniholm, *Origins of the Cold War in the Near East,* 356–57.

57. Jones, *New Kind of War,* 38–41.

58. Winston Churchill, *Triumph and Tragedy* (Boston: Houghton Mifflin, 1953), 669.

59. Kuniholm, *Origins of the Cold War in the Near East,* 402–3.

60. Jones, *New Kind of War,* 30.

61. Max Mazower, *Inside Hitler's Greece: The Experience of Occupation, 1941–1944* (New Haven, Conn.: Yale University Press, 1993); Gabriella

Etmektsoglou, "Changes in the Civilian Economy as a Factor in the Radicalization of Popular Opposition in Greece, 1941–1944," in *Die "Neuordnung" Europas: NS-Wirtschaftspolitik in den besetzten Gebieten,* ed. Richard J. Overgy, Gerhard Otto, and Johannes Houwink ten Cate, 193–240 (Berlin: Metropol, 1997).

62. Kuniholm, *Origins of the Cold War in the Near East,* 226–27.

63. Haris Vlavianos, *Greece, 1941–49: From Resistance to Civil War: The Strategy of the Greek Communist Party* (London: Macmillan, 1992), 23.

64. Matthias Esche, *Die Kommunistische Partei Griechenlands 1941–1949: Ein Beitrag zur Politik der KKE vom Beginn der Résistance bis zum Ende des Bürgerkriegs* (Munich: Oldenbourg, 1982).

65. Vlavianos, *Greece, 1941–49,* 24.

66. William H. McNeill, *The Greek Dilemma* (London: Gollancz, 1947), 94.

67. John Iatrides, *Revolt in Athens: The Greek Communist "Second Round" 1944–1955* (Princeton, N.J.: Princeton University Press, 1972), 20–21.

68. John Campbell and Philip Sherrard, *Modern Greece* (New York: Praeger, 1968), 11–12.

69. C. M. Woodhouse, *Apple of Discord* (London: Hutchinson, 1948), 10–11.

70. McNeill, *Greek Dilemma,* 13ff.

71. C. M. Woodhouse, *The Struggle for Greece, 1941–1949* (London: Hart-Davis, MacGibbson, 1976), 103–4.

72. Albert Resis, "The Churchill-Stalin 'Percentages' Agreement on the Balkans, Moscow, October 1944," *American Historical Review* 83 (1978): 368–87.

73. Woodhouse, *Struggle for Greece,* 149.

74. Barbara Jelavich, *History of the Balkans,* vol. 2, *Twentieth Century* (Cambridge: Cambridge University Press, 1983), 312.

75. Kuniholm, *Origins of the Cold War in the Near East,* 402–3.

76. Evangelos Kofus, *Nationalism and Communism in Macedonia* (Thessaloniki: Institute for Balkan Studies, 1964).

77. Elisabeth Tonkin, Maryon McDonald, and Malcolm Chapman, eds., *History and Ethnicity* (London: Routledge, 1989), 71–88; Anna Collard, "Investigating 'Social Memory' in a Greek Context," in *History and Ethnicity,* ed. Tonkin, McDonald, and Chapman, 89–103; see esp. 98–99.

78. Esche, *Die Kommunistische Partei Griechenlands,* 315–16.

79. Anastasia N. Karakasidou, "Fellow Travellers, Separate Roads: The KKE and the Macedonian Question," *East European Quarterly* 27 (1993): 453–77.

80. Edgar O'Ballance, *The Greek Civil War, 1944–1949* (New York: Praeger, 1966), 132.

81. Milovan Djilas, *Conversations with Stalin* (New York: Harcourt, Brace & World, 1962), 142–43.

82. Jelavich, *Twentieth Century*, 331–32.

83. Kuniholm, *Origins of the Cold War in the Near East*, 402.

84. Esche, *Die Kommunistische Partei Griechenlands*, 317.

85. Kofus, *Nationalism and Communism in Macedonia*, 158–59.

86. Esche, *Die Kommunistische Partei Griechenlands*, 348.

87. D. George Konsoulas, *Revolution and Defeat: The Story of the Greek Communist Party* (London: Oxford University Press, 1965).

88. Kofus, *Nationalism and Communism in Macedonia*, 177f.

89. McNeill, *Greek Dilemma*, 221.

90. Jelavich, *Twentieth Century*, 313.

91. Kofus, *Nationalism and Communism in Macedonia*, 185–86.

92. O'Ballance, *Greek Civil War*, 210.

93. Jones, *New Kind of War*, 36.

94. John L. Gaddis, "Was the Truman Doctrine a Real Turning Point?" *Foreign Affairs* 52 (1974): 346–402.

95. Glenn Paige, *The Korean Decision, June 24–30, 1950* (New York: Free Press, 1968), 54–148, quoted in Kuniholm, *Origins of the Cold War in the Near East*, 419.

96. *The Pentagon Papers*, Senator Gravel Edition, vol. 1 (Boston: Beacon Press, 1971), 615.

97. Gaddis, *We Now Know*, 74.

98. Bruce Cumings, *The Origins of the Korean War*, vol. 1, *Liberation and the Emergence of Separate Regimes, 1945–1947* (Princeton, N.J.: Princeton University Press, 1981).

99. Gaddis, *We Now Know*, 74.

100. John L. Gaddis, *The Long Peace: Inquiries into the History of the Cold War* (New York: Oxford University Press, 1987), 72–73; George C. Herring, "The Truman Doctrine in the Restoring of French Sovereignty in Indochina," *Diplomatic History* 1 (1977): 101.

101. Gaddis, *We Now Know*, 74.

102. Kathryn Weathersby, "The Soviet Role in the Early Phase of the Korean War: New Documentary Evidence," *Journal of American–East Asian Relations* 2 (1993): 425–58.

103. Gaddis, *We Now Know*, 77.

104. Jian Chen, *China's Road to the Korean War: The Making of the Sino-American Confrontation* (New York: Columbia University Press, 1994), 102.

105. Rolf Steininger, "Entscheidung am 38. Breitengrad: Die USA und der Korea-Krieg," *Amerikastudien* 26 (1981): 40–76.

106. Kissinger, *Diplomacy*, 481–82.

107. Michael Schaller, *The United States and China in the Twentieth Century* (New York: Oxford University Press, 1979).

108. Ibid., 98.

109. Gaddis, *We Now Know*, 59.

110. Odd Arne Westad, *Cold War and Revolution:. Soviet-American Rivalry and the Origins of the Chinese Civil War, 1944–1946* (New York: Columbia University Press, 1993), 79ff.

111. Gaddis, *Long Peace*, 164ff.

112. Kissinger, *Diplomacy*, 727ff.

113. Westad, *Cold War and Revolution*, 9ff.

114. Schaller, *United States and China in the Twentieth Century*, 110.

115. Chen, *China's Road to the Korean War*, 72.

116. Shu Guang Zhang, *Deterrence and Strategic Culture: Chinese-American Confrontations, 1949–1958* (Ithaca, N.Y.: Cornell University Press, 1992), 16–17.

117. Ibid., 25.

118. Ernest R. May, *"Lessons" of the Past: The Use and Misuse of History in American Foreign Policy* (New York: Oxford University Press, 1973), 32ff.

119. For a different view, see Gaddis, "Was the Truman Doctrine a Real Turning Point?"

120. Acheson, *Present at the Creation*, 420.

121. Rolf Steininger, *Wiederbewaffnung: Die Entscheidung für einen westdeutschen Verteidigungsbeitrag: Adenauer und die Westmächte 1950* (Erlangen: Straube, 1989), 43ff.

122. William Stueck, *The Korean War: An International History* (Princeton, N.J.: Princeton University Press, 1995), 19–20.

123. Gaddis, *We Now Know*, 82.

124. William J. Duiker, *U.S. Containment Policy and the Conflict in Indochina* (Stanford, Calif.: Stanford University Press, 1994), 29.

125. Robert J. McMahon, *Colonialism and Cold War: The United States and the Struggle for Indonesian Independence, 1945–49* (Ithaca, N.Y.: Cornell University Press, 1981), 56–57.

126. Robert S. McNamara, *In Retrospect: The Tragedy and Lessons of Vietnam* (New York: Times Books, 1995), 16.

127. Andrew J. Rotter, *The Path to Vietnam: Origins of the American Commitment to Southeast Asia* (Ithaca, N.Y.: Cornell University Press, 1987); Ronald McGlothen, *Controlling the Waves: Dean Acheson and U.S. Foreign Policy in Asia* (New York: Norton, 1993).

128. François Joyaux, *La nouvelle question de l'Extrême Orient*, vol. 1, *L'ère de la Guerre Froide (1945–1959)* (Paris: Payot, 1985).

129. Jacques Dalloz, *The War in Indo-China, 1945–54* (Dublin: Gill & Macmillan, 1990), 119.

130. Zhang, *Deterrence and Strategic Culture*, 174–75.

131. Ibid., 172.

132. Dalloz, *War in Indo-China*, 143.

133. Ibid., 130.

134. George C. Herring, *America's Longest War: The United States and Vietnam, 1950–1975* (New York: McGraw Hill, 1996).

135. George T. McKalin, *Intervention: How America Became Involved in Vietnam* (New York: Knopf, 1986).

136. Richard H. Immerman, "Prologue: Perceptions by the United States of Its Interests in Indochina," in *Dien Bien Phu and the Crisis of Franco-American Relations*, ed. Kaplan, Artaud, and Rubin, 1–26, see esp. 7.

137. Michael Schaller, "Securing the Great Crescent: Occupied Japan and the Origins of Containment in Southeast Asia," *Journal of American History* 69 (1982): 392–414.

138. For a detailed treatment, see Lawrence S. Kaplan, "The United States, NATO, and French Indochina," in *Dien Bien Phu and the Crisis of Franco-American Relations*, ed. Kaplan, Artaud, and Rubin, 229–50; see esp. 240.

139. George C. Herring, "Franco-American Conflict in Indochina, 1950–1954," in *Dien Bien Phu and the Crisis of Franco-American Relations*, ed. Kaplan, Artaud, and Rubin, 29–48; see esp. 30–38.

140. Dalloz, *War in Indo-China*, 130–42.

141. Gary R. Hess, "Redefining the American Position in Southeast Asia: The United States and the Geneva and Manila Conferences," in *Dien Bien Phu and the Crisis of Franco-American Relations*, ed. Kaplan, Artaud, and Rubin, 123–48; see esp. 132.

142. Ibid., 126f.

143. Dalloz, *War in Indo-China*, 167.

144. William Roger Louis, "Dulles, Suez and the British," in *John Foster Dulles and the Diplomacy of the Cold War*, ed. Richard Immerman, 133–58 (Princeton, N.J.: Princeton University Press, 1990); William

Roger Louis and Roger Owen, eds., *Suez 1956: The Crisis and Its Consequences* (Oxford: Clarendon, 1989).

145. Herring, "Franco-American Conflict in Indochina," 42–43.

146. Ibid., 35.

147. Ibid., 42–43; George C. Herring and Richard H. Immerman, "Eisenhower, Dulles, and Dien Bien Phu: 'The Day We Didn't Go to War,'" in *Dien Bien Phu and the Crisis of Franco-American Relations*, ed. Kaplan, Artaud, and Rubin, 81–104.

148. Kaplan, "United States, NATO, and French Indochina," 232.

149. Ibid., 240.

150. Denise Artaud, "Conclusion," in *Dien Bien Phu and the Crisis of Franco-American Relations*, ed. Kaplan, Artaud, and Rubin, 269–74; see esp. 274.

151. Immerman, "Prologue," 15.

152. Melanie Billings-Yun, *Decision against War: Eisenhower and Dien Bien Phu* (1954; repr. New York: Columbia University Press, 1988).

153. Artaud, "France between the Indochina War and the European Defense Community," 259.

154. Michael H. Hunt, *Lyndon Johnson's War: America's Cold War Crusade in Vietnam, 1945–1968* (New York: Hill & Wang, 1996).

155. Kaplan, "United States, NATO, and French Indochina," 231.

156. Artaud, "France between the Indochina War and the European Defense Community," 252–53.

157. Kaplan, "United States, NATO, and French Indochina," 230.

158. George A. Kelly, *Lost Soldiers: The French Army and Empire in Crisis, 1947–1962* (Cambridge, Mass.: MIT Press, 1965), 20–21.

159. Alfred Grosser, *Das Bündnis: Die westeuropäischen Länder und die USA seit dem Krieg* (Munich: Hanser, 1978), 122ff.

160. Wolfgang Benz, "Bundesrepublik Deutschland," in *Europa nach dem Zweiten Weltkrieg 1945–1982*, ed. Wolfgang Benz and Hermann Graml, 124–47 (Frankfurt am Main: Fischer Taschenbuch Verlag, 1983), 142; Norbert Frei, *Adenauer's Germany and the Nazi Past: The Politics of Amnesty and Integration* (New York: Columbia University Press, 2002).

161. Dalloz, *War in Indo-China*, 144.

162. Kaplan, "United States, NATO, and French Indochina," 235.

163. Alfred Grosser, *La IVème République et sa politique extérieure*, 3rd rev. ed. (Paris: Colin, 1972).

164. Pierre Gillen, "Le Gouvernement Pierre Mendès-France face aux problèmes Tunesien et Marocain," in *Pierre Mendès-France et le*

Mendèsisme, ed. François Bédarida and Jean-Pierre Rioux (Paris: Fayard, 1985), 317.

165. Lutz Köllner et al., eds., *Anfänge westdeutscher Sicherheitspolitik, 1945–1956*, vol. 2, *Die EVG-Phase* (Munich: Oldenbourg, 1990), 197.

166. Zhang, *Deterrence and Strategic Culture*, 185.

167. Herring, "Franco-American Conflict in Indochina," 45.

168. Geoffrey Warner, "Britain and the Crisis over Dien Bien Phu, April 1954: The Failure of United Action," in *Dien Bien Phu and the Crisis of Franco-American Relations*, ed. Kaplan, Artaud, and Rubin, 55–77.

169. Volker Matthies, *Die Blockfreien: Ursprünge, Entwicklung, Konzeption* (Opladen: Leske & Budrich, 1985).

170. Wilfried Loth, *Der Weg nach Europa: Geschichte der europäischen Integration 1939–1957* (Göttingen: Vandenhoeck & Ruprecht, 1991), 110.

171. Arnulf Baring, *Außenpolitik in Adenauers Kanzlerdemokratie: Bonns Beitrag zur europäischen Verteidigungsgemeinschaft* (Munich: Deutscher Taschenbuch Verlag, 1971).

172. Steininger, *Wiederbewaffnung*, 253ff.

173. Jean Greenwood, "Return to Dunkirk: The Origins of the Anglo-French Treaty of March 1947," *Journal of Strategic Studies* 6 (1983): 49–65.

174. Grosser, *La IVe République et sa politique extérieure*, 193ff.

175. Christoph Andrew, *Théophile Delcassé and the Making of the Entente Cordiale* (London: Macmillan, 1968), 27, quoted in Heinz Gollwitzer, *Geschichte des weltpolitischen Denkens*, vol. 2, *Zeitalter des Imperialismus und der Weltkriege* (Göttingen: Vandenhoeck & Ruprecht, 1982), 199.

176. Paul Noack, *Das Scheitern der europäischen Verteidigungsgemeinschaft: Entscheidungsprozesse vor und nach dem 30. August 1954* (Düsseldorf: Droste, 1977), 34–35.

177. Köllner et al. eds., *Die EVG-Phase*, 231.

178. Armand Clesse, *Le projet de C.E.D. du Plan Pleven au "crime" du 30 août: Histoire d'un malentendu européen* (Baden-Baden: Nomos, 1989), 29–30.

179. Loth, *Der Weg nach Europa*, 91ff.

180. John Gillingham, "Die französische Ruhrpolitik und die Ursprünge des Schumanplans: Eine Neubewertung," *Vierteljahrshefte für Zeitgeschichte* 35 (1987): 1–24.

181. Hans-Peter Schwarz, "Adenauer und Europa," *Vierteljahrshefte für Zeitgeschichte* 27 (1979): 471–523; Gilbert Trausch, "Robert Schuman, le Luxembourg et l'Europe," in his *Robert Schuman: Les racines et l'oeuvre d'un grand Européen* (Luxembourg: Ville de Luxembourg, 1986), 24–83.

182. Hans-Jürgen Küsters, "Die Verhandlungen über das institutionelle System zur Gründung der Europäischen Gemeinschaft für Kohle und Stahl," in *Die Anfänge des Schuman-Plans 1950/51*, ed. Klaus Schwabe, 73–102 (Baden-Baden: Nomos, 1988).

183. Köllner et al., *Die EVG-Phase*, 140–41.

184. Ibid., 190–91.

185. Ibid., 195.

186. Wilfried L. Kohl, *French Nuclear Diplomacy* (Princeton, N.J.: Princeton University Press, 1971), 31ff.

187. Gustav Schmidt, ed., *Großbritannien und Europa—Großbritannien in Europa: Sicherheitsbelange und Wirtschaftsfragen in der britischen Europapolitik nach dem Zweiten Weltkrieg* (Bonn: Brockmeyer, 1989).

188. Wilfried Loth, "Der Koreakrieg und die Staatswerdung der Bundesrepublik," in *Kalter Krieg und deutsche Frage: Deutschland im Widerstreit der Mächte, 1945–1952*, ed. Josef Foschepoth, 335–61 (Göttingen: Vandenhoeck & Ruprecht, 1985).

Index

world market, 46, 119, 201; idea of
    an indivisible, 46
world revolution, 80–81, 89, 91
World War I, 6–7, 12, 17, 21–22, 24–
    26, 28, 30–33, 42, 49, 64, 69–70,
    73, 83–84, 87, 99–100, 103, 117,
    131, 133, 140, 158, 160–63, 203,
    207, 209, 215
World War II, 39, 46–47, 100–103,
    173–96, 205–11, 225, 233
Wrangel, Peter N., 80, 84, 90–91, 206

Yalta Conference (Ukraine, 1945),
    227, 242
Yalu River (North Korea/China),
    224

Yan'an (China), 225
Yegorov, Alexander, 83–84, 92
Young, Owen D., his Young-Plan,
    110
Ypres (Belgium), 31
Yugoslavia, 67, 69, 102, 131, 211, 214,
    217–21; coup d'état (1941), 102.
    See also Montenegro; Serbia

Zaitun (Turkey), 159
Zeligovsky, Lucian, 87
Zhdanov, Andrey, 201
Zhou Enlai, 225
Zhukov, Georgi K., 91
Zurich (Switzerland), 246
Zwischeneuropa, 66